Latvia in transition provides the material necessary to understand present-day Latvia. The author examines the main events, processes and problems of the transitional period of this country from a dependent and Moscow-dominated Soviet Republic to an independent and also interdependent state. The book presents the most relevant and essential aspects of Latvia's history, politics, economics and society. The historical analysis highlights the formative events which are still recalled in Latvian political discourse. The period of awakening is discussed in detail to reflect its world-wide resonance and impact on similar processes in other Soviet Republics. The creation of a new state and the establishment of democracy have forced the elite to cope with a multitude of problems simultaneously. This book describes the approach to politics, market economics and ethnic relations.

Latvia in transition

Latvia in transition

Juris Dreifelds

Brock University

CAMBRIDGE
UNIVERSITY PRESS

Published by the Press Syndicate of the University of Cambridge
The Pitt Building, Trumpington Street, Cambridge CB2 1RP
40 West 20th Street, New York, NY 10011-4211, USA
10 Stamford Road, Oakleigh, Melbourne 3166, Australia

First published 1996

Printed in Great Britain at the University Press, Cambridge

A catalogue record for this book is available from the British Library

Library of Congress cataloguing in publication data
Dreifelds, Juris.
Latvia in transition / Juris Dreifelds.
    p.   cm.
Includes bibliographical references.
ISBN 0 521 47131 1 (hc)   ISBN 0 521 55537 X (pb)
1. Latvia – History – 1991–   I. Title.
DK504.8.D74   1996
947'.430854 – dc20   95-16444   CIP

ISBN 0 521 47131 1 hardback
ISBN 0 521 55537 X paperback

Contents

Tables

Acknowledgments

Many people in Latvia and North America have donated their time, insights, information and ideas during the research and writing of this project. The Klavs Sipolins Foundation with its generous assistance allowed me to spend my sabbatical in Latvia in 1990. Dr. Jerry F. Hough and his East–West Center at Duke University provided me with much stimulation and the clash of ideas which has forced me to refine and re-evaluate many of my concepts. The Association for the Advancement of Baltic Studies has been an invaluable resource. My Baltic colleagues Rein Taagepera and Romuald Misiunas have been important in helping me expand my Baltic horizons.

Introduction

Latvia: a building block for comparisons

After the collapse of the Soviet Union, fifteen truly sovereign countries emerged claiming their right to statehood and to their own approaches to development. Freed from the tutelage of central control they have chosen varying paths and different speeds of political, economic and structural evolution. The directions taken by these former Soviet republics offer an unparalleled opportunity for comparisons – especially because of their shared point of departure from a Soviet environment.

To be sure, the exposure to common Soviet rules and practices did not prevent the existence of vast differences between the republics in economics, educational levels, demography, political culture and other important social variables. Even their paths to independence, attitudes to Communist power and relationships to each other have not been identical.

The gamut of differences in the development of the republics after the breakup of the Soviet Union is indeed very wide. The use of violence in the Caucasus, Moldava, Tadzhikistan and Russia is one of the most visible demarcation lines. The approach to economic reforms is another. The Baltic republics have most closely embraced the "shock therapy" method of change. The Ukraine had still not started on this road by early 1995 and Russia had followed a path somewhere between that of the Baltic republics and the Ukraine.

The need for comprehensive single country studies is evident. It is extremely difficult to make valid generalizations with an incomplete overview of the processes of change, reform and transition. Even the three Baltic republics of Estonia, Latvia and Lithuania, which often appear from a distance to be similar, differ in many respects in policy-making. Probably the most important divergence can be seen in their formulations of citizenship laws which were based on different demographic imperatives. Their political and electoral systems are also vastly different. The pace of economic change, and attitudes towards it, do not

1

coincide. Approaches to privatization, tariff policies, and purchase rights to land have diverged. There is symbolic significance in the fact that each of the republics has chosen to tie its currency to different bases: Estonia has chosen the Deutschmark, Lithuania the American dollar and Latvia the IMF basket of currencies (SDR).

Importance of the Baltic states

It is clear that having knowledge about one Baltic republic does not necessarily allow for a safe generalization about all of them. Never-theless, in many respects their historical development and importance have indeed been very close. The Baltic republics have often been credited with or blamed for starting the process of disintegration of the USSR. In the course of regaining their lost independence the Baltic republics became important role models for other Soviet republics and important catalysts in the *démontage* of socialism and of the Soviet empire. Two Swedish specialists on the Baltic and the USSR, Kristian Gerner and Stefan Hedlund, highlight this role in their book *The Baltic States and the End of the Soviet Empire*. They point out in their introduction why they have focused on the Baltic states to understand the broader picture of the breaking apart of the USSR:

Although constituting a tiny minority of the "Soviet" population, and an almost negligible share of its territory, the Baltic states played a role in the Soviet breakdown which can hardly be overestimated ... What makes the story of the Baltic republics particularly relevant to a deeper understanding of the drama of Soviet disunion, is the fact that this was where it all started.[1]

In this respect it is worth noting that the first anti-Soviet manifestations occurred in Latvia with the "calendar" demonstrations on June 14 and August 23, 1987. The following year the initiative was most successfully carried forward by Estonia and in 1989 by Lithuania. Not surprisingly, *Pribaltika*, as the area is called by Latvia's eastern neighbors, is still widely seen in Russia as the demolition team responsible for the collapse of the USSR.

It is ironic that in spite of their relatively small size these three states have attracted the unmitigated enmity of the Russian military. An October 1994 polling study of 615 upper-level military officers in Russia, commissioned by the German Ebert Fund, revealed the depth of this strange bitterness. In response to the question of whom they considered to be their chief enemy, Latvia was rated first with 49 percent. After Latvia came Afghanistan, Lithuania, Estonia and only then the United States.[2]

The Baltic states have also informally been blamed as key agitators in Chechnya, the Muslim area of Russia that declared its independence in 1991 and was able to maintain its internal rule for several years. The process of demonization of *Pribaltika* has even taken on an ironic historical twist. In an environment of growing realization of the harm done by the Bolsheviks to Russia's historical development together with the new growth of nostalgia and pride in old Russia and its czarist leadership, the critical role of the Balts in this epoch of history is now being resuscitated. Latvian Red Riflemen, in particular, played a pivotal role in helping Lenin's Bolsheviks maintain their power. Latvians opposed to Russian imperialism filled the upper echelons of the Red Army and the Cheka until their demise in Stalin's purges after 1935.[3]

Without a doubt the Baltic republics have become symbolic objects of hostility among the "saviors of the empire" in Russia.[4] At the same time they have become symbols of another sort for many European states. According to the former prime minister of Sweden, Carl Bildt, Russia has a historical opportunity to find a return path to Europe where he claims it should belong. However, in an article entitled "The Baltic Litmus Test," he acknowledges that Russia's relationship to Europe will be measured by its political behavior towards the Baltic states: "If Moscow fully accepts the independence of the Baltic states and fully respects their rights, one can be sure that Russia has entered the family of nations. But if Moscow questions their sovereignty or undermines their independence, that would signal that Russia might once again become a threat to the international system."[5]

If the former Eastern European countries, especially the "Visegrad Four" of Poland, the Czech Republic, Slovakia and Hungary, have been considered the first group of potential candidates from former communist states for integration with the European Union and with other European organizations, the Baltic states have been considered the group immediately behind them. The other states of the former Soviet Union have been relegated much further back in the priority list for European integration in spite of their larger size. In effect, the Baltic republics have been taken "under the wing" of Scandinavian countries which consider their integration into Europe and their independence important ingredients of their own security and of their own long-range regional planning. Furthermore, the entry of Sweden and Finland into the European Union substantially changes the geopolitical significance of Northern Europe and for the first time places this union of states in contiguous geographical contact with Russia.

Many Western countries have become guilty of demonization themselves with respect to the former communist countries. The arch-villain in the pantheon of the enemies of liberalism for many Western academics and politicians has most often been "nationalism" whose multifaceted characteristics have usually been grossly simplified and distorted.[6] Anne Applebaum, deputy editor of *The Spectator* of London, has pointed out one dimension of this problem: "It is now clear that the intense Western fear of nationalism in Central Europe misidentified the problem, and that the attempt to thwart the progress of so-called nationalist parties was a mistake."[7]

The charges of "nationalism" and even "ethnic cleansing" have also been aimed at Latvia and the other Baltic states. A study of the complexity and of the ebb and flow of Latvian nationalism should add a "reality check" to much of the ideologically bound and automatically denounced essence of group ethnic bonding and ethnic politics. Such insights, in turn, may help one understand a large part of the world where ethnic collectivities are a basic source of attachment and a powerful root of self-definition.

For many years the Baltic republics were told that such small states could not survive on their own without the brotherly help and sacrifice of other Soviet republics, especially Russia. Since independence, however, these three countries have been able to achieve a faster, deeper and more successful transformation towards the market system than any of the other former Soviet states. Ironically, today, one of the arguments often used to explain such progress is the small size and lack of complexity of these three states.

The reasons for much of the political and economic progress, however, are not to be found so much in the relative size of these countries as in their unique history compared to that of other republics in the Soviet Union.

Baltic incorporation into the USSR

Although each one of the Baltic states has had a different history, they have experienced a broadly similar fate from the eighteenth century onwards when they were absorbed into the Russian empire. Following the turbulent years of World War I and the Russian revolutions of 1917, all three were able to establish their independence. In 1920 the Soviet Union signed separate peace treaties with each of the Baltic states, recognizing their rights to sovereignty and independence "in perpetuity." Other parts of the Russian empire also broke away and declared themselves independent states, but except for Finland and Poland these states were soon forced back under Moscow's rule.

The Baltic republics were able to remain independent for only two decades. Their sovereignty was disregarded on August 23, 1939 when Estonia and Latvia (eventually Lithuania as well) were illegally placed under Soviet control in the secret protocols of the Nazi–Soviet Non-Aggression Pact.[8] Within one year they were occupied by the Red Army and forcibly annexed to the USSR without overt military opposition. Finland was also "bestowed" upon the Soviet Union by Nazi Germany in these protocols, but its annexation was foiled in large measure by the unflinching resistance shown by the Finns to the Soviet invasion.

The "restoration of Soviet power" in the Baltic began in mid June 1940 with these countries' occupation by the Red Army.[9] Consequently, these members of the League of Nations disappeared from the world stage as countries with the power to exercise their own sovereignty. Indeed, they were the only members of the League of Nations not to regain their independence after World War II. This meant that they lost their right to choose their own way of living and of interaction with their neighbours. In the most basic terms they lost the right to their own history and became mere locations on the map of the USSR. Only half a century later, following the failed coup of August 1991, did all three once again emerge as independent states, active participants in the world community and members of the United Nations. Their renewed importance indeed rests on the fact that they have regained their right to make independent decisions and affect the flow of history.

The relative Baltic advantage

Latvia, together with its Baltic neighbours of Estonia and Lithuania, has faced fewer problems than the other former Soviet republics in setting out on the road to reform. Twenty successful years of independence during the interwar period allowed these countries to establish borders, strengthen national cohesion, raise national consciousness and demonstrate the viability of their economies. The laws, traditions and practices of this period have been an invaluable resource in state-building and in the establishment of democracy and the rule of law. The memory of the successful operation of the market economy has provided faith for many people during the period of privation associated with reforms. Gold deposited abroad before the invasion of the Red Army has now become an invaluable asset for stabilizing local currencies and economies. Even in the realm of foreign policy the three states have been able to regain their diplomatic property abroad and to carry on business in certain embassies which continued to work for Baltic freedom during all the years of occupation.

Independence was easier to attain for the Baltic states because of their particular status in the view of most Western countries. Their incorporation into the Soviet Union was never recognized as legal by these countries, hence demands for their independence were not considered to be interference with the internal affairs of the USSR. In contrast, the Ukraine and Belarus, both of which had seats in the United Nations, were considered by the West as integral and legitimate parts of the Soviet Union.

The Baltic states also benefited from the greater volume of contacts with the outside world because several hundred thousand refugees who fled during World War II ended up in Western countries. About a third of all Balts in 1993 indicated that they had relatives or close friends abroad. Even among the Russian speakers in these countries, 21 percent indicated such ties; in Russia itself, however, only 8 percent claimed Western relatives or friends.[10]

This Baltic diaspora was important in mobilizing world attention concerning the issue of occupation and in bringing information, books and support for relatives in their respective countries. In effect, the monopoly and credibility of Soviet information was diluted throughout the entire Baltic region because of these contacts. This diaspora has also been important after independence in forging links with the West, in introducing specialized skills and in helping develop political and economic initiatives.

In many respects, the Baltic republics resembled the countries of Eastern Europe. Nevertheless, in contrast to Eastern Europe, for almost half a century they were deprived of normal control over state organs and institutions. They did not have their own armed forces or security systems, independent laws or jurisdictions. Most importantly, they had lost control over all the economic levers, such as banking, debt, currency emissions, tariffs, foreign currency reserves, labour movement, wages, prices, location and type of industry, exports, imports and even welfare. Moreover, all economic activity was integrated to serve one Soviet-wide market and was controlled by bureaucrats from Moscow. In sum, the Baltic republics represent unique hybrids among former communist states, differentiated from Eastern Europe on the one hand and the remaining former Soviet republics on the other.

This unique mixture of features has had important consequences in the way in which the Baltic republics have coped with their transition from communist, totalitarian and Moscow-directed Soviet republics to independent, democratic and market-oriented states – the explicit target sought by a majority of Balts. Indeed, the changes already in progress and those contemplated in the immediate future are revolutionary in their scope and impact, and have already required and will continue to require tremendous adjustments in the institutional and psychological realms of populations saddled with very fundamental ethnic and ideological cleavages.

Paul A. Goble, a former special advisor on Soviet nationality problems at the US State Department and a close observer of the Baltic scene, has accentuated the fact that each of the Baltic republics carries with it unique problems. He has outlined their differences in five major areas: cultural, demographic, geographical, economic and political.[11] It is beyond the scope of this study to expound the comparisons in all these fields. A focus on Latvia should provide the building blocks for future comparisons, not merely among the Baltic states, but also among all the countries which used to be part of the USSR.

Residual obstacles to reforms in Latvia

It is clear that post-communist Latvia is not the country of 1939 altered merely by the normal processes of modernization, such as those experienced, for example, by Finland. The obstacles in the way of reforms are formidable. The decades-long discontinuity in the sovereignty of Latvia and its incorporation into the USSR precipitated momentous changes and altered the demographic, economic, political and psychological characteristics of the country.

The changes in demography appear most permanent. The influx of close to a million Russian-speaking settlers after World War II changed the fundamental complexion of the country. By 1989, ethnic Latvians had been reduced to 52 percent of the total population of the republic from 77 percent in 1935. As a result of the deportations, executions, war casualties and outflow of refugees between 1940 and 1950, the absolute number of Latvians living in the republic in 1994 (1391.8 thousand) had not yet reached the levels of 1935 (1467.0 thousand).[12] The differences and lack of integration of the two almost equal language groups are problems presenting challenges in all areas of reform.

Dismantling the legacy of centralized and total state control of production and distribution and creating a competitive market economy is an extremely daunting and wrenching process. It is already leading to unprecedented privations for individuals, as well as societal and political turmoil. This process will not end for many years. The gigantic factories and military industries placed in Latvia by Moscow's central planners to serve a state of nearly 300 million people together with their imported labour will for a long time be a brake on economic progress in Latvia and limit the republic's range of options in meeting the challenges of global competition. The profile of production cannot be changed overnight. Moreover, the positive perceptions of the defunct economic system by a majority of both language groups in Latvia have injected a psychological barrier to change, although socialism itself is no longer seen by many as a viable option.[13]

The dependence for half a century on the caretaker state is difficult to reverse. The selective nostalgia for stable prices, full employment, relatively comfortable pensions, low standards of work discipline, numerous social amenities dispersed through the workplace, subsidized transportation, rents, and food, and other features often tends to induce forgetfulness of the backward and undesirable traits of the communist economy. The frustrations of radical changes and readjustment after independence have placed limits on the pace and amplitude of economic reforms because of the threat of political backlash in a democratic system. Moreover, the long years of fitful economic reforms and crumbling state authority under Gorbachev spawned a Soviet-wide network of organized crime whose leadership is often suspected of having come from the top Communist Party and KGB ranks. Independence and new borders have not decreased the amplitude and penetration of organized criminal groups into broad areas of the Latvian economy, especially in urban areas. The ruthless actions of these "mafiyas" have sapped the will and energy of many honest entrepreneurs who are forced to play by the informal but deadly rules of the mob. Others do not even begin to realize their economic ideas and potential out of fear of the criminal infrastructure and its perceived link to political decision-makers.

The political and legal legacy of central, one-party dominance has provided Latvia with few able politicians and with a population not prepared for the cacophony of conflicting views that is a normal feature of democratic systems. The sudden lifting of political controls has encouraged a hypertrophied growth of unduly malleable, shifting, fractious and constantly dividing political movements, parties and organizations that have generally failed to attract a significant pool of dedicated members. As well, the population has a low degree of political attachment and loyalty, and exhibits a high degree of volatility in party support. While the framework of a democratic system is in place, political instability will probably be a reality for the foreseeable future. Instability will be encouraged in large measure by the growth of quick-fix populism, the presence of uncompromising and ego-sensitive leaders, the low value placed on accommodation and bargaining and other residues of totalitarianism. The new state leadership also has to contend with a high degree of nostalgia for the old Soviet system of one-party government, especially within the Russian-speaking population. In the fall of 1993, 66 percent of Russophones had a positive rating of the political system before independence. In contrast, only 39 percent saw the system created after independence as positive. Among Latvians the ratings were only slightly more positive for the new system than the old one, that is, 43 percent compared to 36 percent.[14]

The psychological legacy of occupation is as yet largely unknown. While there are polls providing insight into the degree and depth of attachment to economic equality, collectivism, state control and uniformity, many other important questions are still unanswered.[15] For example, how deeply did the morality of totalitarianism penetrate the psyche of individuals subject to its devastating power? How many thousands of Latvians were recruited to inform on their neighbors and colleagues? What effect did the playing of stage-managed roles and the wearing of psychological masks over many decades have on the intrinsic nature of personality and on interpersonal trust? What impact did the wholesale reversal, almost overnight, of allegiances by apparently ideologically committed communist functionaries at all levels have on their own self-image and on the perceptions of their countrymen? How much did concepts of morality, honor, pride and selflessness change after the wholesale replacement of one set of officially venerated values by an incompletely understood, ersatz model of "Western" values? The answers are not obvious and available evidence appears contradictory. Nevertheless, the pervasive cynicism found throughout Latvia seems to reflect in part the consequences of the effortless switching of public and personal values.

The secret-police connections forged during the period of occupation are a potentially explosive hazard to Latvian solidarity and even to group self-esteem and survival. If local politicians decide to open files for public viewing the effects will be no less dramatic than they were among former East Germans when many people discovered that even close kinship ties had been breached by the all-pervasive snooping systems of the state. Even more ominously, Russia is holding the bulk of the KGB reports prepared in Latvia and in spite of many requests by early 1995 has not been willing to send them back. The use of blackmail against Latvian officials is an extremely powerful potential lever and threat to independent decision-making in Latvia. For self-protection, Latvia has passed laws which forbid people with KGB connections from working in parliament and the civil service.

Latvia has also been significantly affected by two major features of the USSR: the facts that it was an empire and that it was a totalitarian state. Alexander J. Motyl, a leading American specialist on the post-Soviet transition, stresses the fact that the "ancien régime" was a "totalitarian empire" and that each part of this combination left indelible marks on the psychological profile of all Soviet societies.[16]

Transition from empire and totalitarianism

One of the most important questions in the analysis of transitions is the nature of the original but abandoned system, because new systems inevitably carry residues and baggage from their predecessors.

Latvia was an unwilling member of the USSR for almost half a century, but regardless of the undesired nature of this relationship, Latvian society was profoundly affected and moulded by the Soviet system. It could not do otherwise because Latvians had lost control over almost all channels of public socialization and communication. Only at the individual level, within families and small groups of friends and also through surreptitious and symbolic communications were Latvian values preserved.

The use of the term "empire" for the USSR has until recently not been widely accepted. Most political analysts and historians have had no difficulty in agreeing on the existence of British, French, Spanish or Portuguese empires, but the USSR has generally been treated as a federation wherein a variant of federalism was the overarching model keeping the fifteen republics together. There have been exceptions of course. Robert Conquest has for several decades described the relationships between the centre and the other republics in terms of empire. Similarly, H. Carrere d'Encausse described the Soviet Union as a declining empire during the 1970s.[17] After the dissolution of the USSR the term and the concept of empire have gained wider currency and greater legitimacy, in part because intellectuals of the former Soviet system have used it extensively.[18]

Without question, the lack of any true federalism in the USSR has left one of the major problems for successor states. The leadership of republic organs appointed by the *nomenklatura* had almost no realm of independent jurisdiction in which they could acquire and exercise political skills. Only in the declining days before the collapse of the empire did these appointees seriously begin to consider the accommodation of local demands and inputs. To be sure, the "stage prop" structures of Soviet federalism eventually became convenient channels for the defense of republic interests, but only after the decay of the power centres of the Communist Party had progressed sufficiently and they were perceived to be on the edge of collapse.

The legacy of the reality and perceptions of the USSR as a Russian power structure or empire has left many of the people in the Baltic states identifying "Soviet" with "Russian." Regardless of how eloquently current Russian politicians articulate the distinctions between the new Russia and the former Soviet empire most Balts are wary of Russian power because they do not see these distinctions in the same benign terms. For Latvians (and all Balts) Soviet aggression in 1940 was Russian aggression and this identification and attendant fear have become a major influence on policy-making. The Commonwealth of Independent States might theoretically hold certain benefits for the Baltic states but the fear of Russian domination has precluded any of them from considering such an option. The goals of democratization and marketization in Latvia have been embraced more fully exactly because they are seen as keys to entry into Europe and away from the embrace of Russia.

Totalitarianism

There is no doubt that Gorbachev moved the USSR in the direction of greater freedom and openness and that his policies seriously attenuated the pervasive state controls characteristic of totalitarianism. The system he tried to reform, however, cannot be simply denoted as authoritarian or as similar in character to Franco's Spain or Salazar's Portugal. Indeed, Gorbachev himself described it as totalitarian in an interview with Larry King on American television in 1993. Geoffrey Hosking, a specialist on Soviet politics, believes that "the totalitarian model is capable of affording us a more complete view of Soviet society than any alternative yet propounded."[19] The veteran methodologist of the Soviet system, T. H. Rigby, has come to the conclusion that in the light of the Soviet disintegration experience and the views of former Soviet citizens, the totalitarian paradigm has gained greater credibility in comparison with many other approaches.[20] The most relevant distinction between authoritarian and totalitarian systems lies in the extensiveness and depth of the structural penetration of society by the state and the almost total absence of independent organizations. This point is well argued by Motyl who highlights the quintessential features of totalitarianism:

Unlike other types of states, ideal type totalitarian states not only extend into virtually all of society's nooks and crannies; they also penetrate its institutions "totally", they manage them "completely". The result is that, where totalitarian states exist, civil society, as a bounded collection of autonomous public institutions, is always absent, although *some* social institutions may of course be present.[21]

In his view this "atomization" of society, prevalent under Soviet totalitarianism, has handicapped the leaders of the new states because they have been deprived of normal political, social and economic institutions and resources in their implementation of policies of change. Without reimposing the former total state controls they are left with unfamiliar, undeveloped and unstable conduits or channels of communication and interaction with their own populations. At the same time, as Motyl points out, this atomization has deprived the populace itself of the social and economic bases which would enable it to withstand better the draining and damaging rigours of elemental transformations. The population cannot fall back on the buffers or safety nets of civil societies and market economies.[22]

The atomization of society under totalitarianism has definitely left its legacy in Latvia, but, for several reasons, in smaller measure than in the republics outside the Baltics. Soviet totalitarianism was applied in a systematic way only after World War II, that is many years after this was done elsewhere in the USSR. Latvia endured the harshest period of Stalinist totalitarian terror for less than a decade. In addition, the twenty years of independence provided an antidote against the full effects of totalitarianism. National pride played its part. The bearers of this new ideology were traditionally seen as "uncouth barbarians" and the effects of perceived superiority and ethnic pride created barriers to the Soviet demolition of the old society and the erection of pervasive communist state controls. Latvian culture became a refuge for social bonding and social communications with a powerful network of thousands of folk dancing and folk song groups, as well as other cultural "collectives" joining people in bulwarks of non-Soviet identity. The period of awakening and the mobilization of hundreds of thousands of Latvians for the common cause of independence, beginning in 1987, served as a new matrix of societal linkages and aspirations.

Totalitarianism has left its mark on the population of Latvia, but it has had a greater impact on the non-Latvian ethnic groups than on the Latvian community. A wide network of mediation groups has developed within Latvian society. Municipal networks, social and religious organizations, professional societies and even local media provide Latvians with far greater support and communications systems than are found among Russian-speakers. The Russian ambassador in Latvia, Alexander Rannikh, in an interview with a Riga newspaper stated that he holds Latvia's Russians in very high esteem. At the same time, he found that "The organizational level of the Russian diaspora is very low, it is like that everywhere, and has always been like that." In his view, regardless of even some minimal activity, the pervasive fragmentation of local Russian organizations prevents them from dealing with any serious problems.[23]

Latvian nationalism

Latvian nationalism has been one of the issues most often raised in the Western media as a negative variable undermining Latvia's democracy. For many decades nationalism commonly had a negative connotation. Lately, however, the concept of nationalism has been undergoing rehabilitation. There are still those who claim that "the politics of nationalism are contrary to the essence of the liberal democratic process" and that democracy and nationalism are "a bad fit."[24] Others have accepted the view that "nationalism is inherently neither good nor bad, but a fact of life that shows a capacity for both good and evil."[25]

The American specialist on ethnicity in post-communist Europe, Rasma Karklins, finds the concept of nationalism to be complex, ambiguous and bearing opposing connotations in different societies. The core of nationalism in her view is the self-assertion of ethnic groups or nations. This self-assertion, however, can be benign if it strengthens a group's identity but harmful if it becomes aggressive or engenders superiority. To avoid some of the methodological, definitional and value problems associated with the concept of nationalism and also in order to expand the ambit or scope of the study of politicized ethnicity she prefers using the concept of ethnopolitics. Nationalism in her definition is a subtype of ethnopolitics. In her analysis of Latvia's transition to democracy Karklins found that ethnopolitics was a constructive rather than a destructive force.[26]

Foreign correspondent of *The Times* and Baltic specialist Anatol Lieven, while less positive about nationalism, found it to be a major source of positive change in the Baltic:

The Baltic national independence movements have therefore also been nationalist movements, and must be described as such. Any negative feelings this may awake should be qualified by an awareness of how in the post-communist context, nationalism alone can awaken cynical and disillusioned peoples to a spirit of sacrifice and common purpose. It is perhaps the only force which can return a sense of tradition and roots and local culture to people who have lived under a materialist "internationalism" of the most grey, shoddy, soulless and banal kind.[27]

Motyl also stresses the value of heightened national identity and "non-exclusionary" nationalism. Its role, as he sees it, can be enormous in the deflection and mitigation of the impact of post-totalitarianism and in the construction of civil society. Indeed, he sees benefits of a large-scale commitment to national identity in helping state-building, in strengthening democracy and in helping to overcome the negative side-effects of marketization.[28]

In Latvia, nationalism has been an extremely important ingredient of change. This nationalism, however, has been mostly confined to the Latvian ethnic group, not because it has been exclusionary, but because the changes it sought were not embraced by many non-Latvians, especially by those who settled in the republic when it was part of the USSR. The low levels of Latvian language knowledge within these groups have also been obstacles to participation.

Latvian nationalism, much like nationalism in other groups and countries of the world, has not remained at a constant level but has surged and ebbed with time. It was most powerful during the period of awakening. Since that period, however, there has been a systematic decline in the intensity of this nationalism except during the brief 1991 armed confrontation with the "Black Berets" in Riga. National commitment, to be sure, has not died and is still a prime consideration in the orientation of many people, especially in the right-of-centre parties. Nevertheless, it is surprising to note that the cup of nationalism rather than overflowing could be best designated as "half empty." The sense of dedication, solidarity, selflessness and willingness to sacrifice for the common cause has been significantly eroded. There is a strong tone of cynicism permeating the orientation of many Latvians and a sense that they have been exploited by self-serving individuals under the guise of nationalism. The bitterness and even overt mockery of the "singing revolution" (the period of awakening) and all of its claims to dedication and sacrifice are a powerful current, especially among those most buffeted by the forces of change. The cause for this disillusionment has most often been laid at the feet of corrupt and greedy politicians and bureaucrats. The lack of order and the discontinuities caused by the revolutionary changes associated with the transition have often been linked to the willful connivance of people in power with organized crime and with sinister imperialist forces located in Moscow.

In reaction to the perceived abandonment of the commonweal, the growth of malevolent machinations and the dominance of greed and selfishness, many of the self-identifying patriotic groups and individuals have sought to form a coalition of national forces to create a Latvia where selfless dedication, pride and patriotism could become dominant. Such a coalition of political parties, called the National Bloc, was successfully initiated in the fall of 1994. As well, nationalist parties were successful in the municipal elections of May 1994, especially in Riga, and public opinion polls in early 1995 favored a firmer and more national orientation in policy-making. In spite of these changes, the overall nationalist intensity is not high and nationalist commitment appears to be soft and brittle, with major divisions within nationalist parties, especially on economic reforms. Even if such a coalition were to achieve victory in the next national elections in 1995, it seems probable that the sense of disillusionment would continue after the first few months of euphoria.

It should be noted that high emotional hopes were vested in the Latvian Supreme Soviet in May 1990 and once again in its successor, the Saeima, in June 1993, but in both cases disillusionment was deep and rapid. The scope and difficulties of the problems of transition will no doubt cause disenchantment with the next Saeima, whatever its ideological composition, as they did with previous legislatures of the transition period.

In sum, nationalism has been a powerful ingredient among Latvians providing the energy for Latvia to leave the Soviet Union peacefully and initiate radical changes. After independence, however, the wave of nationalism receded somewhat and lost some of its driving force. To be sure, the attachment to Latvia and to Latvian culture has not dissipated but the emotional intensity of this attachment has become diluted. Even the regrouping of national forces lacks the energy of previous years and in large measure appears guided by pragmatic considerations and strategies. Battle fatigue has overcome the feelings of many, but perceived dangers to the survival of the nation could once again energize people for collective sacrifice and selfless devotion. Perhaps a serious and perceived threat from Russia could be the catalyst for such a resurgence.

Goals of transition

It is certainly impossible to predict at what point the transition is going to be completed and Latvia reasonably defined as a normal, market-based, democratic, European state. No one can as yet foresee at what point of development Latvia will be accepted by such restricted membership clubs as the European Union and NATO.

While the Western-inspired goals of democracy, rule of law, civil society, market economy and independent and viable state institutions have become the most popular end-points for the majority of European post-communist states and a majority of Latvians, such goals are not accepted as priority ideals by all. There are other goals held in higher esteem by certain states and, within Latvia, by certain groups of both the left and the right. Alternative priorities for these groups include stability, preemptive state power, state-controlled change and maintenance or increase of traditional outputs of production in industry and agriculture. Indeed this alternative set of goals appears to attract many of those dissatisfied by the discontinuities and perceived instability brought about by the reorientation to democratization and marketization.

There is as well a third set of goals which may include elements of the other two but which has found resonance within a vocal minority in Latvia and the other Baltic republics. Its message, often found in sloganeering speeches of right-of-centre groups, demands the following: de-occupation, de-communization and de-colonization. In effect, these demands envisage the total departure of all personnel of the occupying armed forces, the KGB and other organs of repression, the dismissal of all senior personnel associated with the ruling Communist Party from Latvian state organs and political institutions, and the encouragement of the voluntary departure of Soviet-era settlers who moved to Latvia after June 17, 1940 when Latvia was occupied by Soviet forces.

Time frames of transition

It should be stressed that the period of transition has not been continuous but has had different phases marked by certain dominant features and developments. It may thus be useful to distinguish four separate stages within the period of transition that permit a more nuanced overview of the processes of change. The first or "awakening" phase occurred between the fall of 1986 and the election of the Latvian Supreme Soviet in May 1990. The event which triggered this phase embraced interrelated issues of ecology, history, public participation and the power of republic-level organs of decision-making. The campaign to save the Daugava River from flooding by the Daugavpils hydroelectric scheme began after the publication of a highly critical article on this subject by two individuals in the October 14, 1986 edition of the Latvian literary newspaper *Literatura un Maksla*. The scope of grass-roots participation, the apparently independent nature of this initiative and the success of its demands were certainly unusual features in a communist totalitarian state. This event energized a previously apathetic society and prepared the ground for the other major steps of the period of awakening which led to the progressive growth of national consciousness among the Latvian population. These turning-points included the first open demonstrations by the dissident group Helsinki '86, at the Latvian Freedom Monument on June 14 and August 23, 1987, the unusually candid and iconoclastic Congress of the Latvian Writers' Union on June 1–2, 1988, and the founding of the Latvian People's Front on October 8–9, 1988.

The several years prior to May 1990 were marked by the growth and complexity of independent group activity, mediation between different non-state interests and between different ethnic groups, and the involvement of hundreds of thousands of individuals in the democratically administered People's Front and in many of its campaigns and demonstrations.

The organization of campaigns for the democratically contested elections to the USSR Congress of People's Deputies in the spring of 1989 as well as for the various municipalities in Latvia in December 1989 and the Latvian SSR Supreme Soviet in the spring of 1990 was a critical learning experience for many people in the ground rules of democracy. The selection and coordination of candidates by the Front, the building of platforms and positions of consensus among a wide spectrum of organizations running under the banner of the Front, and the mobilization of the electorate using various media sources set a tradition for the non-violent achievement of desired collective goals. Another feature is worthy of note. At least one year before the election of the Supreme Soviet in May 1990, the "old" Latvian SSR Supreme Soviet, as a result of pressures from the People's Front, had become attuned to popular demands and endorsed an unusual array of legislation, widening the sphere of democratic and national rights and reintroducing the national symbols of independent Latvia.

During the second phase, between May 4, 1990 and the full declaration of independence on August 21, 1991 (in the dying days of the Moscow coup), the newly elected legislature, controlled by the People's Front, acknowledged Latvia's sovereignty and proceeded to expand the sphere of rights and powers of the republic as well as to strengthen human and ethnic rights for all inhabitants under its jurisdiction. In this "sovereignty" phase Latvia was able to achieve an unprecedented measure of economic self-determination and began to control the movement of goods across its borders. It also began to cooperate bilaterally and multilaterally with other Soviet and even non-Soviet states without explicit permission from Moscow. Legislation was passed moving Latvia closer to rule of law and economic marketization.

The advent-of-independence period, from August 1991 to the election of the Fifth Saeima in June 1993, without question involved the greatest rate of progress towards Westernization goals. The total rupture of the lines of command from Moscow and the new freedom to determine options in all areas of economics and politics laid the most important foundations for the launch of reforms. As well, the constitution of 1922 came into force in its entirety. Western *de facto* recognition of Latvia together with offers of advice and aid from many countries and the IMF helped strengthen the momentum for renewal.

The period of constitutional legitimacy began after the Saeima accepted the 1922 constitution in its entirety. In practical terms, the years after June 1993 were focused on reconstruction and normalization. The Saeima introduced the last major steps toward legitimization and normalization of the Latvian state and its government including the parliamentary election of its president. The electoral rules of the interwar republic were applied and binding rules of procedure were accepted for the cabinet and the Saeima. While the previous legislature had been elected by all adult residents of Latvia, including the Red Army, the electorate for the Saeima included only those who themselves or whose parents (at least one) had been citizens of Latvia prior to the occupation of June 17, 1940. The political parties elected to the Saeima began to engage in politics in a more disciplined and predictable way although more than a half-dozen deputies had bolted or were expelled from their parties within a year of the elections. The upper ranks of the bureaucracy were reviewed and filtered for competence and previous KGB links, and generally the strengthening of professionalization and the rule of law allowed for the routinization of relations in business and between people and various branches and departments of municipal and national administration. The status of non-citizens was established and the requirements for citizenship were explicitly legislated. The occupying Red Army, which had by decree become the Russian Army, left Latvia at the end of August 1994. About twenty thousand retired officers, however, remained.

The process of change continues. For some people it is too slow but for others too rapid. Nevertheless, the goals of Westernization have not been abandoned and none of its elements have been jettisoned. The next election to the Saeima in October 1995 may bring new political forces to the fore, but all viable political parties appear to differ only in details and pace of implementation rather than basic goals and direction.

Outline of the book

Latvia, a country larger than Portugal, Holland and Denmark and slightly smaller than Ireland, is not well known, because until recently it offered very little that was exciting for a scholar to write about. The communist system provided only superficial material about what was going on in economics, politics and society. Today there is an avalanche of information, much of which is accessible only to those familiar with the Latvian language.

In approaching the analysis of Latvia no single model of change was chosen to interpret available information. The main criterion for topic selection has been perceived relevance of subjects to understanding the processes and attitudes involved in Westernization reforms. This study therefore does not pretend to be an exhaustive examination of all facets of Latvian life and politics.

In all aspects of the study of communist and post-communist Latvia there is one major caveat that needs to be strongly expressed. Statistics provided by state organs vary widely in quality. Unfortunately there are as yet no satisfactory screening mechanisms and in the selection of data one can only rely on judgment and an intimate knowledge of the context within which they apply.

The first two chapters set out the formative historical events that impinge on present-day consciousness and politics in Latvia and analyze the factors precipitating the period of awakening and the flow of events leading to Latvia's declaration of intent to separate from the USSR. The third and fourth chapters delve into the essential goals of transition, the processes establishing Latvian independence, democracy, the rule of law and a market economy.

The chapter on demography, language and ethnic relations treats the underlying strains in ethnopolitics, the most serious area of dispute and concern within the republic and the one with the greatest potential consequences for the peaceful evolution of Latvian society. Indeed, this topic has become the focal point of international attention.

There are other areas of life in Latvia which should be explored such as religion, environment, culture, health, education, social values, crime and the directions of the government in foreign affairs and defense. No doubt these will receive the deserved attention of scholars now that there is normal access to materials and that Latvia is once more an independent republic with the right to choose its own way of living and of interacting with its neighbors.

1 Historical residues and impact on present-day politics

In the struggle for Latvia's independence, history became a major vehicle for destabilizing communist rule. The first protests of 1987, which initiated the awakening in Latvia, were exercises in historical recall and were widely designated as the "calendar demonstrations." Demonstrators attempted to open doors to realities of the past that the Soviet regime had forcibly closed. These realities included the deportations to Siberia of tens of thousands of citizens on June 14, 1941 and March 23, 1949, the signing of the Molotov–Ribbentrop Pact of August 23, 1939 and the declaration of Latvian independence of November 18, 1918. The memorandum of the first Congress of the Latvian People's Front raised these as well as other historical issues such as Latvia's incorporation into the USSR in August 1940 and the purges of the Latvian "national Communists" in 1959. Soon, as well, the entire period of independence and the role of its most famous politician, Karlis Ulmanis, were placed on the agenda of important issues and analyzed at length in the public media. An editorial in Latvia's newspaper *Cina* on January 1, 1989 summarized the extraordinary impact of history in Latvia: "No branch of knowledge has gained such public attention during the last year among the most varied professions and age groups – as history. Never has there been such a need for a close relationship between historians and the nation, never have the events of the past so palpably resonated with the present."

The above points of tension in history became the peaceful weapons of the nationally mobilized Latvian people in their pursuit of independence. The awakening period has often been called the "singing revolution" because of the absence of violence and the importance of Latvian traditional music during a large number of the manifestations which touched the emotional chords of so many who had formerly given up hope of independence. In contrast the revelations and challenges of history, while also raising emotions, were clearly aimed at the intellect; they assailed the legitimacy of the existing Soviet elite in Latvia and built the foundation for a new Latvian national elite. This battle of historical interpretations is important in order to uncover the significance of debates, testimonies and revelations which otherwise might remain obscure and confusing.

The highlights of history offered by the media have another important aspect. Historical events create the building bricks of collective memory. Their dim and oftentimes contradictory and even mythical dimensions have a direct bearing on what present-day populations support or are averse to, and on their behavior. Rudyard Kipling noted in his famous maxim that "the game is more than the players of the game and the ship is more than its crew." Indeed the relationship between different groups of people and especially their relationship to events in the past in many important respects shapes their destiny.

The distorted and highly ideological treatment of history by the ruling Soviet elite became a point of contention in the entire USSR. The first articulations of this unease surfaced in literary works. During the early eighties the concept of "mankurtism" became very popular in Latvia and elsewhere in the USSR. It was created by Chingiz Aitmatov, one of the most renowned Soviet and Kirghiz writers of that time, in his novel *A Day as Long as Centuries*. Mankurts were a mythical group of Kirghiz people who had been captured and turned into slaves. Their will-power and memory of past events and even of their parents had been taken away by a tortuous process of brainwashing. A Latvian playwright made this novel into a play in 1984.[1] The message was not lost on the Latvian readers and audience. Indeed, "mankurtism" was widely used as a synonym for the way in which the Soviet people had been cut off from their historical memory as the result of a conscious conspiracy by the Communist elite. With the advent of glasnost, Gorbachev himself invited republics to fill in the blank spots of history. His motivation was admirable. He hoped that truth would prevail over obfuscation and lies. Yet he did not foresee the power of the forces this truth would unleash.

History is more than a detached register of significant events of the past. History can be a weapon, a club, as mentioned earlier. It can also be a source of strength and of mobilization, a focal point of intense emotions; it can help define friends and enemies and break down walls or build them up. It can be the cement that keeps a nation together or the dynamite that can shatter the unity of empires. To be sure, anyone intent on discovering all the varied, subtle and changing relationships between a people and its perceived history is bound to fail. Yet a broad, even if indistinct, outline of these relationships is a necessity for anyone trying to understand the behaviour of collectivities and even individuals.

The following review of certain historical experiences is not an attempt to provide a comprehensive history of Latvia and the Latvians.

Its focus is on the major formative events which have become sources of controversy or have a continuing impact on the politics and sociology of present-day Latvia.

Early history and the advent of independence

Until about 1300 Latvia was a collection of independent kingdoms with two basic ethnic groups. The first settlers in this territory were Finno-Ugric peoples variously called Livs, Livonians or "Libiesi." Their language, related to Estonian or Finnish, has all but disappeared as a result of many factors including the plague during the Middle Ages and assimilation to the Latvians.[2] The other group, the Latvians, arrived in the present territory several thousand years ago.[3] Their closest ethnic cousins were the Lithuanians, the ancient Prussians, the Galinds and the Jatvingians. The latter three groups became extinct many centuries ago. Their extinction as well as the fate of the Libiesi was a popular and oft-repeated threat posed to Latvians in their struggle for survival.

After the German-led crusaders had conquered the territory of Latvia by 1300, there was a succession of foreign regimes in charge of various parts of the country during the next six hundred years (the Vatican, Denmark, Prussia, Poland–Lithuania, Sweden and Russia).[4]

Peter the Great was the first to expand Russian influence into Latvia. As a result of his victories against Sweden he was able to attach northern Latvia, including Riga, to the empire in 1721. Half a century later (1772) Russia appropriated the south-eastern part of Latvia and in 1795 was able to lay claim to the western part, the semi-autonomous Duchy of Kurland which had been a protectorate of the Polish–Lithuanian kingdom.

For more than two hundred years Latvians experienced a unique mixture of elites. The German-speaking "Baltic Baron" nobility was dominant in economic, cultural, social and local political life while the Russian bureaucracy was in charge of higher politics and administration. Resentment by Latvians was much more intense of the Germans than of the much less visible Russians except during periods of overt Russification.

Serfdom in Latvia ended half a century before it did in the rest of the empire (1817–19). The German clergy in their attempts to gain the loyalty of Latvians and to further their religious convictions became actively involved in the spread of elementary education. As a result of their efforts Latvia attained one of the highest rates of literacy in the Russian empire. The presence of a reading public spurred the growth of newspapers, journals and books and helped familiarize Latvians with then current ideas in politics, economics and life styles in western Europe as well as in Moscow and St. Petersburg.[5] Latvia's geopolitical situation and ice-free ports attracted business and trade and led to a rapid growth of urbanization. By 1913, Riga for example had a population of half a million.

In the second half of the nineteenth century Latvians became conscious of their ethnic heritage. The intensity and scope of Latvian professional cultural endeavors (art, books, theatre, song festivals) welded together and mobilized a nation. This period led to a heightened national consciousness and to the development of a Latvian elite interested in the furtherance and survival of its national culture against the inroads of both Germanization and Russification. This period is known as the first Latvian awakening.

Riga, the capital city of Latvia, became one of the leading trade centres of imperial Russia with large factories (some with 20,000 workers) and a multi-ethnic work force. It was one of the busiest railroad centers in the empire and its port in 1913 claimed 17.2 percent of all trade logged by Russian ports. In this respect it was ahead of St. Petersburg. In fact, all of Latvia's ports claimed 24.5 percent of the total volume of shipping trade in the empire.[6] The rapid pace of industrialization and rigorous conditions of work, together with access to Marxist-socialist literature, created a rise in radicalism in the working class comparable to that of Moscow and St. Petersburg. By the end of the nineteenth century many ideological currents found adherents in Latvia, but socialism prevailed among the working classes.[7]

The dramatic events of 1905 in Latvia radicalized not just the workers, but also the peasantry. The killing of seventy peaceful demonstrators by Russian troops in Riga on January 13, 1905 was followed by massive strikes and eventually by arson against hundreds of manor houses and the execution of Baltic German nobles. In retaliation, the imperial army shot about 3,000 revolutionaries and sent many to Siberia. Close to 5,000 were forced to flee abroad (including the later president of independent Latvia, Karlis Ulmanis). In 1905 almost all segments of Latvian society were united in their anger at the Russian reaction and German barons.

The 1905 experience and its aftermath set the stage for radical action in 1917 and in the words of an American historian forced a large part of the Latvian intelligentsia to "seriously question Latvian membership in the empire."[8]

Between 1915 and 1917 over half of the Latvian population was dislocated as a result of World War I and the advance of German troops. Many of these refugees settled in north-east Latvia but a large proportion went to Russia to distance themselves from the front lines and the ideological conflicts that were beginning to arise. The refugees in Latvia were traumatized, living without their own homes, with no work, and according to a Latvian historian "the war quite naturally created the apocalyptic landscape which provided a fertile ground for the millennial Bolshevik visions to mature."[9] Indeed, for several years the north-eastern part of Latvia, teeming with refugees and Latvian riflemen, became a strong base for Bolshevism. Bolsheviks won local elections in the Vidzeme Land Council in 1917 (66.4 percent) and most of the other local elections. The vote for the All-Russia Constitutional Assembly between November 18 and 21, 1917 has become a landmark in Latvian history. While in the entire empire (which was by then in Bolshevik hands) less than a quarter voted for the Bolsheviks, in north-eastern Latvia they received 71.9 percent. Participation had also been relatively high with a two-thirds turnout of eligible voters. Within the dozen Latvian rifle regiments on the Northern Front, support for Bolshevism was an astounding 95 percent.[10]

Not all Latvians favored Bolshevism, however. The Latvians living under German occupation saw an opportunity to begin the creation of a new democratic and independent state and on November 18, 1918, a week after Armistice Day, a group of leading Latvian representatives, from Social Democrats to rural Conservatives, declared Latvian independence. At the time this declaration had a tremendous impact, but mostly in the symbolic realm. The German authorities, still in charge, hampered the newly created Latvian provisional government particularly in its right to recruit its own armed forces. In fact, this provisional government was forced to flee from German troops, finding safe refuge on a ship guarded by the Allied naval squadron near the port of Liepaja.[11] This multiparty democratic provisional government faced many more months of tribulation before it was able to begin the serious work of economic reconstruction. It had to face many enemies besides the Germans and their lingering troops. There were also Russian troops, the so-called "whites" who were ready to fight for the restoration of Russia's sacred borders, that is borders which included Latvia. The greatest threat, however, came from the Latvian Bolsheviks.

In December 1918 a Latvian Bolshevik government under the leadership of Peteris Stucka took the reins of power in certain parts of Latvia and on January 3, 1919 took control of Riga and other Latvian territories not occupied by the Germans. A noted American historian, Stanley W. Page, has captured the contrasts in the ideological orientation at that time of the two northern Baltic republics in his chapter headings "Latvia chooses Bolshevism" and "Estonia rejects Bolshevism."[12]

The Latvian Bolshevik republic lasted less than six months, until the end of May 1919. It was forced to retreat in disorganized haste in part because of German and Estonian military advances but largely because it had alienated itself from the local population. One of the most eminent personalities of the Latvian Communist Party during this period, Linards Laicens, delved into the reasons why within a year Bolshevik popularity in Latvia plummeted from "at least 75 percent" to "less than 15–20 percent" by May 1919. In his view the following were the principal factors of alienation: "... unnecessary terror, forced communization, the complication of the agrarian question, bureaucratization, appropriation of privileges, unnecessarily rapid nationalization of trifles." According to Laicens, "Soviet Latvia" fell mainly because of internal collapse as a result of the loss of support and of trust from the working people.[13] This trust and support were never re-established. In the elections of independent Latvia the vote for Communist-backed parties never exceeded 10 percent.

Those Latvian riflemen who joined the ranks of the Bolsheviks eventually became the foundation of the Red Guards and Lenin's principal trouble-shooters in Russia. The first commander-in-chief of the Red Army, J. Vacietis, came from Latvia, as did many of the top generals, Cheka organizers and Bolshevik political luminaries.[14] Their efforts were pivotal in the dissolution of the empire, and this dissolution was a key for the emergence of the independent Baltic republics. In his memoirs published in 1922–4 Vacietis explicitly noted the connection:

Many still do not appreciate just how significant the slogan "Free Latvia" was for the Latvian Riflemen. The Latvian *strelnieki* as a group were, and continued to be, nationalist in the best sense of the word ... The Latvian *strelnieki* understood well that if reaction were to return to Russia, all power in the Baltic region would likewise return to the reactionaries. Thus, in struggling against Russian reaction, the Latvians gained freedom for the Balts, providing the foundation of a free Latvia.[15]

It is important to note that in 1940 and after 1945 the Bolshevik occupation regime attempted to gain sympathy and popular support from Latvians by propagandizing the link between communism and Latvians in the years 1917–20. They highlighted the critical role in the Russian Revolution of the Latvian Red Riflemen (albeit in a selective way), the significance of the Latvian vote for the All-Russia Constitutional Assembly and the "achievements" of the first Latvian Communist government. Because of this link to the past, the imposition of a communist system in 1940 was declared the "renewal" of Soviet power. The evident loss of appeal of Bolshevism, of course, was never ever raised. The book by Laicens was kept in the "special library fund" behind locked doors. For as long as possible, as well, little publicity was given to the fate of most of the famous Latvian revolutionaries and Red Riflemen. Their wholesale execution by Stalin was made public only during the awakening period, although individual luminaries had been selectively rehabilitated in the 1960s. Over 73,000 of about 200,000 Latvians living in the USSR were killed during Stalin's purges.[16] During this period many Latvians in the USSR tried to hide their ethnic roots for fear of suffering the fate of other co-nationals. Even Janis Kalnberzins, the Communist Party leader in Latvia in 1940 and 1945, was on the list of those to be executed during the 1930s. He was then doing illegal Party work in Latvia and could not immediately heed the request to return to Moscow, and soon thereafter he was arrested by the Latvian government. This saved his life. His wife and father, however, were killed in these purges.[17]

While formal Latvian independence had been declared on November 18, 1918, *de facto* independence came only in January 1920 when Polish and Latvian troops were able to clear Latgale of Communists. A new constitution was adopted on February 15, 1922 and the first parliament, or Saeima, assembled in November 1922. On August 11, 1920, in the Treaty of Riga, Russia, i.e., the "Federated Socialist Republics of the Russian Soviets," extended *de jure* status to Latvian independence and renounced "voluntarily and for eternal times all sovereign rights over the Latvian people and its territory."[18] Ironically, diplomatic recognition was delayed by Great Britain and France until 1921 and the United States until July 27, 1922 because of "the hope entertained by the Allied Powers in general and by President Wilson in particular that Bolshevism could be destroyed and the territory of the former Russian empire left intact."[19] It thus appears that only the continued presence of Bolshevism in Russia finally allowed the Great Powers to countenance independence for the Baltic republics. On September 22, 1921, together with its sister republics, Latvia was admitted as a member of the League of Nations.

Independent Latvia

During its twenty years of independence Latvia was able to establish itself as a successful state. This period is categorized as the second awakening. Among its key characteristics, three are particularly relevant:

(1) Economic viability
(2) Treatment of minorities
(3) Political instability and the 1934 *coup d'état*

Six years of war interspersed by occupations and invasions had devastated large parts of Latvia and the economy was in shambles. Most of the industrial infrastructure had been hauled to the interior of Russia, and agriculture had been lacerated by six years of continuous war action. Fields were replete with trenches, undetonated ordnance and the rusting paraphernalia of war; animals, especially horses, and seed grains had been requisitioned for transport or food and were scarce; even timber was often an unsafe asset because of the many lodged bullets and shrapnel which endangered saws and sawyers. Armed bands and crime were rampant. According to the Royal Institute of International Affairs:

Everything had to be built up from the very beginning; not only a new constitution, but new law courts, new schools, and even new central and local government bodies had to be set up; and every activity was hampered by the relative inexperience of leaders who up till now had always been in opposition, and by the virtual disappearance of the former Russian and German official classes.[20]

One of the principal moves in social and economic stabilization was agrarian reform which appropriated land from German and Polish landlords and distributed it to landless peasants. This move has been recognized as a major ingredient in minimizing the appeal of communism and even in the declining influence of socialist and other left parties and in the stabilization of labour. It did, however, create a serious conflict with the local German minority which appealed to the League of Nations claiming abuse of human rights.[21]

The loss of the Russian market was a major blow to the economy. Nevertheless a combination of state-run marketing and export boards for agricultural and forestry products and the widespread implementation of cooperatives and joint ventures between state and private industries slowly created a base of powerful economic units. The Latvian currency, the lats, became relatively stable. While the Great Depression created many hardships, the period 1935 to 1940 witnessed rapid economic growth. All this was achieved without any foreign aid and almost without any foreign debt. According to Latvian historian Alfreds Bilmanis, by 1939 Latvia had made "a rapid swing away from depression" into an era of "unparalleled prosperity." In 1938 national income was over 2 billion lats, compared to 745 million in 1932. The total national wealth at the end of Latvia's independence period was 9 billion lats or about 3,000 per capita.[22]

On the whole Latvia's economic achievements were on the level of those of Finland.[23] While there was minor unemployment for industrial and service sector workers during the early 1930s, later in the decade there was a shortage of farm workers, who had to be imported from

Poland. It is ironic that the three Baltic republics exported, in total, one-half of the amount which the USSR did in 1938.[24]

One aspect of the economy, however, has received broad criticism from some, although high praise from others. The trend to ever greater direct state involvement in many areas such as heavy industry, building materials, electricity, tobacco, brewing, confectionery, textiles, insurance and food processing strengthened the economic influence of Latvian bureaucrats. In some cases the state created monopolies or quasi-monopolies for its own production units. The Royal Institute of International Affairs warned in 1938 that the pursuit of what they called "State capitalism" could discourage potential investors. Nevertheless, one result of this policy was to allow a greater Latvian role in the economy.[25]

Very progressive welfare programs and other systems of support by the state lessened social tensions. There was a great stress placed on higher education. In its proportion of students in the population, Latvia rated second in Europe (after Estonia). The European part of the USSR, in contrast, was last of twenty-five countries.[26]

Perhaps one of the most important indices of achievement in the economic realm was the placement of 10.6 tonnes of gold by the Latvian government for safekeeping in the United States, the United Kingdom, France and Switzerland.[27] Further, there was a broad consensus among Latvians themselves that Latvia's economy was doing very well. This reservoir of goodwill was often mocked by the Soviet press in its attempts to demolish the image of this period with headlines such as "About the Old, 'Good' Times."[28] Its approach was to focus on the period of the Great Depression and its attendant problems of unemployment and farm auctions.

The economic hardships during the first years of independence have been used by many in making comparisons with the economic crisis of post-communist Latvia in 1995. Many of the financial and fiscal strategies of those days are being analyzed carefully. The example of Finland is used to divine what Latvia could have achieved if it had not been occupied by the USSR. Most importantly, the gold sent abroad by Latvia for safekeeping is now considered an essential anchor for the stabilization of an independent Latvian currency.

For the Soviet regime, Latvia's economy during independence was characterized only in negative terms. Ironically, even as they castigated czarism, the Soviets reiterated how much better Latvia had been as a part of Russia rather than as an "agrarian appendage" of Western imperialism. Its statistics almost invariably tried to demonstrate that independent Latvia had not even achieved the production levels of 1914.[29]

Treatment of minorities

The supportive treatment of minorities was one of the major achievements of the independence period. Latvia accepted many Russian, Jewish and other refugees fleeing from Bolshevism in the USSR. The population of Russians increased from 118,023 in 1920 to 237,809 in 1930 and of Jews from 60,892 to 94,388.[30] By law all citizens of Latvia were given equal rights. The state allowed for school autonomy by creating councils for the larger minorities which had complete control over types of schools, programs of instruction and other matters. Minority primary schools were maintained by the state and secondary schools received grants.[31] However, in May 1934, after the *coup d'état* by Ulmanis, some restrictions on choice of educational institutions were decreed, reflecting the growing dominance of defensive nationalism and political conservatism. Latvian children, including children with one Latvian parent, had to attend Latvian-language schools. Jewish education was placed under the control of the religiously strict and conservative Agudat Israel, rather than allowed to reflect the mosaic of its many different cultural elements. Until 1934, German and Russian languages had been accepted in state and commercial services alongside Latvian, but under the new law Latvian was decreed as the only written or spoken language in such institutions except in districts where over half of the population spoke another language.[32] Again, before 1934 all ethnic groups were free to publish books, journals and newspapers in their own language. Even minority churches such as those of the Old Believers received subsidies. After 1934, however, minority groups together with Latvians were restricted in the range of their political expression. Even after the establishment of these restrictions Latvia provided far more state support for its minorities than most countries of the world. It should be noted that in the neighboring USSR all Latvian cultural institutions, including schools, theatres and publications, were abruptly ended in 1937.[33]

It is ironic that with the arrival of the forces of "internationalism" in Latvia after 1945, all minority schools were closed or transformed to Russian ones.

Political instability and the coup d'état

Latvian political institutions and electoral systems were patterned on those chosen by the Weimar Republic. The acceptance of proportional rather than majoritarian elections turned out to be a political blunder. A most disruptive situation arose because of the incredibly large number of political parties which vied for power in the elections to the Latvian parliament, the Saeima. Only two of the parties competing in 1920 were still in contention in 1931 (the Latvian Social Democrats and the Latvian Farmers' Union). No single party was able to obtain a majority in any of the four elections held during Latvia's independence period. In the last democratic elections, in the fall of 1931, a total of forty-four parties and groups competed. Even ethnic minorities were split into numerous small factions: the Jews and Russians each had six parties or groups, the Poles and Germans each had two, and Lithuanians had one. Among the hundred deputies elected to the Saeima in 1931 there were representatives from twenty-seven different parties or groups (eleven deputies were the sole representative of their electoral group). The largest party, the Social Democrats, garnered twenty-one seats and the main opposition party, the Farmers' Union, obtained fourteen seats. In the period up to the *coup d'état* by the Prime Minister, Karlis Ulmanis, in May 1934, Latvia had experienced eighteen parliamentary governments. Between each of these coalition structures there were "crisis days" when open and covert wheeling and dealing over votes, cabinet posts and coalition partners occurred.[34] This political instability and the machinations and bargaining for personal and minority advantages created among many people a sense of frustration and disgust with politics and, unfortunately, with democracy. Thus when Karlis Ulmanis set aside the constitution, proclaimed a state of emergency and ordered the dissolution of the Saeima on May 15, 1934 there was little protest.

Ulmanis himself has become an object of ongoing controversy. He had been one of the key leaders in the creation of independent Latvia, had served many times as Prime Minister and held this post at the time of the *coup d'état*. He was an agronomist who had studied at the University of Nebraska and had been forced to flee from Latvia in 1905 because of his revolutionary activities. Since then he had come to represent the interests of the Farmers' Union, the second strongest party in the Saeima. His policies were welfare-oriented, with a stress on strengthening Latvian culture and economic initiative. Until 1940 there was widespread support for his policies although he had suspended all municipal councils and had not brought in a new constitution as he had promised. Not a single person was executed or shot for political reasons during his period of rule. However, persons of the extreme left and right were incarcerated for brief periods of time.[35]

Compared to other dictatorships in the world, his was truly mild. It should be remembered that in Eastern Europe most countries suffered the same fate and that democracy as a process had not gained unconditional supporters.

Soviet propagandists made much of the "fascist" dictatorship of Ulmanis. Yet he had never been an ideologue and certainly had not sided with Germany. During the Ulmanis period the radical nationalist group called the *Perkonkrusts* (swastika), which copied several of the Nazi ideas current at the time, was disbanded and a number of its leaders and followers were arrested. It was under his "watch" that the Red Army troops were granted bases in Latvia, and when the Communists took power he remained in his post and provided a smooth transition until arrested and deported. He died in Turkmenia in 1942 and in 1995 efforts were still being made to find his remains and return them to Latvia.[36]

This political history of independent Latvia is very important because the Supreme Council voted in 1992 to reintroduce the old Latvian constitution and, with minor changes, the electoral system of 1922. Estonia and Lithuania have worked out new constitutions which depart from the Weimar model.[37]

Ulmanis himself has become a powerful symbol of selfless dedication to Latvia and his memory is being refurbished even by organizations with high concentrations of ex-Communists. They realize that the once vilified dictator still has tremendous appeal among Latvians, especially in rural areas, and that their association with Ulmanis can provide long-term political dividends. At the same time, the historical experience of such a dictatorship, even if beneficial in many respects, has been used in debates as a political tocsin to warn against possible repetitions.

World War II

The war years were particularly tragic for Latvia's population. Latvia was occupied first by the USSR (from June 17, 1940 to June 27, 1941), and then by Nazi Germany (until the day of capitulation, May 8, 1945). This, of course, preceded the occupation by the Communist regime which continued until September 1991. These were events which had an important impact on the evolution of Latvia or became focal points of public debate, especially during the period of awakening when Gorbachev's policy of openness allowed formerly untouchable or distorted subjects to be discussed from many viewpoints.

The first year of Bolshevik occupation

Two events in particular which are tied to Latvia's loss of independence and the first year of Bolshevik occupation were in the forefront of the first demonstrations by Helsinki '86 in the summer of 1987:

(1) The Molotov–Ribbentrop Pact of August 23, 1939 and its secret protocols, and its role in the mythology concerning Latvia freely joining the Soviet Union.

(2) The deportation of thousands of civilians on June 14, 1941.

On the eve of World War II Latvia's fate was determined at the bargaining table by representatives of Stalinist Russia and Hitler's Germany in spite of the fact that Latvia was an independent state and was not theirs to give or take. Yet, in the setting of a world paralyzed by fear and apprehension, no help was offered or received, leaving both Hitler and Stalin convinced that they could proceed with the creation of new "facts on the ground" in Europe. The definition of spheres of interest began at the August 23, 1939 meeting between the foreign ministers, Joachim von Ribbentrop of Nazi Germany and the newly appointed Vyacheslav Molotov of the Stalinist USSR. The secret additional protocols of this pact placed Latvia and Estonia in the Soviet sphere of dominance. Later, on September 28, after the USSR had occupied Poland, Lithuania, which had initially been assigned to Germany, was added to the other two in exchange for other territories and sizable sums of gold.[38] The Baltic states were not the only victims. Finland, the larger part of Poland, Bessarabia (part of Romania) and other smaller areas were placed in the Soviet fold in this grossly illegal territorial pact.

As its first move, the Soviet Union forced Latvia to accept 30,000 troops after the latter was coerced into signing a Pact of Defense and Mutual Assistance with the USSR on October 5, 1939. Similar treaties were forced on Estonia and Lithuania. Finland, however, refused to accept such a demand and valiantly fought the Soviet army in the famous Finnish Winter War after it was attacked on November 30, 1939. The USSR was expelled from the League of Nations for this unprovoked attack on Finland.[39]

The coming of Soviet occupation was clear to Hitler, however, who proceeded to withdraw into the German fold all those of German origin living in the Baltic states. In most instances these Baltic Germans could trace their ancestry back over 700 years in the Baltic area. As a result of this action about 63,000 people left Latvia and 22,000 left Estonia.[40]

At a time when world attention was concentrated on the imminent collapse of Paris to the Nazis, the Soviet Union sent out ultimatums in the middle of June 1940 to all three Baltic countries. Moscow demanded a change of Baltic governments to ones capable of assuring the proper fulfilment of the previously signed Pacts of Mutual Assistance. Moscow also demanded the free entry of unlimited troops to secure strategic centres. These ultimatums were worked out for each state separately and in the case of Latvia only eight hours were allowed for reflection. Under the circumstances all three states, isolated and seeing no signs of support anywhere in the world, capitulated to these demands and allowed the entry of new Soviet troops. The Red Army entering Latvia brought with it a special emissary, Andrei Vyshinskii, to oversee the takeover of government positions by collaborators willing to follow the instructions of the Kremlin. Vyshinskii had learned political choreography during his staging of the infamous Moscow show trials of Stalin's enemies. The initial creation of a "People's" government was assigned to a Latvian professor of biology, Augusts Kirhensteins. In this carefully scripted political theatre, elections were deemed necessary for the legitimation of the changes. On July 14 and 15, the elections, which were held simultaneously in all three Baltic republics, provided equally absurd results of over 90 percent participation and support for the Communist slate of 99.2 percent in Lithuania, 97.6 percent in Latvia and 92.2 percent in Estonia. Of course, in all three cases, only one slate was allowed on the ballot. It should be noted that attempts by a group of prominent non-Communist Latvians (Atis Kenins and others) to get on the ballot were unsuccessful.[41] Most of these brave individuals ended up in Siberia or were shot. Within one week of the elections Latvia's president, Ulmanis, was sent to Voroshilovsk. He died in prison in 1942. The next scene in this previously arranged play was to have representatives of the newly elected People's Assemblies plead for the incorporation of their respective republics into the USSR. Not surprisingly, these requests were granted in the first week of August, 1940.

The first year of Communist occupation was traumatic for the local population, most of whom had been totally isolated from events in the giant country next door, had read only isolated bits and pieces about the horrors of Stalinist Russia, but were all of a sudden thrust under its direct power.[42]

This first Bolshevik occupation was capped by a coordinated act of terror against totally innocent and helpless civilians whose crime it was to have been successful and loyal citizens of Latvia. According to historian Alfreds Bilmanis, "especially marked for extermination were the government officials, members of the intelligentsia, and army officers."[43] Latvia's elite and leadership were deliberately separated from the whole nation for easier manipulation of the remaining masses. The rounding up of 14,693 people for deportation to Siberia began at midnight on June 13–14, 1941 and was mostly completed by six in the morning in the cities, although in several rural areas the operation continued into the evening of June 14. Among those placed in 824 railroad cattle cars were 5,154 women and 3,225 children. Men were separated from their families and sent to gulag camps where almost all perished. Women and children were sent to primitive villages in Siberia where many died from exposure, disease, starvation and the enmity of local peasants who were told that these people were "fascists." During this year of occupation about 35,000 people were "repressed," that is, deported or shot.[44] According to available documents the June 14 action was to have been followed by several more, but these were cut short by the German attack on Russia under "Operation Barbarossa," and the occupation of Latvia by Hitler, ironically Stalin's former partner who had given him rights to the Baltic States in August 1939.

For almost five decades the June 14 deportations and the Molotov–Ribbentrop Pact were forbidden subjects in the USSR. The official Communist explanation concerning Latvia's acceptance of communism and voluntary entry into the Soviet Union was based on an elaborate edifice of historical falsification. According to the Soviet version of events, Latvia was in a revolutionary situation in 1940 as a result of the ongoing economic crisis and the increased alienation of the Ulmanis "fascist" regime from the people. The working class under the leadership of the Latvian Communist Party overthrew the hated bourgeois regime and installed an anti-fascist People's Government. No civil war or foreign intervention was possible because of the existence of Soviet armed forces on Latvia's territory. Within a month the People's Government pleaded to be accepted into the USSR and thereafter Latvia became a contented member of the fraternity of progressive states whose future prosperity was assured by the shared assets and rational division of labor that only communism could provide.[45]

It had been clear to opponents of the Soviet occupation that the elaborate edifice of mythology about the supposed revolution of the working class of Latvia would be seriously shaken if it could be shown that Stalin and Hitler had made a deal about the Baltic republics in August 1939. Much energy was expended to that end in all three Baltic republics. The issue was certainly the Achilles' heel of the Soviet version of revolution in the Baltic. The first people publicly to draw attention to the Pact were Latvian youths who undertook, at great risk, to organize demonstrations for August 23, 1987.

On the fiftieth anniversary of the Pact, August 23, 1989, the Baltic republics organized one of the most effective publicity campaigns ever held. Up to two million people, holding hands, created a human chain, from Vilnius, through Riga to Tallinn. This emotionally captivating scene was widely described not just by the Baltic media but also abroad. Hardliners in the Kremlin felt that the Balts had strayed beyond the bounds of acceptable behavior and several weeks of tense rhetoric ensued.[46]

As a result of Baltic pressure Gorbachev had created a commission to investigate the Pact on June 1, 1989. The report on the Pact was presented by its chairman and Gorbachev's closest advisor, Alexander Yakovlev, to the Second Congress of the USSR People's Deputies on December 23 and 24, 1989. As a historian he was very aware of the impact of this document:

The secret protocol of 23 August 1939 reflected precisely the inner essence of Stalinism. This is not the only one, but one of the most dangerous delayed action mines from the minefield we have inherited and which we are now trying to clear with such difficulty and complexities. It is necessary to do this . . . Sooner or later the truth will win out on God's earth and deception will be unlocked.[47]

The original of the secret protocol given to Molotov had by then not yet been located and the German original had been lost after the aerial bombing of an archive center. Before the bombing, however, all important documents had been microfilmed by the staff of these archives and were captured by the Americans. The absence of the original copies was one of the major reasons why many deputies disputed Yakovlev's conclusions. He offered five points of proof which made the existence of the document highly believable. Eventually the original Russian copy of this infamous document was located.

It is striking that the Pact "reclaimed" most of the old territories of the czar for the "internationalist" and "revolutionary," but at heart still empire-oriented, Mother Russia. If class considerations alone had prevailed, would Eastern Europe not have enjoyed the same status as the Baltic republics and Moldava? Why didn't the leadership and population of Eastern Europe join the USSR with great enthusiasm? Wouldn't China have been a solid addition to the Union of Socialist Republics? These issues and questions, however, were understandably never seriously raised within the USSR, and less understandably were neglected within mainstream Western Sovietology.

Nazi German occupation

Operation Barbarossa, the German attack on the USSR, began on June 22, 1941. Four days later German troops had crossed the frontiers of Latvia. The Communist forces were driven out of Latvia in extremely rapid fashion in part because of help from the local populace. The deportations which had occurred less than two weeks earlier and the fear of more such actions had induced a widespread sense of inchoate terror within the Latvian population. Historically Latvians had been very ambivalent in their attitude to Germans (having fought them in World War I and having opposed them as the ruling land-owning class). In this new context, however, the feeling of having been saved from immediate death and deportation created a public mood of relief.

The Nazi regime, however, had its own agenda, which did not include the restoration of Latvia's independence. According to secret documents of March 1943 found in German archives, Latvian territory was to be repopulated by Germans from the Reich. The fraction of Latvians deemed most Nordic and "desirable" according to caliper-style measures of physiological features and genetic heritage were to be allowed to remain and to become assimilated to the German race in a gradual process lasting several generations. The inhabitants of eastern Latvia, the Latgallians, were lumped together with Lithuanians as undesirable elements not worthy of assimilation. The bulk of Latvians were to be expelled and resettled in adjoining Slavic lands.[48]

The regime which without any qualms had ceded the Baltic republics to Stalin's Russia began its totalitarian rule with no regard for the needs and traditions of the local population. Latvia's minorities including Jews, Gypsies and some Slavs were rounded up and many were eventually shot. Over 70,000 of Latvia's Jews were killed in a series of officially organized, cold-blooded and merciless mass shootings in the forests surrounding Riga and other large cities. Latvian youths were illegally drafted into the armed forces and sent to the front lines in central Russia. Others were rounded up and sent to labor camps in Germany. Many people were arrested and shot. Nationalized property and lands, with minor exceptions, were not restored to their owners. Nevertheless when the Red Army re-entered Latvia (Riga falling on October 13, 1944) hundreds of thousands of Latvians fled to the coastal areas and headed for Germany or Sweden. This massive outflow of refugees was driven by the traumatic memories of the year of Bolshevik terror.

Romuald J. Misiunas and Rein Taagapera, in their historical review of the Baltic states after 1940, have summarized the reason why Baltic resistance to the German occupation was not particularly widespread or well organized: "Compared to most occupied nations of World War II, the Baltic nations were in the unenviable situation of facing not one, but two occupying powers. Of these, the one coming second had an unfair advantage: it did not have to destroy the national elite, because the first had done the dirty work. Therefore it generated little resentment."[49]

Three issues are particularly relevant for this period of German occupation:

(1) The relationship between Latvians and Jews.
(2) The exodus to the West of several hundred thousand Latvian refugees.
(3) The military draft of Latvian youth into the German and Soviet armies.

Latvians and Jews

The first Jews settled in Latvia sometime in the sixteenth century at the time of the advent of Polish rule on Latvian territory. By the end of the nineteenth century the Jewish presence in Latvia was proportionately larger than in almost any other national area of the world. In 1897 there were 142,315 Jews who accounted for 7.4 percent of the total population of Latvian territory. There were particularly high concentrations of Jews in the cities of Latgale.

Latvian folklore reflects a multitude of images about the Jew, and especially of the itinerant Jewish tradesman, but none is inimical or hateful.[50] Gertrude Schneider, a specialist on the Jewish holocaust in Latvia, has noted that for centuries Jews had found a good life in Latvia:

Despite occasional setbacks over the past four centuries, the Jews in Latvia had enjoyed a better life than Jews in the neighbouring countries. Even the pogroms raging in the Russian empire around the turn of the century hardly touched the Baltic states. The influx of Jews from the affected areas was great and by 1914 there were 185,000 in the territory of Latvia, a number greatly reduced during World War I.[51]

There was cooperation and camaraderie between Jews and Latvians during the period 1905–20, especially in the various working-class movements and organizations. During the period of independence, relations between the two groups were socially somewhat distant (with almost no intermarriage or assimilation) but functionally cooperative at the political and state policy level. A Latvian-born Jew, Frank Gordon, claims that "the two decades of independent Latvia's existence are remembered by both Latvians and Jews as the 'good years.'"[52] According to Mendel Bobe in *The Jews in Latvia* the Jewish community was able to thrive in Latvia: "Attempts were made here and there to undermine the rights of the Jewish Community in Latvia. In spite of this, Latvian Jewry was a lively national entity in all respects: education and culture, economics and finance. It had its own charitable and social welfare institutions, political parties of every kind with their youth clubs, sports association, press, etc."[53] Changes did occur after the *coup d'état* in 1934, however. Bobe notes the limits on the Jewish press and on cultural autonomy, which fell under the monopoly direction of the right-wing Agudat Israel. These limits mainly changed the balance of forces within the Jewish community and diminished political rights, as they did for all groups including the Latvians.

The war brought tensions which were exploited by both occupation regimes to their own advantage. The war years have left a legacy in many circles of bitterness and mutual accusations about the behavior of Latvians and Jews which is still relevant half a century later. In each case it appears that behavior is criticized without regard to its historical context. Many Latvians were upset by the jubilant way in which some Jewish individuals and groups received the Communist army of occupation in June 1940 and by their visible participation in the Soviet militia. Many Jews have criticized the seemingly tolerant stance of certain Latvian individuals and groups towards the Nazi regime and the participation of some in extermination units called the *Sucmani*.

A former Latvian parliamentary deputy, J. Lejins, observed that "Soviet tanks rolled into Riga and were greeted with ovations and flowers by many Jews."[54] Dov Levin, a Jewish specialist on the Sovietization of Latvia, has also noted this behavior and its effect on Latvian attitudes:

The inimical attitude of the Letts towards the Jews increased during the first few days after the entry of the Red Army into Latvia. One of the causes of this was the abundant enthusiasm and sympathy with which the Red Army was welcomed by Jews in many areas – principally by Communists and left-wing youths, but also by "ordinary Jews". There were instances where Jews took part in the safeguarding of Red Army units and the prevention of hostile acts against them by Lettish military organizations.[55]

The context for such behavior is evident. There is little doubt that Latvian Jews were painfully aware of the fate of their co-religionists in Germany, in occupied Poland and in other Nazi-occupied areas. Indeed, Jewish refugees from Nazism had been received by Latvia prior to the Communist occupation.[56] Jews also knew that in the choice between two totalitarian regimes the Communist one at least did not involve the certainty of death. To many Jews the occupation by the eastern regime was widely seen as the lifting of an imminent death sentence. At a time when all of Europe was being carved up by these two powers the option of an independent neutral Latvia did not appear to be, or was not seen as, a very viable one.

To many Latvians this enthusiastic reception and perceived collaboration with the regime of occupation was seen as treasonable. Dov Levin has noted the tension: "The conspicuous position of Jews in the new regime and its political and administrative apparatus caused the Letts to identify the whole of the Jewish community with the hated Soviet regime which had been imposed upon them by the Red Army. During this period, anti-Semitic feeling increased among the people so that a tense atmosphere prevailed between Jews and Letts."[57]

In parallel fashion, individual Jews have criticized the jubilant way in which Latvians received the Nazi army of occupation in June 1941 and the seeming collaboration of many Latvians with the regime. Max Kaufman in *The Jews in Latvia* notes that "the Latvian population of Riga welcomed the Nazis in their Sunday garb."[58] Here again the context becomes important. Just two weeks earlier Latvians had experienced the terror of deportations and executions and many knew that further deportations were planned. Most Latvians, moreover, were convinced that no regime, regardless of its reputation, could be worse than that of the Bolsheviks. Hence the entry of the German army was seen by many as the end of indiscriminate death and brutality. Later, of course, tens of thousands of these Latvians suffered at the hands of the Nazis. Nevertheless, the bitterness of seeing some Latvians among those who participated in the holocaust or in the Nazi administration created widespread anti-Latvian orientation among Jewish survivors of the holocaust. This is exemplified by the comments of Kaufman, a Latvian Jew who lost his entire family to Nazi murderers:

The destruction of Latvian Jewry will remain an eternal stain on the Latvian and German peoples. Future generations must not forget the barbarities of the wild beasts. The voice of our brethren will rise forever from the earth. History is very cruel and at times it repays what a people deserves. It is in this context that I venture to say that Latvians will be repaid for their complicity in the extermination of Jews, and for stabbing retreating Russian forces in the back. With its millions of citizens, the huge neighbour to the east is flooding Latvia with its citizens; and Latvians are bound to become a minority in their own country in the not-too-distant future.[59]

The Jews suffered an immense tragedy, and so did the Latvian state by the loss of its Jewish citizens. During this time of occupation the infrastructure of the Latvian state no longer existed. All policy was made by the German Nazi administration. The acts of individual Latvians engaged in murderous activities can only be judged on a case by case basis. These Nazi executioners certainly were not delegated by, nor did they represent, the Latvian nation as a whole. The same can be said about individual Jews who worked with the Soviet apparatus of repression. Under certain conditions potential murderers can be found and activated in every large group of human beings. There were some brave Latvians who helped Jews escape.[60] Some lost their lives in the process. Oppressed Latvians were no more able to stop the execution of the Jews than the Jews or Latvians were to stop the deportations of Latvians to Siberia.

The reality is that Jews also suffered under the Communists and Latvians under the Nazis. At this juncture of history neither group was given the choice of an independent Latvian state and a peaceful, normal society.

During the forty years of Communist occupation Latvian–Jewish relations normalized with little visible tension between them. To be sure only a small fraction of Latvian Jews returned to the republic; most had been killed by the Nazis while others chose to leave for Israel or remain in other parts of the USSR. The majority of postwar Jews in Latvia came from other republics and they were more attuned to the Russian-speaking community. Nevertheless, relations between the two groups were correct and cooperative at the professional level, with still some distance maintained at the social level. According to Frank Gordon, who worked as a journalist in Riga, "... based on direct experience, I can state that in Russian-occupied Latvia, anti-semitism among Latvians is practically nonexistent."[61] The majority of Jews came out in favor of Latvian independence, especially in early 1991 at a time when tension between Moscow and Riga was high.[62]

It is noteworthy that the first Jewish high school in the postwar USSR was established in Riga, and contains over 500 pupils. The Jews also have their own youth organizations, a documentation center, a sports association, and several synagogues.[63] Support for Jewish culture and education by the newly independent state renewed a policy which had existed in independent Latvia but which had been cut short by the half-century of occupation by foreign powers.

Latvian refugees in the West

The 120–150 thousand Latvian refugees living in the West have become and still are an important ingredient in Latvian politics and culture.[64] The Communist regime for many decades tried to counter the political influence of Latvian refugees who left in 1944 and 1945. Initially the refugees were depicted as "fascists" or "fascist collaborators" who had fled out of a fear of justice for their deeds. As contacts between relatives broadened, this all-inclusive label became more conditional until it was allowed that many had been merely duped by the Nazi regime to leave.

The cultural legacy of Latvian refugees, with minor exceptions, was for a long time placed beyond the cultural pale in Soviet Latvia. The rediscovery of hundreds of Latvian writers, artists, academics and entrepreneurs by the official media was a key ingredient of the period of awakening. Thousands of Latvians living abroad have come back to offer their contributions in many fields. Their claims to nationalized land and enterprises have been seen by some resident Latvians as a potential boon to the economy but by others as the reassertion of a new class of property-owners with only minimal ties to the daily realities of Latvia.

The impact of several hundred thousand people leaving Latvia was immense. The departure of the bulk of the intelligentsia and the best-educated citizens seriously depleted the pool of experienced personnel suitable for positions of leadership. It also left a vacuum in many areas of life, breaking the continuity so necessary for creative endeavors.

The military draft

The Nazis and Bolsheviks both dragooned Latvians into their respective armed forces. According to international law of that period it was forbidden by those occupying a country to mobilize its population into the ranks of the military and engage it in active war duties. Such legal trivia, of course, were of little consequence as both regimes tried to work out schemes which would technically give them a free hand in this respect. Under Nazi rule, Latvian youths were given a choice of being sent either to labour battalions or to the Latvian Legion to fight the Bolsheviks (avoiding the draft could result in execution). The Legion was chosen in a proportion of 3 to 1.[65] There was a reason for this. Latvians felt that having their own divisions could lead to a better bargaining position to defend Latvia's interests, especially during a period when German retreat was becoming a reality. They hoped to take over power once the Nazis left, repeating the scenario of World War I when Latvia regained its independence. Most soldiers who fought on this front believed themselves engaged only in a struggle against the Bolsheviks and for "Mother Latvia" and not for the survival of the Third Reich. They were not Nazi sympathizers and many documents of the Third Reich indicate a widespread anti-Nazi orientation in Latvian ranks.[66] The major mobilization of Latvians began only in November 1943 with peak strength reaching about 60,000 men. According to some estimates the total of men mobilized or recruited as volunteers during the German occupation was about 150,000. A large contingent of about 20,000 were made prisoners of war in Western Allied zones. After the capitulation of May 1945 about 80,000 were left in Soviet hands. The rest, numbering about 50,000, were war casualties.[67]

The two Latvian divisions fighting on the Kurzeme front on several occasions were placed opposite Latvians fighting in Communist battalions. Many of these individuals, as well, had been drafted from among those who fled the Nazi occupation and those on Communist-occupied Latvian soil who had not yet been drafted by the Germans. Quite literally brother had to fight brother.[68]

The debate among Latvians today is whether Latvians could afford to be cannon fodder for any foreign army. The Lithuanians evaded the German draft quite successfully. The demographic losses from the various wars on Latvian territory have been enormous. The World War II losses left indelible imprints not just on Latvian natality tables but in creating a tremendous disproportion between men and women. The postwar proportion of three women for every two men set the stage for family instability and strengthened the male-dominated political culture for another half-century.

Most of the individuals who fought in the German armed forces and were captured by the Soviets ended up in Siberia. Those who survived, as well as their relatives, had to carry the black mark of having supported the enemy. This meant that another large contingent of people was automatically excluded from any positions of leadership and influence. This blackballing, together with the outflow of refugees and the deportation of Latvia's elite, was a major factor preventing the formation of a stronger resistance to Sovietization and Russification. It appears, as well, that these "lessons of history" have made Latvians much more conscious of preserving their numbers and avoiding dramatic deadly conflicts whether ideological, ethnic or international.

Postwar communist occupation

Several aspects of the postwar occupation period, which lasted until August 1991 (or, in the eyes of some, August 1994 when the last Russian-organized troops left Latvia), have become focal points of debates:

(1) The existence and nature of guerilla war.
(2) The March 1949 deportations and collectivization.
(3) The actions and fate of the Latvian "national Communists" led by Eduards Berklavs and purged in 1959.
(4) The nature and scope of non-violent opposition and dissent.

Postwar guerillas

The guerilla war in Latvia involved almost a decade of fierce fighting and the loss of many lives. Those fighting against the occupiers received almost no help from abroad and were forced to rely on their own resources and to set up their own coordination mechanisms. Without a strong coordinating centre and with no store-houses of new weapons, the scattered bands of Latvian fighters were at the mercy of their well-organized and well-supplied exterminators. The Communists brought in their best anti-partisan specialists and successfully infiltrated many of the nationalist fighting organizations, in the process even creating entire infrastructures of "fake partisans."[69]

Even more deadly in its effects on Latvian partisan morale was the loss of hope in Western intervention. During this decade of struggle many countries including Czechoslovakia and China fell under Communist control with little serious counter-effort from the West. This had a seriously negative impact on the pursuit of armed opposition. Most people are not suicidal and they will not risk their lives unless they are convinced that their suffering is going to have a positive impact. Thus the guerilla war was forced to wind down. Many Latvians, intent on helping their country, chose other methods of operation which involved fewer risks.

What is clear about the postwar action of partisans is that it hampered and seriously slowed down the Sovietization of the countryside. People were afraid to undertake official functions because they could be shot. The former First Party Secretary of Latvia, Augusts Voss, has described the intensity of this struggle: "In many rural districts, nationalists organized armed bands, terrorized and robbed local inhabitants and murdered Soviet and party workers. But the party and Soviet organs were able to become organized in spite of the ferocious opposition of the reactionary bourgeois nationalist elements."[70]

With the recent opening of Party and government archives it is clear that even in the summer of 1953, after Stalin's death, "underground bourgeois nationalist" organizations were still active. According to the First Secretary of the Latvian Communist Party (LCP), Janis Kalnber-zins, there were still, in June 1953, 13 known groups of "bandits," 133 individually working "bandits" and 77 "illegalists" in Latvia. He pointed out that in spite of "widespread repression" against this underground it continued "to exist and to commit murders." Kalnber-zins readily admitted that a part of the population supported this nationalist underground. In his analysis, the eradication of this opposition was hampered by the distortions and arbitrariness of nationality policy and the non-Latvian character of those fighting on the government side.[71] Indeed, the battle lasted well into the 1950s.

The presence of such a large contingent of guerillas fighting without any support from abroad and with a totally uneven balance of forces is another index of the depth of antagonism felt by Latvians toward the forcible loss of independence.

1949 deportations

The March 25, 1949 deportations, which were aimed at eliminating Latvian "counterrevolutionary inimical elements" were another indication of Latvian resistance and of forcible repression of the Latvian population by Soviet power. Parallel deportations were enacted in Estonia and Lithuania on the same date.

These deportations differed from those of 1941 in several respects. The bulk of those rounded up were farmers and their families rather than the intelligentsia and elite which had suffered proportionately more in the earlier deportations. The scope of arrests was much larger with 40,334 people involved. Included were 18,801 women and 10,590 children under the age of sixteen. In many cases family members were kept together and sent to isolated villages in Siberia. The rate of survival of these people was also higher.[72]

An insight into the actual mechanics of the deportations has been provided by Edvards Karnats, who was a member of a district Executive Committee at that time:

A day before the deportations, cars arrived. From Cesis an envelope had been sent with the list of deportees. It was sealed shut and on it was written the time in the morning when it could be opened. A representative of the Party Committee was present to watch so that the letter with the names of kulaks would not be opened prematurely. The campaign started early in the morning and continued all day, not much baggage could be brought along – only the necessities ... Those who remained, however, immediately joined the *kolkhozes*.[73]

Often the supposed kulaks, on the day of arrest, were not home or had managed to escape to the woods. Since the quota had to be filled or overfilled, other persons were simply taken in their place.[74]

A most poignant illustration of the brutal nature of the Communist administration concerns the case of the treatment of children from the first deportations. After World War II, in 1947, several daring Latvian activists managed to overcome all bureaucratic obstacles and bring back to Latvia from Siberia over a thousand children who had been deported in 1941. Many were sent to orphanages, others were adopted by relatives and friends of the family. In March 1949 most of these children were once more on the list of deportees and once again suffered the trauma of Siberian exile. Many spent several months in passage and had to endure brutalities and harassment from their tormentor guards for whom they were merely children of fascists, to be abused in whatever manner desired.[75]

The paralysis of people in the face of overwhelming power was once again demonstrated as it had been in the first deportations and in the killing of Jews and Gypsies in Latvia. The presence of nationalist partisans did not alter the situation. As well, many t ousands of Latvians were consciously coopted by the regime to help in the round-up.

The deportations were a cold-blooded policy choice made by the forces of occupation. In their plans this was supposed to break the back of the national resistance and to facilitate the process of collectivization. Their calculations were partly correct. Latvia became collectivized before the end of 1949.[76] The underground, while it fought valiantly for many years, was seriously weakened because many of its supporters were deported and because collectivization made it more difficult for individual farmers to provide help. The deportations also deprived the Latvian countryside of its most able farmers. Many of them found lonely graves in the hinterland of Russia. Others returned broken in body and spirit and afraid to apply common-sense solutions to simple problems for fear of contravening the wisdom of the Party. All were made pariahs who carried their "black mark" of deportation in their files and were lorded over by representatives of the Party, often individuals who had participated in their arrest.

The repetition within Latvia of the Soviet program to eliminate the kulaks in the USSR during the 1930s brought with it endemic paralysis of agriculture in Latvia. To paraphrase Marxist jargon, these deportations sowed the seeds of the destruction of communism.

The 1949 deportations were the major but not the only instance of Soviet violence against local inhabitants after the war. According to First Party Secretary Kalnberzins, a total of 119,000 people were "repressed" in the period 1945 to 1953. Of these, 26,500 were arrested by state security organs, 2,321 were killed as bandits, 43,702 were deported as "kulaks" and "supporters of bandits" and another 46,350 were arrested by organs of the militia and procuracy.[77] For comparative purposes it should be noted that equivalent proportions of the population applied to the United States would have involved over 20 million people.

The 1959 purge of national Communists

After Stalin's death the intensity of repression decreased somewhat. During the ensuing leadership struggle some of the contenders catered to regional and republic interests and for several years thereafter nationality demands received more attention and support. Within Latvia the thrust for more Latvian-sensitive policies was initiated and organized by a group of Latvian Communists under the leadership of Eduards Berklavs, the Deputy Chair of the Council of Ministers. Berklavs and his supporters passed regulations restricting in-migration, requested future

knowledge of the Latvian language by Party and government functionaries, and planned to limit the growth of industry requiring large inputs
of labor. Attempts were also made to rationalize production by slowing
down the growth of industries using high inputs of expensive imported
metals and other raw materials, and by speeding up the input of
consumer goods and of construction to improve the social infrastructure. Increased funding was planned for agricultural machines, urban
and rural housing, schools, hospitals and social centers rather than for
"truly grandiose projects."[78]

These programs were not well received in Moscow and a purge of
about 2,000 "national Communists" was initiated in July 1959. Many of
the most gifted individuals in Latvia, among them people who had
fought in the war against fascism, lost their former positions and had to
endure continuous harassment. Ironically, not all of these "nationalists"
were Latvian. The very popular Minister of Agriculture during the
Berklavs period was Aleksandr Nikonov, a Latvian-born Russian: he was
also fired and forced to leave the republic. He eventually became the
President of the USSR Academy of Agricultural Sciences, Deputy
Chairman of the USSR State Committee of Agro-industry, and
agricultural advisor to Gorbachev. He received the prestigious Order of
Lenin from the USSR Supreme Soviet Presidium for "great achievements in the development of agricultural science." Only in August 1988
was he rehabilitated by the Latvian Communist leadership, receiving the
title of "Latvian SSR Honored Agricultural Worker" for great merit in
the development of agriculture "in the republic."[79] A Latvian historian,
I. Apine, has summarized the "negative legacy" of this period: "Within
a few years there was a significant removal of cadres at all levels.
Experienced and capable workers at the peak of their creative power –
party and Soviet activists, scientists, journalists – were fired from active
political and economic endeavours. Their intellectual potential was lost
to the republic."[80]

The fate of Berklavs and his movement was used by the Third
Secretary of the Latvian CP, Anatolijs Gorbunovs, in arguing for a
slower pace of reforms in Latvia in 1987.[81] Berklavs himself was exiled
from Latvia and left the Communist Party. Upon returning to Latvia he
was one of the leaders of the Latvian underground opposition having co-
authored the 1972 letter of seventeen Latvian Communists which
received considerable notice in the wider world and was claimed to be a
CIA concoction by the Soviet establishment.[82] In 1988 he became one
of the key founders of the Movement for Latvian National Independence
(LNNK) and as a deputy in the Latvian Supreme Council and Saeima
has defended Latvian nationalist interests. His own experience in 1959

led him to prognosticate that only the collapse of the USSR would lead to Latvia's independence.[83]

Non-violent opposition and dissent

Until the demonstrations of June 14, 1987 it appeared that the Latvians had been much less restive than their neighbors in Estonia and Lithuania. One of the major Latvian veterans of opposition to Soviet occupation, Gunars Rode, claimed in 1979 that Estonian and especially Lithuanian "nationalistic activity" was much higher than in Latvia. In his view the contacts of the latter republics with fellow nationals abroad were much closer and more practical. Both, as well, were able to forge a closer alliance with the dissidents of Russia.[84] Lithuanians even had their own *samizdat* "Chronicle" to reflect their national struggle for independence. Another Latvian veteran of the prison camps, Viktors Kalnins, provides additional insight. Among youths in political prison camps in the early 1960s, Latvians were dominant.[85] An American Latvian specialist on the question, Uldis Blukis, ventured an assessment of the numbers involved in 1982: "We can confidently claim that the number of national activists in Lithuania reach at least several tens of thousands, in Estonia, thousands but in Latvia, tens."[86]

It appears that Latvians were very active guerilla fighters up until the mid 1950s; they were daring trailblazers for national rights under the Latvian national Communists led by Berklavs in the late 1950s; this momentum for Latvian survival continued into the early 1960s and is highlighted by the arrest of the "Baltic Federation" group in 1962. From then on until the advent of Helsinki '86 Latvian resistance was much less visible than in the other Baltic republics. Only from 1975 and the Helsinki human rights proclamations and the start of Latvian language programs on Radio Liberty (beamed from Munich, West Germany, and financed by the United States) did the embryonic infrastructure of a new opposition form. But even then it was somewhat anemic and small in numbers.

There are several reasons why the Latvian opposition was less visible and vigorous than that of the other Baltic republics, especially after the early sixties. One of the most obvious difficulties for Latvians was contact with the West or non-Soviet world. Estonia with its geographical proximity to Finland even enjoyed Western television broadcasts from Helsinki because Finnish is closely related to Estonian. Regular ferry connections, bringing thousands of Finnish tourists, facilitated the organization of resistance and contacts with the West. Lithuanians had the superb organization of the Catholic Church to rely on. The Church was in constant contact with the Vatican and with the West. Moreover, Poland, one of the most restive and relatively free satellite republics, with a powerful Catholic Church of its own, was next door.

Another major factor limiting Latvian dissent was demographic reality. From the early 1960s there was a veritable avalanche of in-migration from other Soviet republics. Latvians became a minority in most urban areas and were diluted by a foreign and much more pro-regime population which was able to monitor any "deviations" by their colleagues, from factory floor right up to the highest echelons of power. The pervasive mood among new arrivals was to distrust the motives of Latvians and to accuse them of nationalism or even fascism at every opportunity and during many minor conflicts. Thus Latvians harboring any ambitions to advance in their jobs were consciously and subconsciously "bending backwards" to prove that they were enthusiastic "internationalists," that is individuals devoted to the welfare and dominance of everything Russian and Soviet. Latvians had few urban areas where they formed a significant majority and could develop a national *esprit de corps*. The urban intelligentsia was swamped by foreigners. In rural areas the scattered pattern of farmsteads and collective farming was not conducive to effective conspiratorial action. Rural areas, moreover, had very few people of the "thinking class," who could initiate a subtle and long-range opposition campaign. For decades, as well, rural areas had experienced extremely serious social problems and degeneration which were amplified by the widespread abuse of alcohol.

Latvia was also much more oppressed than the other two republics. Policies of all kinds were much harsher, reflecting the greater consolidation of reaction and Communist dogma. This reflected the reality of post-Berklavs Latvia. The vengeful, reactionary and intolerant policies and staffing practices of Latvian CP First Secretary Arvids Pelse and his successor, Augusts Voss, prevented a more rational and wide-ranging consideration of local demands. In effect, they appointed mostly trusted Russians and mediocre Russian-born Latvians whose attitude to Latvia was at best neutral. In Latvia the forces of repression were much more visible and given much greater power. It was common knowledge among Balts that plays or literary works acceptable in Tallinn or Vilnius would be censored or vetoed in Riga. "Big Brother" was bigger, meaner and more petty in the middle Baltic republic. A prominent Latvian author, Andris Kolbergs, has described in a series of articles the depth and pettiness of harassment writers had to endure. Nothing was too small or insignificant for those intent on excising the consciousness of Latvian identity and mechanically blending this national group into a bureaucratic vision of the new "soviet man." One example among many illustrates the repressive attention to detail permeating this campaign of historical exorcism. According to Kolbergs even the inclusion of the word "Latvia" or "Latvian" was deemed to be counter-revolutionary:

If the manuscript contained the word Latvia, then the editor, knowing that the manuscript was to be reviewed at a further three much higher levels of authority, for his own and the author's safety definitely changed "Latvia" into "republic" and "Latvian" into "Rigan" [citizen of Riga]. Because the ruling policy was that Latvians did not have a history – with minor exceptions, for example, the Red Riflemen – [and that] Latvia never existed and also soon probably no Latvians would exist.[87]

In Latvia the government, the local party and the KGB formed a cosy seamless web of Russian-speaking camaraderie, reinforced by periodic drinking and hunting parties and other bonding practices, and by the widespread illegal appropriation of dachas and other desired objects. Latvia's Communist elite was Russian-oriented, bereft of talent but suspicious and heavy-handed. In Estonia and Lithuania natives were much more prominent in the hierarchy of power and the KGB had to contend with structures which provided a counter-force to its optimal programs of repression. In Latvia its reach extended to every organization. It successfully infiltrated nationalist organizations. Some of these informers were widely known throughout Latvia but the more effective ones remained undiscovered. In Lithuania the KGB attempted to infiltrate the Catholic Church and to stop the Lithuanian "Chronicle." Except for a few minor gains they failed in their goal. In Latvia, the Catholic Church had to contend with a serious breaching of its lines.[88]

It is revealing that when the first opposition groups of the awakening period came on to the stage there was a widespread suspicion that they were organized or led by KGB confidence persons. This suspicion surfaced publicly over the origins of the People's Front in late 1990. The arguments focused more on exactly when the KGB had lost control of this organization rather than on the issue of whether it had been involved at the outset.[89] A determined minority in the *Pilsonu* (citizen) faction still maintains that the "whole thing," including the 1990 elections to parliament and the declaration of independence, was nothing but a very involved ploy of the KGB. Others counter that the *Pilsoni* themselves were KGB tools created to demolish the legitimacy of Latvian power.

Be that as it may, a legacy of suspicion remains because of the effectiveness of repression for those many decades. It could be noted, however, that the czarist secret police, the Okhrana, under General Sergei Zubatov infiltrated the Russian labor movement prior to the Russian Revolution so that many of the strike leaders turned out to be its own agents' including the famous Orthodox priest, Father George Gapon.[90] In the end Zubatov's agents played their game only too well and the mobilized masses could no longer be stopped.

The most intriguing reason for passiveness and even active cooperation with the oppressor lies in the psychological realm. Only recently have psychologists begun to explore the odd behavior of people faced by overwhelming power and the threat of death. The kidnapped daughter of an American press magnate, Patty Hearst, became seemingly a willing accomplice in the various bank robberies and other acts of violence initiated by her captors. This same behavior in the case of normal people in a prolonged armed robbery of a Swedish bank has led to the term "Stockholm syndrome" to describe this evidently perverse bonding between victim and outlaw. In Latvia, Soviet power was much more visible and ubiquitous. Latvia had more Red Army troops and was the headquarters for the Baltic military region. The KGB, as pointed out earlier, was much harsher and more forceful in its methods. Latvians were a minority under stress. Could all of this have created a powerful psychological impact leading to the unfolding of the Stockholm syndrome on a larger geographical scale?

Certainly Latvian society was entering a very dangerous period which left little energy for collective dynamism and vigorous opposition. During the three decades of accentuated repression, Latvians appear to have entered a period of collective stress, marked by a loosening of the social bonds that bind members of a nation together. Real problems facing the survival of the Latvian nation were no longer addressed in the media. It seems that people had become conditioned to accept the inevitability of the status quo and, in behaving according to the Stockholm syndrome, many in the intelligentsia had joined the ranks of the oppressors in voicing support for policies of Latvian denationalization. The Latvian nation was moving inexorably toward that point where national dissolution and extinction could become irreversible.

The two foremost and best-known authors in Latvia, Janis Peters and Mara Zalite, both voiced this concern in their addresses to the Latvian people at the beginning of the awakening. They claimed that if the third awakening did not succeed then Latvians would never rise again.[91] Both individuals were very conscious of the precariousness of the Latvian social fabric and were aware of the deep wounds in the Latvian collective psyche and spirit.

In spite of the process of denationalization within Latvia which continued into the mid 1980s, Latvians became the trailblazers for changes in national consciousness and republic sovereignty for most of the other Soviet republics. The impetus for this initiative appears to have included the sense of frustration and hopelessness induced by the continuously decreasing Latvian proportion in the population, the marginalization of Latvian language in everyday life and the rebirth of a new environmentalism which precipitated a much more negative view of Soviet developments in Latvia.

2   The Latvian national rebirth

On June 14, 1987, for the first time since the end of World War II, several thousand Latvians publicly commemorated the infamous Soviet deportations of innocent civilians to Siberia which had occurred forty-six years earlier, on June 14, 1941. The Helsinki '86 organizers wanted to reclaim Latvian history and reclaim the truth about the period of Soviet occupation and its officially expurgated "blank spots." This demonstration was a probe of the boundaries of glasnost and of the reaction of the forces of repression. The event became a major catalyst of the Latvian reawakening and emboldened other Balts to mark the next, and even more sensitive date, August 23, 1939 when the Molotov–Ribbentrop Pact with its secret protocols divided the Baltic and Eastern Europe into spheres of Nazi and Soviet control.

Latvians were the first to openly confront Communist authorities in the Baltic in 1987. They were the first to pick up the torch in a unique political relay race. While they were the trailblazers in 1987, the following year the Estonians took over leadership in testing and expanding the boundaries of glasnost and in confounding the system of repression. The Lithuanians appeared to be slow off the mark. But then, in 1989, Lithuanian dissent exploded, carrying that country to an unconditional declaration of separation from the USSR in March 1990, a declaration which, however, it partially retracted in the summer of that year.

Within Latvia itself the Helsinki '86 group was forced away from centre stage of the nationalist revival by the more legitimate, experienced and broader-based organization of the Latvian intelligentsia – the Latvian Writers' and Artists' Union. It helped strengthen and focus the newly resurgent national emotions and perceptions and guided this leaderless movement into the organizational confines of the Latvian People's Front (LPF). The People's Front then became the main moving force of Latvian political development and attracted to its ranks many of the best thinkers, organizers, planners and tacticians from the Communist establishment as well as from the "informals" who had not been coopted into the Party ranks. This assembly of unusually talented but politically dissimilar activists set aside their differences and pooled their resources to concentrate on gaining state autonomy and control over the levers of national survival. The dynamics of the process, however, led them into the front lines of the struggle for national independence.

The Latvian experience of confrontations with the regime was highly regarded by dissident groups in other republics. Ukrainian, Moldavan, Belorussian, Armenian, Georgian and Azerbaydzhan democrats and nationalists came to Riga to learn first hand the techniques of successful organization.[1] Among many Russian "empire savers," however, Latvia and *Pribaltika* were seen as the epicentre of their problems, with their ascribed powers for trouble-making growing almost to mythical proportions. The period of awakening in Latvia included an extremely wide and increasingly active mobilization of a majority of Latvians and to a lesser extent a fraction of non-Latvians. This level of high-intensity participation reached its culmination in the elections to the Latvian Supreme Council in March and April 1990. With the May 4 declaration of Latvia's sovereignty and of its desire to move towards *de facto* independence, there was a sharp drop in political activism. People returned once more to their jobs, families and gardens. In the following five years, political exhaustion was followed by political disillusionment, fractionalization and cynicism as well as by economic disarray and severe privation. The solidarity and shoulder-to-shoulder intimacy of the period of awakening have not been rekindled except for the brief period of the barricades in January 1991. Thus the three-year period 1987–90 can be seen as unique in its characteristics and in its accomplishments. Even though some critics describe this period somewhat disparagingly as the "singing revolution," it was a deeply touching time for hundreds of thousands of people and it has become an important turning-point in Latvian history and has affected the development of Latvian political culture. In that respect the abstention from violence was probably one of the greatest contributions.

The process of rebirth

The process of rebirth among Latvians began slowly at first, with a reassertion of their commitment to the Latvian heritage and a concern with ecological issues. The first in a chain of events that spurred rebirth was the revival of folk-culture groups.

The first folk-culture groups to be revived in Latvia were among the almost extinct Livs, an indigenous ethnic group whose cultural patterns closely resemble those of the Estonians. These groups had already been in existence for three years when a more formal Latvian-oriented folk-culture group was organized in 1976, calling itself the Skandinieki. According to one of its founders, Helmi Stalts, this group was inspired by the success of folk-culture groups in Estonia and Lithuania. Despite warnings that "they would not come to a good end," the Skandinieki began touring all regions of Latvia, reviving local songs, legends and traditions, and convincing people that "we have no right to rupture [our link] with the folk song, the folk wisdom that has been nurtured for hundreds of years, from generation to generation." They railed against the faint-heartedness of their generation and exhorted it to pass on the torch of Latvian consciousness to the younger generation, so that "our children will not have to curse us."[2] The folklore movement thus became part of the Latvian struggle for national self-esteem, for the reclaiming of one's roots and for the strengthening of the family through involvement of people of all ages in a common endeavor.

As folk-culture groups began to mushroom throughout Latvia during the early 1980s, they met strong resistance from the Latvian Ministry of Culture and various functionaries. According to Stalts, the officials' "fierce opposition" to these groups grew out of their perception that "beneath the song there lies something much more powerful." Folklore had the unique ability to awaken pride in being Latvian and to destroy inferiority complexes by highlighting the fact that Latvians as a nationality "also have significant values."[3]

At about the same time that folk-culture groups were becoming popular, a small movement dedicated to the repair of old churches and architectural monuments and to environmental protection began to impress people with its members' dedication and hard work. The founder of this movement, Arvids Ulme, a forester and poet in his mid-thirties, admitted later that "we clearly understood that our efforts were primarily directed at raising the consciousness of the general public."[4] (By 1987, this movement had grown into the Environmental Protection Club, one of the most visible activist organizations in Latvia, which later gave birth to many other organizations, including the Latvian National Independence Movement.) The first leader of the People's Front, Dainis Ivans, in October 1988 described the seminal role and effect of environmental groups:

In Latvia everything began with the movement to save the environment. The Environmental Protection Club was formed. Individual fighters arose – prophets who were guided by the conviction and unbending faith in the justice [of their cause]. Slowly ever more people joined and assembled around it. It seemed as if people were slowly arising from deep slumber. The people became active in the discussion of the most varied social and political questions. The big awakening had started.[5]

Then came the US-Soviet Conference on mutual relations organized by the Chautauqua Institution, the Eisenhower World Affairs Institute, and the USSR–USA Society, which took place September 15–19, 1986 in Jurmala, Latvia. US representatives at this meeting reaffirmed their government's commitment to a policy of non-recognition of Soviet annexation of the Baltic republics and criticized the Soviet Union's Baltic policy. By showing the Latvians that the world had not forgotten them, the US representatives helped lift spirits, heightened expectations for a reevaluation of Latvia's status within the USSR and added impetus to the national revival.[6]

In October of the same year, Latvians from all walks of life participated in a campaign to stop the construction of a hydroelectric dam on Latvia's largest and most cherished river, the Daugava. They feared that the project would be destructive of farmlands, animals, plants and rural settlements, and that it would disrupt the river's ecosystem. Popular mobilization was achieved by the independent initiatives of two men – journalist Dainis Ivans, then a thirty-two-year-old former school-teacher, who was later elected President of the People's Front, and Arturs Snips, a thirty-eight-year-old computer specialist and writer, who had worked at a hydroelectric station. Their article condemning the project appeared in the October 14, 1986 issue of the Latvian literary newspaper *Literatura un Maksla*. It energized a previously apathetic society, which responded with demonstrations, meetings, and tens of thousands of letters protesting about the dam. In early November 1987, the USSR Council of Ministers passed a decree to stop construction of the dam.[7] For the first time in nearly half a century, Latvians savored a collective success. The attitude of subservience and feeling of powerlessness began to dissipate as a new ebullience and hope permeated society, especially its younger members.

In 1987, Latvian activists became trailblazers within the Soviet Union, feeling out and even stretching the boundaries of glasnost with their calendar demonstrations. These demonstrations, which received extensive media coverage throughout the world, including the USSR, were seen by many in the West as the litmus test of Gorbachev's sincerity and seriousness in implementing liberalization. The demonstrations were organized by a small human rights group, formed in the summer of 1986 by three workers from the city of Liepaja, calling itself Helsinki '86. The purpose of the demonstrations was to commemorate publicly the events of June 14, 1941 (the mass deportation of Latvians to the Soviet Union), August 23, 1939 (the signing of the Molotov–Ribbentrop Pact) and November 18, 1918 (the proclamation of Latvian independence) – three turning-points in Latvian history that had been distorted or ignored in official publications.[8]

Helsinki '86 hoped that by commemorating these events, it could highlight the fact that an independent Latvia, founded in 1918, had been forcibly annexed by the Soviets in 1940 without the consent of the people and contrary to all tenets of international law, and that tens of thousands of Latvians had lost their lives in the gulags. It hoped thereby to undermine the legitimacy of Soviet rule in Latvia. Although Soviet authorities could readily blame Soviet deportations of Latvians on the excesses of Stalinism, they could hardly hide the fact that Hitler "gave away" the Baltic republics to Stalin, and that this set the stage for the Soviets' forcible incorporation of Latvia into the Soviet Union. It also hoped to discredit the official Soviet interpretation of Latvian history, namely that a socialist revolution in Latvia in 1940 had led to the voluntary incorporation of the republic into the Soviet Union.

The public commemorations of significant historic events precipitated systematic harassment of demonstrators by authorities, particularly during the celebration of Independence Day. Nevertheless, the demonstrators persisted, displaying ingenuity and courage.

The calendar demonstrations of 1987 were mostly organized by the Latvian working-class youth, without much support from the intelligentsia. They became widely publicized and laid the foundations for the coming mass movements that developed in Latvia and the other Baltic republics. They were certainly a catalyst in the reawakening of the Latvian intelligentsia, which by the spring of 1988 took on the leading role in articulating Latvian national grievances. By bringing about a sense of national rebirth among all sectors of society, the organization at the forefront of these demonstrations, Helsinki '86, eventually forced the Communist Party to reconsider its interpretation of Latvian history and its attitude to the demonstrations. By 1988, when demonstrations were repeated on the same three dates, some more progressive Party officials and prominent Party media commentators stood shoulder to shoulder with the demonstrators, even though they came from opposite ends of the political spectrum. On November 18, 1988, an officially sanctioned concert was held in the theatre where Latvia's independence had been declared seventy years earlier.[9]

Intellectual activism

A major sign of renewed public activism on the part of the intelligentsia came on March 3, 1988 during an executive meeting of the Latvian creative unions. The meeting had been called to discuss the tragic consequences of Stalinism in Latvia and the responsibility of the creative intelligentsia in dealing with this issue. The chairman, Janis Peters, invited the artistic community to explore the subtler manifestations of Stalinism, which aims to "prevent independent thinking, forbid an attachment to a nation and a language and ... destroy historical memory and cultural heritage." As a result of this meeting, two commissions were created for the purpose of commemorating and rehabilitating victims of the personality cult, that is, of Stalinism.[10]

Three weeks later, on March 25, the creative unions organized a widely publicized demonstration at the Cemetery of the Brethren to commemorate the 1949 deportations of more than 43,000 Latvians to Siberia. This demonstration effectively overshadowed a parallel demonstration at the Freedom Monument organized by the more radical Helsinki '86 and other "informal" groups that had led the previous three calendar events. It should be noted, however, that organizers of the demonstration at the Freedom Monument were at a disadvantage: not only were many of them, notably those heading the human rights groups, harassed by the KGB and militia and prevented from attending the event, but also their demonstration was not accorded the publicity given by the media to the one organized by the creative unions.

Defining themselves as the moderate opposition, the creative unions were able to both fulfill grass-roots desires for self-expression and assuage Communist Party apprehensions concerning their program. As a result, they succeeded in providing an officially sanctioned demonstration at the cemetery that people could attend without fear of possible consequences. The media and union organizers worked together to elicit a positive mood at the demonstration and to stress the need for mutual support, healing and national bonding. More than 25,000 people from all walks of life joined a procession, carrying candles and expressing long-suppressed grief.[11] Another step on the road to psychological recovery had been taken.

The creative intelligentsia opted for the road to political emancipation several months later at the June 1–2, 1988 Latvian Writers' Union plenum which followed on the heels of a similar plenum in Estonia. Attended by the leaders of other creative unions and by widely respected intellectuals, the plenum had been called to formulate a response to the theses drafted for the Nineteenth CPSU Conference, scheduled for the end of the month in Moscow. The speeches delivered by several dozen prominent intellectuals at this gathering were extremely blunt and crossed a threshold of political expression and openness not breached at an official gathering in Latvia for over half a century. These speeches were later published in Latvian newspapers together with the plenum's daring resolution that soon became a blueprint for subsequent national demands in the republic.[12] This resolution, of many subheadings, demanded the implementation of human and nationality rights and asked for the recognition of Latvia as a sovereign and national state with its own symbols but still within the Soviet federation. It demanded a review of critical turning-points in recent Latvian history and especially of the incorporation of Latvia into the USSR. Language and ecological issues were also prominent in this document expressing formerly repressed Latvian collective aspirations.

The People's Front

The plenum resolution spurred a coalition of seventeen nationally prominent intellectuals, clergymen and human rights activists, many from the Helsinki '86 group, to form on June 21, 1988 an organizing committee for a Latvian People's Front. However, Peters and the leadership of the creative unions moved quickly to thwart this effort and to put organizational initiative in the hands of individuals less visibly affiliated with protest and opposition groups. Later, the President of the People's Front, Ivans, would explain the situation thus: "The first variant was signed in the name of Helsinki '86 and other informal groups. My signature was also there. But evidently someone did not like the surnames and organizations listed under this invitation. Hence a 'new' document was published – in reality the same text only with the signatures of different people."[13] Under the guidance of a collective "brains trust" led by Peters, mobilization was begun at the grass-roots level and People's Front support groups were created during the summer months. New sectors of the intelligentsia were tapped, with prominent lawyers, philosophers, sociologists and economists being increasingly recruited for the People's Front.[14]

The People's Front was not meant to replace already-existing organizations, but to serve as an umbrella organization for them. Indeed, the various organizations and informal groups in Latvia helped shape the profile of the People's Front. Foremost among them were the Latvian Environmental Protection Club (VAK), or the Green Movement as it is often called, the then newly formed Latvian National Independence Movement, and Helsinki '86. During the months of the Front's gestation, the VAK and the Latvian National Independence Movement organized many consciousness-raising events, which helped create a new spirit of activism.

The VAK, which for several years had devoted its time mostly to improving the environment and refurbishing cultural monuments, became more politicized in 1988. Several of its activities gained national recognition, and respect for the movement grew among a wide circle of Latvians.

Also active during the Front's gestation was the Latvian National Independence Movement. Many of its members had worked underground for several years and were members of VAK. On June 17, 1988, several of these individuals met to debate the founding of the movement. On July 10, the movement held an open meeting at the Arcadia Gardens in Riga to attract new members and greater public support. The Voice of America and Radio Free Europe had carried news of the impending meeting, and as a result many people attended the meeting to learn more about this organization's platform. Several hundred people then joined the Latvian National Independence Movement. The event was covered by Soviet Latvian radio and television.

The most visible leader of the independence movement was Eduards Berklavs, the former vice-chairman of the Council of Ministers who had been purged in 1959 because of his supposed "Latvian nationalism."

For its part, Helsinki '86 was also active during this period. However, its ranks had split into several factions, and a number of its founding members had been forced by the authorities to emigrate to the West.

The founding congress of the People's Front, originally planned for the very beginning of October, took place on October 8–9 so as not to coincide with a similar Estonian congress in Tallinn.[15] On the eve of the congress, a rally attracting several hundred thousand people was held in Mezaparks and a euphoric mood enveloped many participants. The mood was created by the sight of countless Latvian national flags and the sound of patriotic speeches and long-forbidden songs.[16] For the first time since Communist rule was introduced in Latvia, authorities granted permission for a church service in the Domas Cathedral. The service was held on the second day and was broadcast on radio and television.[17] The two young ministers who officiated at the event, Juris Rubenis and Modris Plate, were members of the religious rights organization Rebirth and Renewal, and active supporters of the People's Front. Their actions in organizing this religious event were greatly opposed by the timorous old-guard Lutheran leadership.

The more than a thousand delegates elected by the various organizations to attend the congress represented over 110,000 subscribing members of diverse social origins and political beliefs. About one-third were Communist Party members; the others came from such organizations as the Environmental Protection Club, Helsinki '86, the Latvian National Independence Movement, and Rebirth and Renewal. The occupational background of the delegates was varied as well: 20 percent were engineers and mechanics; 16 percent were teachers and professors; another 16 percent were factory workers and drivers; 3 percent were journalists; another 3 percent were cultural workers; and 2 percent were artists.[18] As could be expected, the overwhelming majority of participants were Latvians.

Among the achievements of the congress was the passage of several resolutions and the election of a Governing Council consisting of a hundred representatives. The resolutions incorporated most of the ideas promoted by the creative unions in early June, but included several additions, among them a call for Latvian "economic sovereignty" within an integrated Baltic region and the abolition of all special privileges for high-ranking officials.[19] Soon after the congress, the Governing Council elected a thirteen-member board with Dainis Ivans as president. They also elected chairmen for nineteen specialized committees and an executive chairman.[20]

The proceedings of the congress were televised and precipitated bitter reactions from those comfortable with the status quo. Taking their cue from similar movements in Estonia, many opponents of the Latvian revival (mostly Russian-speakers) banded together to create the Latvian International Working People's Front – or "Interfront" – to counter what they perceived to be aberrations from traditional party norms and previously "ideal" ethnic relations.[21]

Paradoxically the more active the Interfront became, the more it helped mobilize Latvians and other ethnic groups, especially in rural areas, to join the People's Front. As one would expect, the two organizations attracted support from different linguistic groups. A poll taken in late 1988 indicated that 48 percent of Russians in Latvia expressed a "need" for the Interfront, compared to 6 percent of Latvians. The People's Front enjoyed the support of 74 percent of all Latvians, but of only 10 percent of Russians in the republic.[22]

Early challenges

The elections of the All Union Congress of People's Deputies, held in the spring of 1989, offered an opportunity for the Front to extend its political influence. Its coordination and information efforts helped elect a majority of reformist candidates.[23] The message of strength sent to those who opposed the Latvian reawakening was unmistakeable. For many in the leadership, however, this was only a successful rehearsal for the coming elections to the republic's Supreme Soviet.

Greater Baltic solidarity and cooperation were forged at what has been considered an "historically significant" assembly of the leadership of the three Baltic popular fronts in Tallinn, May 13–14, 1989.[24] Among the many participants were representatives from almost all the democratic movements and organizations in the USSR. Delegates from Hungary, Czechoslovakia, Bulgaria, Finland, Sweden and West Germany, as well as numerous foreign and Soviet correspondents, were witnesses to this "lesson in parliamentary discussions."[25]

The assembly produced seven radically worded and jointly signed declarations outlining the goals and orientations of the three movements. These declarations called for the implementation of genuine economic independence, the condemnation of Soviet policies in 1939 and 1940, and the denunciation of Stalinist genocide against the Baltic states. They were supplemented by promises of cooperation with other democratic movements of the USSR and by statements of concern for the Karabakh Committee, whose members had been arrested. A key declaration spelled out the Baltic states' "aspirations" for sovereignty in a "neutral and demilitarized Baltic-Scandinavia."[26]

The declarations represented the first agreement in Soviet history to be signed by independent groups from three Soviet republics without the participation of Moscow. According to Esther Fein in the *New York Times*, on May 15, 1989, "the action taken today . . . marks the first time these groups have appealed for an international forum to decide their status, basing their claims on the illegality of the Stalin–Hitler pact." The leader of the Latvian People's Front in his Tallinn speech minced no words in assessing the achievements of this Baltic Assembly: "We have built the foundations for a common Baltic home, the home we will build in the future; and with the documents approved today we have undermined the foundations of another dwelling; this dwelling is called totalitarian imperialism."[27]

A Soviet doctor of jurisprudence, Reyn Myullerson, implied in an article in *Pravda* that the Tallinn resolutions were aimed at the complete separation of the three republics from the Soviet Union.[28] His analysis was insightful.

Political radicalization

The political program of various organizations in Latvia became radicalized in late spring of 1989. Setting the new tone was the Latvian National Independence Movement. Its founding program adopted in February 1989 was deemed to be anti-constitutional by Latvian Communist authorities. Consequently an extraordinary congress was called three months later to "rectify" the points of discord. While some cosmetic changes were introduced, the movement's basic orientation to

Latvian independence remained unaffected. This congress received wide television and press coverage and inspired thousands of viewers to join the organization. More importantly the articulate stand of the Independence Movement was a catalyst for the People's Front executive. On May 31, the board of the LPF voted unanimously to publish an appeal calling for a discussion of complete independence for Latvia. This appeal appeared on the front page of the June 21, 1989 issue of *Padomju Jaunatne* together with a preamble explaining the reasons for this serious step.

According to the appeal, Latvian attempts to find true accommodation for their republic within the Soviet federation were being stymied by very powerful centralizing political, economic and ideological forces, as well as by reactionaries within the republic who were prepared to use brute force (as had been done in April in Tbilisi, Georgia) in order to maintain the status quo. The appeal also pointed out that the proceedings of the USSR Congress of People's Deputies highlighted the tremendous gap between what the conservative majority would allow and what the Latvian republic was demanding.

The hundred-member Governing Council of the People's Front ratified the board's appeal on June 10. The ratification caught the Communist Party by surprise. Gorbunovs denounced the action, arguing that only the government had a right to initiate referenda and that the appeal went directly against the Front's own founding documents.[29] Nevertheless, the appeal to independence enjoyed wide resonance in the Latvian population.

The goal of the restoration of Latvian independence was fully legitimized by the Second Congress of the People's Front which met on October 7–8, 1989. Over a thousand delegates voted for this measure as well as the ideals of a parliamentary democracy and of a mixed market economy. At this point there was no turning back to anything less than full independence unless, of course, force and terror were brought in by the Communist rulers.

The Communist Party of Latvia

The lack of bloodshed on the road to independence can be partly attributed to the leadership and the reform-minded section of the Latvian Communist Party. Many Party members, especially among Latvians, became strong reformists affected by the overall mood of change prevailing in the rest of the nation and by the unfolding developments in Eastern Europe. They wanted to keep up with and even preempt the new popular demands in the hope of modernizing and revitalizing a spiritless and ossified organization. Many of their collea-gues, especially within the majority Russian-speaking group, were much more inclined to resist changes and continue the traditional – and for them comfortable – Soviet lifestyle and Russian dominance. It should be noted that Latvians formed only 39 percent of the Latvian CP. Initially the Latvian Communist Party strained to accommodate both its Latvian-oriented reformist members and its Russian-oriented tradition-alists, but this did not satisfy either faction. Flare-ups between the two groups surfaced during selection of delegates for the Nineteenth CPSU Conference and in the Latvian Communist Party's Central Committee plenum of June 18, 1988.[30]

The Latvian Party leaders Janis Vagris, Anatolijs Gorbunovs, Vilnis Bresis and Ivars Kezbers were able to mobilize reformers in the Party-controlled Supreme Soviet of Latvia to effectively introduce many laws and regulations to accommodate Latvian cultural, linguistic and demo-graphic demands. The reformers introduced a regulation to limit further in-migration from other republics; they helped pass a language law which made Latvian the official language of the republic and envisaged the broadening of Latvian language use in schools, government services and commerce. They legalized the old symbols of independence such as the flag and anthem of independent Latvia and later made them the official symbols of the state. As well, they introduced former national holidays including St. John's Day (June 24), Independence Day (November 18) and Christmas. They fought with Moscow for economic sovereignty for Latvia. Latvia was the first to introduce alternatives to the Soviet military draft. It also led the way in starting ethnic schools for many of its minorities.[31]

According to Ivans, the President of the People's Front at this time, there was a great deal of informal cooperation between the Front and the Latvian-oriented section of the Communist Party leadership. Two individuals in particular, Vagris and Bresis, were kept informed on the struggles within the Party, and when required the Front organized wide-spread demonstrations to press the stagnant wing of the Party into accepting innovations.[32] To be sure, part of the success in carrying through the controversial reforms rested on the still-existing notions of party discipline. This, however, was eroding rapidly at both ends of the spectrum.

Influenced no doubt by the clear actions of the Lithuanian CP and by the rapidly evolving attitude of Latvian society, a group of eight reformist Communists from the Central Committee and thirty-two local Party secretaries publicized an appeal "to Latvian Communists" on No-vember 27, 1989 which called for a revolution in the traditional guiding concepts of the Soviet party and in the organization of the USSR.[33] These reformist pioneers wanted nothing less than the wholesale restructuring of values which had hitherto underlain the CPSU. They demanded a politically, economically and organizationally independent Latvian CP which would have the right to form relationships with other Communist parties on the basis of mutual respect and equality. The Latvian CP was to renounce its constitutional guarantees on the monopoly of power and become an integral part of the parliamentary Latvian state system. Internally, the paralysis of centralization and centrally based discipline had to be replaced by consensus, freedom of discussion, guarantee of minority rights and the doing away of the existing *nomenklatura* system. The appeal's greatest impact for most Latvians, however, was its call for an independent and democratic (although still socialist) Latvia formed in accordance with the will of the nation. The appeal concluded with a demand for a spring 1990 convocation of the Latvian CP Congress, because each day of delay, it was claimed, only helped to slow down the pace of reconstruction of society.[34]

This appeal had a wide resonance within the Latvian wing of the Party. There was an increase in the polarization of what reformists called the *gaisie speki* (the bright forces) and the *tumsie speki* (the dark forces). An active attempt to organize the "bright forces" was initiated by the Latvian CP Third Secretary, Ivars Kezbers, who called several meetings independent of the regular Party hierarchy and without its overt blessing. In spite of these efforts, the Communist Party was losing its credibility among Latvians, and several prominent members, including Dainis Ivans, President of the People's Front, publicly called for the self-liquidation of the Party. In the view of these latter reformers, all property of the Party, the whole of which had been illegally obtained at the expense of the people, should be handed over to the Latvian state to end the struggle between the two Party wings. Given its links to the CPSU and its large apparatus, the continued existence of the Party was deemed to be a potential threat and could "at any time" endanger Latvian democracy, independence and unity.[35]

The defection of Ivans and other outstanding personalities from the Party pushed the reformers to more resolute action. Within three weeks of Ivans' exit from the Party on February 24, 1990, over one thousand reformist delegates met in Riga to consider the founding of an independent communist party. At this conference, discussions focused on two alternatives for action. Should the break from the CPSU be accomplished right away or by degrees, that is, should the Latvian party follow the example of Lithuania or the more measured pace of Estonia? The supporters of a rapid break won. They argued that any delays would lead to the loss of many more members and that the reformists had no hope of attaining changes at the regular Party Congress against an antagonistic majority. The date for the founding congress was set for April 14, 1990.[36] Soon thereafter, on March 6, the Latvian CP Central Committee Plenum decided to hold the Twenty-fifth Party Congress on April 6 to try to pre-empt the need for a parallel communist party by passing radical resolutions of its own.[37]

First Secretary Janis Vagris, in an interview prior to the congress, expressed his opposition to the "slamming of doors" against the CPSU because "we could also lose many powerful levers of influence which could help in the advance towards Latvia's independence." In a very prescient analysis he dismissed the future prospects for a new breakaway communist party which in his view could obtain support neither from the countryside nor from the working class. It certainly would not attract the 40,000 Party members within the ranks of the Latvian People's Front. A dependence only on the urban intelligentsia, however, would probably not "affect the political life of the republic." His own position was a compromise envisaging the activation of true territorial federalism principles within a union of Soviet communist parties.[38]

The Twenty-fifth Congress of the Latvian CP only hastened the departure of the reformists from Party ranks. The conservative wing under the guidance of the Riga section and having control over a majority of delegates was able to set the tone for this congress. After failing to find compromise solutions the reform wing, composed of 263 delegates (one-third of the total), walked out never to return to the fold of the Latvian CP. The remaining 518 delegates chose Alfreds Rubiks, a hardliner and a Latvian of Polish origin, as First Secretary.[39]

Meanwhile on April 14 the "national" communists held their own congress, composed of 90 percent Latvian delegates, and elected the former Ideological Secretary, Ivars Kezbers, as leader.[40] Now Latvia had two communist parties: the Communist Party of Latvia and the Independent Communist Party of Latvia. The remnant of the old party was preponderantly non-Latvian and many in its top leadership were Russified Latvians. Rubiks' party of hardliners hastened to excommunicate officially the leadership of the Independent Communist Party. Kezbers, on the other hand, sent a complaint to Gorbachev claiming that the other party was composed of stagnants opposed not merely to perestroika, but also to the USSR General Secretary himself. The Independent Party was also worried about the fair division of property, funds and printing presses.

The split resulted in front-page resolutions by both parties. Long articles by both sides explained why "compromise was impossible." The

Russian-language press gave more space to Rubiks' party while the Latvian press printed more articles from the "independents."

Rubiks maintained control of the *apparat*. He also began to consolidate his position by neutralizing or taking control of reformist organs or structures within or under the aegis of the Latvian CP. For example, the Riga city newspaper, *Rigas Balss*, was shut down temporarily because its ideology was found to deviate from that of the conservative Latvian CP. Under the leadership of Rubiks the Party effectively consolidated and mobilized its forces to counter the inroads of the "national" communists and of the People's Front.

Elections for independence

March 17, 1990 was set as the date for the first round of elections to the Latvian Supreme Soviet. Latvian organizers realized the significance of these elections. A failure to garner two-thirds support for the cause of independence would be seen as a traumatic outcome for Latvian survival as demonstrated forcibly by the front page of the LPF weekly newspaper *Atmoda*: "Now or Never." In his editorial in this same newspaper the chairman of the LPF, Dainis Ivans, noted that the alternative to their victory was "totalitarianism and the strengthening of Party authoritarianism in Latvia." He concluded with the rousing appeal: "Let us vote for freedom, let us vote for the future, believing in and trusting each other. May God help us in this responsible moment and day."[41] Never before had Latvians gone out in such numbers to work for an election. Mass rallies and concerts were held to maintain the enthusiasm of workers. The Latvian media provided a detailed and unremitting coverage of LPF candidates and opinions.

The election campaign was heated and emotional. The LPF tried to describe the tragedy if a two-thirds majority was not achieved whereas the opposition tried to spread panic among non-Latvians, suggesting various forms of nationalist retribution including forced evacuation to Russia would be instituted if the Latvian "nationalist" group won.

On average 1.7 candidates contested the vote in 201 electoral divisions. In the first round, 170 deputies received a majority and were elected, 14 divisions had to organize run-off elections, and 16 had to reopen nominations for new elections. (One further division was thought to have suffered illegal practices and was being investigated.) By May 8, 1990 the Electoral Mandate Commission was able to offer profiles of 197 elected deputies.

Only fifteen of the deputies had previously served in the Supreme Soviet of Latvia, an eloquent testimonial that the old guard had been thoroughly trounced and replaced. This was a body of highly educated, middle-aged men: There were only 11 women; 180 of the deputies had a tertiary-level education; and only 6 were under the age of 30. The most popular age groups were 30 to 40 (54), 40 to 50 (59) and 50 to 60 (68). The most common professions were engineering (23), law (16), economics (13), journalism (12) and medicine (9). Ethnic origin was also diverse: 138 Latvians (70 percent), 42 Russians (21 percent), 8 Ukrainians, 3 Jews, 2 Belorussians and one each from Polish, Greek and German roots.[42]

On May 4 the vote for Latvian independence was watched with bated breath by most Latvians, because right up to the final tally there had not been a clear assurance of a two-thirds majority. While 134 had been the critical number required the resolution on Latvian independence received support from 138 deputies. Soon thereafter the Latvian Supreme Council chose Ivars Godmanis as Chairman of the Council of Ministers and Anatolijs Gorbunovs as Chairman of the Presidium.

This election in Latvia proved to be a relatively democratic contest in spite of the active participation of the army of occupation. One could observe many of the same rhetorical excesses and image manipulation techniques often found in veteran democracies in the West. Most significantly this election did provide a mechanism for the smooth replacement of old establishment elites by new individuals, more oriented to democracy and independence.

The general impact of rebirth

Within three years the Latvian reawakening had deeply affected many areas of life and changed old relationships. Without a doubt, its most significant impact was to strengthen Latvian national consciousness and pride. The reintroduction of independent Latvia's national symbols; the rehabilitation of many formerly discredited authors, politicians, scientists and other national figures; the reinterpretation of Latvian history – especially of the independence period; the public recognition of the sufferings of Latvian deportees in Siberia and of all those maligned by Stalin's system of terror; and hundreds of smaller developments all created a Latvian population conscious of its own status as a recognized European nation with unquestionable rights to its own sovereign state.

While the legitimacy of Latvian nationhood grew, the legitimacy of Soviet power among Latvians plummeted, mostly because of revelations about the secret protocol to the Molotov–Ribbentrop Pact and about the subsequent occupation and annexation of the Baltic republics. These revelations amply demonstrated to middle-aged and younger generations the illegality of Soviet control over the republic and of policies of Sovietization. A further blow to Soviet legitimacy was Latvian exposure to Western culture and its standard of living which called into question the credibility of Soviet boasts of economic, scientific and other achievements. The closing in the summer of 1988 of most resort beaches in Jurmala, the incredible bureaucratic bungling of the construction of even minimal purification devices for Riga, and the general lack of progress in solving acute air and water contamination problems throughout the republic served as powerful testimonies that the Soviet system did not work.

The veritable mushrooming of independent societies, movements and groups was another result of the national revival. The organizations with the greatest potential significance for the future were perhaps the ones representing minority ethnic groups in the republic. The People's Front's initiation and support of Jewish, Polish, Ukrainian, Belorussian, Gypsy and other cultural societies and clubs, and Interfront's snubbing of them, caused fissures within the "Russian-speaking" group and led to the formation of less homogeneous and reactionary groupings within its ranks.

Freedom of the press is a cornerstone of true democracy and a bastion against totalitarianism. The majority of the media in Latvia became increasingly iconoclastic and broadened the scope of their coverage. Tolerance of pluralism created more favorable conditions for religion. The mainstream press carried numerous articles and interviews on religion, reflecting a budding interest in man's "spirituality." Bible studies were introduced in certain schools, and Christmas and Easter were officially recognized once more, increasing the visibility of religion. Young clergymen successfully challenged and helped restructure a formerly moribund Lutheran Church. The People's Front emerged as a major source of support for freedom of conscience. The religious publication it initiated, *Svetdienas Rits* (Sunday Morning), was widely disseminated and complemented the journals published by the Lutheran and Catholic churches.

Contacts and interaction with the West also boomed, and became a major factor in educating Latvians about alternative concepts of politics, economics and human rights. There was a tremendous growth in the interaction levels with Latvians abroad.

The psychological attitude of Latvians as a nation very definitely improved, especially as fears of imminent assimilation abated. However, the gains of Latvians in the areas of their greatest insecurities were often perceived as threats by the non-Latvians, unwillingly confronted with formidable but as yet ill-defined changes in every aspect of their lives.

Impact of awakening on non-Latvians

The awakening led to a reversal of direction in three main areas of Latvian vulnerability: immigration, language and cultural-historical heritage. This sudden reversal, however, had a serious impact on the Russian-speaking cohorts within Latvia. The reassertion of Latvian national rights changed the accepted rules of the game for hundreds of thousands of individuals who had settled in what to them was merely another region of the USSR to seek a better life for themselves and their families. Moreover, until recently their presence had been officially welcomed.

The Russian-speaking group had never felt the need to organize itself as a minority lobbying for specific demands and concessions. And for good reason. The republic's Communist government met most of their needs, and besides, their major orientation was to Moscow rather than to Riga. They saw themselves as a part of the majority of Russians in the USSR and not as a minority group in Latvia.

The Russian-speaking collectivity was very diverse in its ethnic origins and in many of its traditions and orientations. The ethnic Russian group itself was not united politically, nor was it united in its attitude to Latvian demands and to independence. One of the clearest lines of demarcation in 1990 was correlated with the length of residence in Latvia. Those who had been born in the republic or who had been living there several decades were much more sympathetic to Latvian aspirations.[43]

The biggest cleavage among the 1.28 million non-Latvians by 1990 was without doubt a political one. The intransigent and reactionary wing rooted in several overlapping organizations including Interfront and the Latvian Communist Party attracted between 20 and 30 percent of all non-Latvians. At the opposite end of the spectrum and of about equal size were those supporting the Latvian People's Front; among these were many intellectuals and democrats. The largest group, in the middle, found itself swayed by events and by the appeals of one or the other group.

It is important to note that the widespread fluency in Russian of Latvians allowed for continual communication between people of different groups. This linguistic bridge mitigated the extremes of both the purist revival groups and the Russian-speaking reactionary saviors of the empire. As well, certain individuals in leadership positions, such as Gorbunovs, who were trusted by both Latvian and non-Latvian groups helped to ease tensions.

Ethnic tensions aroused at the beginning of the period of awakening had subsided significantly by the end of that period in 1990. At this time as well, there appeared to be a weakening of purist and extremist sentiments and of their representative organizations in the republic's population. Both the International Front, on one side, and the Latvian Citizens' Committee, on the other, lost considerable appeal.

Conclusion

The period of awakening ended the apathy of hundreds of thousands of people. Its promises of peaceful change toward independence brought Latvians together in a rare embrace of solidarity. The visions of the future of the Latvians were highly optimistic. The belief in their own powers was almost limitless. The Latvian nation saw itself recognized on the world stage and reflected in the world media. It was credited with having started the dissolution of the Soviet empire. Its spokesmen were sought out by international reporters to comment almost blow by blow on the significance of one action or change after another. The Latvian horizon was expanding at a very rapid pace. The future held the promise of political independence, wise government management, economic abundance and mutual trust. It was a period of emotional soaring; it brought the opportunity of seeing the outer world and its glittering and seductive plenitude, either directly or with the help of uncensored television and journals. Soon it was hoped Latvia would be part of the West again and all of the latter's trappings would surely follow.

The non-Latvians were at first perplexed and antagonistic toward the changes occurring around them. In a surprisingly short period the majority of them adapted to the new political circumstances. Their vision of the future, however, was much less optimistic.

The two large linguistic groups began the new period of transition to sovereignty on May 4, 1990 with differing agendas and priorities, but the significant split among the Russian-speakers allowed for new and powerful coalitions in the struggles against Moscow. Once power was transferred from the Communist-directed Supreme Soviet to the independence-minded Latvian Supreme Council, Latvians quickly returned to the routine of everyday life. Their future now was in the hands of a Latvian-dominated legislature and cabinet, and the expectation was that they would lead Latvia back to Europe, back to civilization. The problems along this road were not yet grasped or foreseen.

3   Regaining independence – establishing democracy

The strategy of independence

The election of the Latvian Supreme Council did not by itself guarantee independence for Latvia but it did create a feeling among most Latvians that a major step had been taken in a process whose conclusion could only be independence. The turbulent period leading up to the elections was in itself an important catalyst in changing the goals and expectations of most people. Within the span of one year, from June 1989 to June 1990, support for unconditional independence among Latvians rose dramatically from 55 to 85 percent. This support continued to increase so that by March 1991 it had reached 94 percent.[1] There was very little sentiment within the indigenous Latvian population for any compromises short of independence. Disillusionment with the USSR had gone too far and the vision of self-rule was too appealing for Latvians to content themselves with anything less than a final break with the empire. Among non-Latvians, however, support for independence in June 1989 was only 9 percent, rising threefold to 26 percent by June 1990 and to 38 percent by March 1991.[2]

In spite of the firm commitment to independence most Latvians expected this change to happen gradually over a period of several years, and the general public as well as the Latvian political leadership was taken by surprise at the rapid developments following the attempted coup of August 1991. It is important to note, however, that even without the failed coup the probability of attaining independence was high because of the general pace of developments within the USSR and, most importantly, because of the collective strategy pursued by the Latvian People's Front and other allied organizations, a strategy which they themselves designated as "soliti pa solitim" or one small step at a time. This strategy entailed the application of constant pressure and the acceptance of limited moves to expand the perimeter of sovereignty without provoking Moscow into a full-scale retaliation or reversal of gains already made.

The strategists of the Front used many points of leverage to achieve their goals and neutralize or blunt Moscow's reactions. One of the most important ones was the exploitation of Gorbachev's liberal policies and his attempts to build a new image for the USSR in the world. In the context of perestroika and glasnost Latvian activists were able to reach the world media and important world leaders and explain the nature of their demands and counter the missives from Moscow's "agitprop" department. Together with other Balts they were on the front lines of change, hence they were newsworthy. Some of their leading personalities were sought out by the media and by Western politicians. The Balts also had an articulate constituency of *émigré* relatives in leading Western countries and particularly in the USA. They were able to mobilize support from Western legislatures and leaders, thus threatening limits on Soviet countermoves.[3]

Of all the fifteen republics in the USSR, the three Baltic ones were treated as a special case by most world countries because their forcible annexation into the USSR in 1940 had not been recognized as legal or *de jure*.

The indigenous population of Latvia had also been mobilized and unified to a remarkable degree. Strategic demonstrations organized by the People's Front at critical turning-points in political relations between Latvia and Moscow were able to attract impressive numbers, sometimes surpassing half a million people. On many occasions, as well, the entire Baltic cooperated to send strong signals to Moscow. One of the most impressive demonstrations, widely covered in the West, was the organization of the "Baltic Way" human chain on August 23, 1989 which linked over 2 million people from Tallinn, Estonia, through Riga to Vilnius in Lithuania. Petitions with over a million signatures in Latvia alone strengthened the image of resolve.[4] All these widespread popular actions made it clear to Moscow that limited clampdowns against small groups of individuals would not be sufficient to curtail the moves to independence. Only a frontal large-scale military assault could have possibly worked in the short run to neutralize Baltic activism, but this was not an option the Kremlin leadership under Gorbachev wanted to pursue at the time. Many hardliners in Moscow, however, did suggest exactly such a course of action to preserve the empire. At times these hardliners had great influence in forging Moscow's policies, but the countering influence of democratic forces within Russia and other republics was growing. These forces for change supported the right of the Baltic republics to choose their own future including the choice of sovereignty, and, most importantly, they firmly opposed the use of violence. The Second Congress of the USSR Democratic Union which was held in Jurmala, Latvia in January 1989 clearly supported the right of the Baltic nations to determine their state structures and their sovereignty.

An unexpectedly strong ally for the Baltic cause of independence was Boris Yeltsin. Yeltsin, as newly elected leader of the Russian Congress of People's Deputies, initiated the process of direct negotiations with Baltic leaders on a broad range of topics. On August 1, 1990 Yeltsin spoke before the Latvian Supreme Council and stressed that "Russia has taken a stand next to the Baltic States, and the center will have to take this into account."[5] His most critical intervention occurred during the January 1991 armed assaults in Latvia and Lithuania when he called on Russian soldiers not to fire at civilians. He also personally went to Tallinn in the middle of this crisis on January 13, to sign agreements accepting Estonian and Latvian sovereignty and calling for an international conference on the Baltic crisis. Agreements with Lithuania were signed later.[6]

The elected Latvian representatives in the USSR Congress of People's Deputies, together with the other Baltic deputies, were another force of change. They were able adeptly to represent and argue for greater Baltic political and economic autonomy in a forum which was televised for public viewing throughout the USSR. Being in the centre of controversy these deputies also had many opportunities to explain the Baltic point of view to the central Soviet media. One of the major achievements of the Baltic deputies was to initiate the creation of a commission to investigate the details and legality of the Molotov–Ribbentrop Pact of August 23, 1939.

While the Balts on their own had been able to change many of the traditional bonds of empire, their example and that of Eastern Europe affected many other regions of the USSR and together these newly awakened republics with a nascent or refurbished national consciousness were a power that could no longer be contained by existing appeals to empire solidarity and Communist unity. The mythology which had bound the empire together was being battered by new revelations and new channels of information. Gorbachev's removal of the curtain of isolation exposed the gaps between claimed socialist achievements and socialist reality.

Within Latvia it is clear that the old Latvian SSR Supreme Soviet was an important catalyst for change because its vestigial institutional levers of power were reactivated by a reform-minded group within the leadership of the Latvian Communist Party. Indeed, a large part of the agenda of this body of the *ancien régime* was set by the People's Front. The leader of this Front, Dainis Ivans, rightly pointed out that by the latter part of 1989 Latvia had two governments, "the nominal power of the Communist Party and old structures and the real power of the People's Front."[7]

The Latvian SSR Supreme Soviet, however, had many limitations because of its dependence on Communist Party ideology and discipline. The eventual split in the Party in the spring of 1990 between the nationalist-oriented faction and the more numerous hardliners would have paved the way for a return of this institution to the forces of reaction. Thus, the election of the new parliament, the Latvian Supreme Council, which excluded the hardline Communists from power, preempted the return to power of the "empire savers," and allowed the much fuller and more sophisticated use of an institution which held legitimacy, at least initially, among the power-wielders in Moscow and the Latvian population. Without a doubt the new Latvian Supreme Council became the main vehicle for the achievement of independence.

The Latvian Supreme Council as instrument of independence

The elections of March–April 1990 significantly changed the configuration of power in favor of independence forces. The People's Front had won a clear majority of seats and its only opposition came from the predominantly Russian-speaking and reactionary *Ravnopravie* (Equal Rights Party). Most significantly, the opposition from the radical nationalist Citizens' Committee abated because this organization was now seen as redundant for Latvian aspirations. It had previously garnered over a million signatures of support for its cause because people were afraid that the institutional channels for independence could be blocked or thwarted. The Committee provided a back-up position. Indeed, the vote on independence was barely above the required two-thirds margin. The plummeting of support for the Citizens' Committee was in marked contrast to the situation in Estonia where a similarly named organization became an important ingredient in national politics.[8] The Latvian committee never achieved popularity, but ironically many of its ideas were absorbed into the mainstream of Latvian politics as popular perceptions shifted towards a more assertive view of citizenship and of the Latvian state.

The first major decision by the Latvian Supreme Council on May 4 was the reassertion of the claim that the Latvian Constitution of 1922 had never been legally abrogated and had been valid in law or *de jure* right through "to this moment." The resolution explained the illegal nature of occupation, terror and the anti-constitutional actions of the "Working People's Bloc" in 1940. The joining of Latvia to the USSR in

1940 could only have been decided by a free referendum which was never held. "As a consequence, the inclusion of the Latvian Republic into the Soviet Union, from the precepts of international law, is not in force and the Latvian Republic still exists *de jure* as a subject of international rights recognized by over fifty nations of the world."[9] Moreover, the Latvian SSR Supreme Soviet (*sic!*) decided that the basic concepts of international rights had priority over norms of state rights; that the July 21, 1940 declaration which joined Latvia to the USSR had been invalid from the moment of its inception.

In an attempt to be conciliatory to Moscow and avoid the harsh reaction elicited by Lithuania after it had declared full independence several months earlier on March 11, which had led to an economic boycott, the Latvian Supreme Soviet made it clear that the renewal of Latvian Republic state power *de facto* would come into force only after a transition period which would end with the assembly of the Latvian Saeima (parliament). The length of this period was not specified. As well, only four key sections of the 1922 constitution were to apply immediately. These sections pronounced Latvia an independent, democratic republic whose sovereign power rested with the Latvian nation. In addition, one section specified that the Saeima was to be elected by secret ballot through universal, equal, direct and proportional elections.[10]

The President of Lithuania, Vytautas Landsbergis, was present at the Latvian legislature at this historic moment. He had come to encourage the Latvian Supreme Soviet to follow Lithuania's lead of a complete break with Moscow. Latvia chose to be more conciliatory by providing a period of transition, a path also taken by Estonia. In order to defuse any potential misunderstanding and economic or armed conflict, an official letter from the Latvian parliament was sent to Gorbachev praising him for his brave reforms and indicating that the renewal of independence could not be achieved "in one day or even in one year." The May 4, 1990 declaration, it stated, "only slightly nudges ajar the gates to the period of transition – for an honest dialog and the working out of guarantees corresponding to our mutual interests." The letter included a paragraph summarizing the stages of development that had been experienced by Latvia: "Moving towards justice, the political process in Latvia, as in Lithuania and Estonia, has gone through two primary stages – the period of national awakening and the period of state self-awareness. During the autumn of last year we began the third period, which derived logically from the first two – the renewal of direct state independence."[11]

Within ten days, on May 14, Gorbachev reacted by declaring the

Latvian resolution to be null and void because it contravened the constitutions of the USSR and of Soviet Latvia. However, no economic boycott was instituted as had been done for Lithuania. The Gorbachev decree did encourage a motley crowd of several thousand "saviors of the empire" including many Soviet military cadets and retired officers to attempt to storm the Latvian Supreme Council building on May 15, 1990. Their attack was stopped by local police and ironically by the "Black Berets" or OMON, a special riot militia created by the relatively reform-minded Soviet Minister of the Interior, Vadim Bakatin. In tandem with this action, the Russian-dominated Latvian Interfront had called a nationwide strike which received, however, only moderate support in the country.[12]

The leaders in the Kremlin had to face other fissiparous developments in the USSR which deflected their single-minded attention from the Baltic area. The most important at this time was the election of Boris Yeltsin as chairman of the Russian Congress of People's Deputies in May followed on June 12, 1990 by the declaration of state sovereignty of the RSFSR. Ukraine also set out its desires for autonomy and civil rights on July 16. Soon thereafter, on July 20, Gorbachev outlined a new proposal for federation to be worked out into a final "Union Treaty" with the participation of all republics. The Baltic Council, a body through which all three republics often coordinated their external policies, almost immediately rejected participation in the new union proposed by Gorbachev.[13]

Hardline offensive

On August 2, 1990 Iraq invaded Kuwait and the USA engaged in a flurry of diplomatic negotiations which included the courting of the USSR. With world attention focused on Iraq, Soviet saviors of the empire successfully pressured Gorbachev to adopt a firmer stance and to reverse some of the gains made by liberals and by Soviet republics. Several moderate ministers in Moscow were dismissed. A key change involved the replacement of the relatively flexible Minister of the Interior, Vadim Bakatin, with the KGB-trained Latvian, Boris Pugo, who at one time had been First Party Secretary in Latvia.

As well, the Moscow-based All-Union Interfront organization was allowed to coordinate and strengthen its various branches in the different republics. The Foreign Minister, Eduard Shevardnadze, was so perplexed by the moves toward apparent dictatorship that during the Supreme Soviet session of December 20, 1990 he announced his resignation, claiming publicly that there was an imminent threat of dictatorship.[14]

In Latvia the new mood of empire restitution was very pervasive. The new hardline offensive was signalled on September 14 when the Black Berets, who had now become the mercenary arm of the Latvian Communist Party, occupied the headquarters of the Latvian State Prosecutor to prevent the building from falling under republican jurisdiction. Then, on November 9, these same mercenaries with the help of uniformed Soviet marines took over the municipal offices in the resort city of Jurmala. Between December 5 and 18, nine organized explosions occurred in Riga in an attempt to create a sense of chaos and to bring about the imposition of Soviet "presidential rule" in the republic. To hasten this process the First Secretary of the Latvian CP, Alfreds Rubiks, helped activate the All-Latvia Committee of Public Salvation to take over power in order to restore "law and order."[15]

Meanwhile, in the fall of 1990, the Latvian government continued to press the limits of its sovereignty by establishing customs offices on its eastern borders to slow down the flood of uncontrolled exports. It became engaged in several skirmishes of jurisdictional legitimacy.

During the month of January 1991 the hardliners became more confrontational. On January 2, the Latvian Press Building was occupied by the Black Berets on the pretext that the building was the property of the pro-Moscow Latvian Communist Party. Only Communist newspapers were allowed to remain. Most Latvian newspapers experienced tremendous difficulties and were forced to turn to unsuitable regional and other small-scale publishers to survive. The main offensive, however, began in Lithuania on January 11 with the takeover of strategic buildings in its capital city. Two days later, in a bloody confrontation between Soviet armed forces and demonstrators defending the Vilnius television and radio tower, 14 people were killed and over 600 injured.[16] The Latvians began their own preparations for defense, with heavy equipment and concrete road-blocks covering the approaches to key government and media buildings and especially the Supreme Council building in central Riga. Barricades and bonfires became the symbol of the determination of Latvians to protect their gains towards independence. On January 20 the Black Berets, in an attempt to occupy the headquarters of the Ministry of the Interior in Riga, killed five people, one of whom was a well-known Latvian television cameraman. A dozen people were wounded.[17]

The attempted putsch in Latvia did not succeed, in large part because the Soviet army did not participate and because the population of Latvia had shown such determination, even resolving to fight armor with stones if necessary. They, of course, could not have stopped any determined armed occupation of strategic points. Nevertheless, the reverberations of world-wide public condemnation and Boris Yeltsin's vocal opposition (including his appeal for Russian soldiers to refrain from shooting), and his signing of inter-state treaties which recognized Baltic sovereignty, forced Soviet decision-makers to halt the operation.

The January incidents had a far-reaching impact on the progress toward Latvia's independence. They created unusual solidarity among Latvians from all walks of life and from all political persuasions. They also alienated many Russians and other non-Latvians living in the republic from Rubik's Communist Party, the Interfront and the Salvation Committee. Indeed, according to Maris Caklais, then editor of *Literatura un Maksla*, every fourth person on the barricades defending the inner city against armed intervention was a Russian or a Russian-speaking individual.[18]

The governments of the Western world were now much more sympathetic to the Baltic cause of independence and during February both the Latvian Foreign Minister, Janis Jurkans, and the Prime Minister, Ivars Godmanis, were received by the leaders of over a dozen countries. The Soviet leadership began a temporary retreat from its hardline approach having gained nothing and having lost much sympathy throughout the world and also within the USSR where the media, especially the independent and non-Soviet controlled outlets, tried to present a fair appraisal of the situation.[19]

The changed mood in the republic and Gorbachev's initiation of a union-wide referendum precipitated the organization of a non-binding Latvian referendum for March 3, 1991 which asked simply "Are you for a democratic and independent Republic of Latvia?" Participation in this referendum reached a surprisingly high rate of 87.57 percent, and 73.68 percent voted in the affirmative. To reach such a high favorable vote, at least 33 percent of non-Latvians had to have voted with the majority of Latvians. Gorbachev's referendum, held throughout the USSR two weeks later, found very little support in Latvia; very few people participated.[20]

During the next five months, preceding the August putsch, the Black Berets became particularly active in the harassment, takeover and demolition of customs posts in all of the Baltic republics. They were also involved in random shootings, kidnapping and murder of citizens. The Red Army, on the other hand, focused its attention on fulfilling the draft quotas which had decreased to 10.9 percent of the theoretical number required for the spring draft in Latvia – compared to a 25.3 percent success rate for the fall draft. A number of conscientious objectors were detained.[21]

The coup of August 1991

The coup was preceded by a warning on August 16 from Soviet reformer, Alexander Yakolev, who had been censured and ordered to be expelled by the CPSU Control Commission the preceding day. He warned that Stalinist hardliners in the Communist Party were plotting a *coup d'état* and "preparing social revenge."[22] Three days later, on August 19, the coup was declared by an eight-member State Committee for the State Emergency led by USSR Vice-President Genady Yanayev. The coup did not succeed, but its consequences were truly far-reaching. Latvia declared its total and immediate independence on August 21, thus putting an end to its "transitional period."

During the several days of hardline control in Moscow, the scenario played out in Latvia was very similar to that of the attempted coup in January 1991 with Black Berets once again occupying strategic buildings and Latvian Communist Party First Secretary Rubiks, in charge of the All-Latvia Committee of Public Salvation, declaring his readiness to take over power and form a new government. This time, however, the Red Army undertook a more active intervention role with General Fedor Kuzmin announcing on August 19 that the Baltic military district was taking over control of the Baltic republics. Red Army troops were also used for the takeover of the Latvian Council of Ministers building and the Riga radio station on August 20. But this military advance was short-lived. Already on that day General Kuzmin, sensing the imminent collapse of the hardliners in Moscow, reassessed the situation and pulled his troops back from the Council of Ministers building, released captives and even apologized for the takeover of the buildings. Kuzmin informed the Latvian government that he was not a member of Rubiks's emergency committee and would wait for further instructions. The next day his troops abandoned another six strategic points which they had occupied.[23]

The Latvian Supreme Council went into emergency session on August 19 and declared its solidarity with President Yeltsin and his call for a general strike. Contingency plans were made for governments in exile and appeals were broadcast for citizen protection of parliament buildings and other key locations. The Latvian Supreme Council's declaration of total independence on August 21 was recognized the following day by a Western country, Iceland, which had already declared its willingness to do so even before the coup. Thereafter, many countries also decided to recognize Baltic independence. Russia recognized Latvia's independence on August 24. The United States accepted Baltic independence *de facto* on September 2 and the USSR Congress of

People's Deputies (Gorbachev) recognized it on September 4. Latvia, together with the other two Baltic republics, the two Koreas, Micronesia and the Marshall Islands were admitted as new member states of the United Nations on September 17.[24] Recognition of Latvian independence was now assured.

The challenges of real independence

The advent of independence after the failed Moscow coup in August 1991 caught the new Latvian elites by surprise. To be sure, this change helped solve some painful problems of jurisdiction, but it also thrust the new state into the rapid maelstrom of major discontinuities or veritable revolutions whose disruptive dimensions had not been grasped even by the most prescient Latvian analysts.

The discontinuities with the previous fifty years of Soviet rule could not be neatly tackled one at a time. Latvia had to face a war on many fronts. From an autocratic single-party rule, it had to establish a democratic political system with all its attendant contradictions and unfamiliar political cacophony and public posturing. As well, in establishing democratic rule, Latvia was forced to confront the explosive issue of who was entitled to participate in the democratic selection process, that is, who was qualified to obtain full citizenship rights.

The second area of change in the democratization of Latvia involved the wholesale reorientation of both citizens and state institutions toward a process of non-arbitrary rules and laws and away from traditional Communist morality of which the guiding dictum was that the ends justify the means.

The reconstruction of civil society in the wake of totalitarian practises required a judicious balancing of the private sphere with the needs of the collective sphere. It required rigorous formal mechanisms for the maintenance and defense of clear boundaries between the two. As well, the establishment of a civic culture depended on informal, but no less significant, public support for, and acceptance of, due process.

The third front of action was the rebuilding of a nation whose institutions, laws and policies had been carefully coordinated and choreographed by the centre of the empire in Moscow. While symbolic vestiges of a state had been allowed to exist within a framework of false federalism, the real infrastructure of a state had to be created *de novo*.

The fourth area of discontinuity, and the one with the greatest immediate consequences for all levels of the population, was the need for a new economic orientation.

Establishing democracy

The Supreme Council: from savior to villain

The Latvian Supreme Council was initially embraced wholeheartedly by Latvians as a vehicle for the establishment of their rights and the republic's independence. Over two-thirds of the deputies were Latvians and 131 of the total 201 were affiliated with the Latvian People's Front (LPF). Not surprisingly, in a republic-wide poll in April 1990 (even before the Supreme Council's first session), 77 percent of Latvians indicated satisfaction with its composition. Among non-Latvians the situation was reversed: only 32 percent were satisfied with the composition of the new parliament and 57 percent were dissatisfied. A poll taken one month later, after the Council had met, indicated that among Latvians 90 percent supported the LPF parliamentary fraction, whereas only 34 percent of non-Latvians did so. *Ravnopravie,* the mostly Russian-speaking fraction in parliament, on the other hand, was supported by 47 percent of non-Latvians and only 7 percent of Latvians.[25]

The differences in support between Latvians and others for the Supreme Council did not change significantly during 1990. Support for the Council by both groups rose dramatically, however, as a result of the armed confrontations in Riga at the beginning of 1991. The subsequent monthly decline in support for the Supreme Council among both groups found the Latvians and non-Latvians, ironically, almost equally contemptuous of this body (table 3.1).

Table 3.1. *Positive evaluation of the Latvian Supreme Council (percent)*

		Latvians	Others	Difference
1990	September	76	30	46
1991	January	98	67	31
	June	71	46	25
1992	January	36	23	13
	June	34	20	14
	September	19	11	8
	December	11	6	5
1993	May	10	6	4

Source: Brigita Zepa, "Public Opinion in Latvia in the Stage of Transition. The Dynamics of Views of Latvians and Non-Latvians," *EMOR Reports* 2:3, July–September 1992; *Druva,* October 31, 1993.

Decline of the Latvian People's Front

There were many factors which attenuated support for the Council. One of the most important reasons, however, was the decline in the popularity, power and leadership of the Latvian People's Front, especially of its parliamentary wing.

For most Latvians the Supreme Council was associated with the dominance of the People's Front – the one organization that was expected to lead Latvia to better times and independence. The LPF, however, was never a homogeneous body but had been consciously formed as an umbrella organization for harnessing the energies of many divergent interests and groups. Most deputies had been nominated by local organizations which displayed differing mixtures of political sentiment. As a consequence the great majority of LPF deputies were affiliated with at least one other political organization, and some members could even claim three or more different affiliations.

In the history of political movements, there is a clear tendency for such omnibus coalitions of interest groups either to become political parties with inner discipline and limitation of political affiliation (e.g., the Congress Party in India) or to disintegrate and form or join other political groups or parties (Solidarity in Poland).

In the Latvian case, the organization of the movement suffered serious decapitation after most of its able leaders and organizers were elected to the Supreme Council and harnessed themselves to the taxing job of making laws and governing in unfamiliar surroundings. The links between the elected deputies and the mass organization atrophied as a result of two tendencies. The rank-and-file individuals who had been mobilized during almost three years of meetings, rallies, petitions and contestations, and who were emotionally exhausted, turned their attention to other pressing aspects of work and life which had been neglected for the sake of a higher cause. This cause, in the eyes of most, had not yet been fully achieved but seemed to have been put in the hands of trusted representatives. The second tendency was the slow withdrawal of most deputies from contacts with the grass-roots and a marked decrease in their zeal and devotion to work. Most of them did not feel the need to go back to their constituencies on a regular basis to listen to petty problems or to the criticisms and frustrations of people experiencing formidable changes. They began to realize very soon that being a deputy entailed tedious work and that the problems they faced could not be solved as easily as they had initially believed. They also felt misunderstood or ignored by the media, and exhaustion and burn-out became endemic.

The parliamentary leadership of the LPF had also been weakened. Dainis Ivans, the first leader of the Front, elected in the fall of 1988, had become exhausted by March 1990 and only reluctantly agreed to run for parliament. He refused to become the head of the Supreme Council and was elected as First Vice-Chairman, a position he filled with little relish. Because of the vacuum of leadership in the Front even the seats of power in the Council of Ministers were filled with minimal coordination, the process involving a small group of activists rather than the entire LPF caucus. Much of the initiative of cabinet recruitment was left to the nominated cabinet Chairman, Ivars Godmanis, a physicist who had never been in politics before. Most of the ministers appointed to his cabinet and most of his advisors were specialists from the *nomenklatura* of the Communist era. Only a few were solid LPF supporters. This approach was purportedly taken in order to provide expertise, continuity and stability in government. Within half a year of his election as Chairman, Godmanis stopped meeting with the parliamentary brain trust of the LPF and made decisions on his own or only with his cabinet.[26]

Further erosion in the stature and cohesion of the LPF deputies occurred in the summer of 1991 when the leader of the LPF fraction in parliament, Janis Dinevics, decided to accept the position of minister and became a member of government. According to Ivans, by abandoning his post Dinevics lost his political influence and "at this point the political nucleus that had entered parliament together with the People's Front, was totally shattered."[27] Ivans offered his resignation as First Vice-Chairman of the Presidium on December 11, 1991 because he felt isolated and unable to change things in parliament. He had wanted to call new elections after the August putsch but was not successful. His resentment and discontent and at times bitter language assured his rapid decline in the eyes of the people and in the process loosened the popular bonds with the LPF even more.[28]

With the discipline and power of the LPF quickly waning and with the single most powerful uniting bond of the movement, the achievement of independence, already realized, strains over policy disputes became catalysts for the formation of new fractions within parliament from September 1991. One of the key fractions, Satversme (Constitution), was created because several dozen deputies were adamantly opposed to the proposed revamping of the 1922 Latvian constitution to reflect new changes and realities, although this had been one of the accords accepted on May 4, 1990. As well, they opposed any expansion of Latvian citizenship beyond those associated with pre-occupation Latvia. In effect, Satversme became the guardian of what its members considered "due process" and generally represented the conservative point of view. Soon, as well, the Rural Deputy Group broke away from the People's Front to push more resolutely the viewpoint and demands of rural areas.

The leadership of the LPF movement itself was overtly expressing its discontent with the parliamentary wing. Romualds Razuks, the Chairman of the Front, made a scathing address at the LPF's Fourth Congress on November 15, 1991, criticizing those deputies who had abandoned the People's Front and also the slow pace of reforms and the self-seeking nature of many representatives.[29]

The movement's disintegration began in earnest during 1992. The strains between the Front's membership and its parliamentary wing became so great that delegates at the Fifth Congress on October 24–25, 1992 demanded that the parliamentary fraction stop using the Front's name because it had already abandoned its program.[30] The fall-out of this internecine battle became very visible during the election to the new parliament on June 5–6, 1993. The LPF representatives headed by Godmanis failed to pass even the 4 percent threshold to win any seats in the Saeima. It is noteworthy that the Solidarity movement in Poland also failed to pass the 5 percent threshold during elections held in the fall of 1993.

Other causes of the decline

A most important factor in the loss of support for the Supreme Council was the rapid deterioration in living standards among the population. After Latvia's attainment of full independence the legitimacy of the Council as a transitional body began to be questioned. There were those who called for an immediate election to begin a new chapter of political development but most deputies, feeling the volatile mood of the population and not being prepared to face the electorate, resisted such a move. Moreover, there was still much confusion and polarization over the issue of the constitution, citizenship rights and the method of selection to the Presidency. Ilmars Bisers, one of the most senior leaders of the LPF, offered a harsh assessment of the Latvian political situation in mid December 1992, claiming that "In politics we can observe the same downslide and anarchy as in economics: there is a threat of a total disintegration of the political system."[31]

Indeed, the lines of responsibility and rules of interaction between the Supreme Council and the cabinet were often unclear and *ad hoc*.[32] For example, until September 1991 no minister could be selected from the legislature unless the chosen deputy resigned his seat. In September 1991, Godmanis decided arbitrarily to increase linkages with parliament by quickly pushing through an amendment in the legislature which allowed for the appointment of deputies to cabinet without the need for them to relinquish their seat. He then selected four Supreme Council deputies to head the Ministries of Defense, Welfare, Forestry and State. The relationship of these ministers to their duties in the legislature was unclear. Similar problems and conflicting lines of responsibility were created with other appointments of deputies to government ministries or institutions.

As the elections for the new legislature came closer, some deputies desired to strengthen their anti-establishment image and to dissociate themselves from the existing power structures. They attempted to dismiss the Premier and some of the more prominent cabinet ministers through votes of confidence, but in the process created more confusion and instability. Several ministers indeed did resign.

There were other problems which the Council had faced even earlier but which had accumulated over time and eventually helped sap the legitimacy of this legislative body.[33] Many deputies were elected thinking that representation would require only part-time attendance and that they could continue to practise their professions or maintain their jobs in a style similar to that for deputies of the old Supreme Soviet which met only twice a year and then for only a few days. Over a third of deputies were indeed classified as part-time parliamentarians. Not surprisingly attendance at parliament and commissions was sporadic. According to one source, out of the 16 to 18 members in each commission only about 3 to 4 were "really working."[34]

The Supreme Council had to bear the normal duties of a legislature but in addition it was saddled with cumbersome, detailed executive-type functions. It had direct jurisdiction over such bodies as the Environmental Protection Committee, the Radio and Television Committee, the Latvian State Bank, the Procuracy and the State Control Committee. As a consequence, it was often bogged down in details, thus limiting the time and energy available for the larger questions associated with unusually difficult economic and social problems.

Deputies were faced with a lack of support staff and other amenities considered necessary in Western legislatures. No minutes of proceedings and voting were published although individual deputies had access to them. Most of them did not have personal offices or secretaries and had to wait in line for scarce goods along with the rest of the population. On the other hand, the few perks with which they were provided often created a populist backlash in the general population and in the media.

A much more difficult problem arose regarding the public perception of deputies. Many of them were seen to be corrupt. In part this perception was reinforced by those deputies working as directors or owners of private firms. Such apparent conflict of interest was ruled unacceptable in the summer of 1992, but the damage had already been done. In addition, one of the most common theories of corruption and conspiracy concerned Club 21 which had been founded under the initiative of deputies Janis Krumins, Valdis Birkavs and others to allow a forum for informal interaction between parliamentarians, business representatives, diaspora Latvians and interested activists.

A certain degree of fraction discipline prevailed until August 1991. After that month's watershed event and the beginning of a new polarization on the future of Latvian constitutional developments, however, deputies felt themselves to be much less constrained. The operation of new parliamentary fractions loosened the bonds of discipline for all. The rapidly decreasing popularity of the Council of Ministers and of Godmanis created an even greater environment of free "conscience" voting.[35] The high turnover within the Latvian cabinet reflected the general malaise at the top. Over the three years between 1990 and June 1993, only four of the twenty-three original members of cabinet remained.[36]

The Supreme Council was the body to determine the voting procedures, the voting date and the structure of the future replacement parliament. A majority agreed to continue with the traditions of interwar Latvia and to elect a hundred-member Saeima. To preserve historical continuity this new legislative body was to be elected using the proportional party-list method rather than the constituency method used in the spring of 1990 for the election of the Supreme Council. The new legislature was to be the Fifth Saeima, thus proclaiming its continuity with the last legally elected parliament of Latvia, the Fourth Saeima. The Fourth Saeima had been illegally dismissed by Prime Minister Karlis Ulmanis after his takeover, on May 15, 1934. Thus this bridging of historical time involved a hiatus of fifty-nine years. The electorate for this election included all those who could prove citizenship ties to pre-occupation Latvia, that is to the period prior to June 17, 1940. According to registration data, 78.8 percent of such citizens were of Latvian origin. Among the major ethnic groups in Latvia the percentages of eligible citizens were: Gypsies 90.1, Poles 61.7, Jews 45.4, Russians 39.1, Belorussians 20.1, and Ukrainians 6.3.[37]

In a departure from the election laws of 1924, however, the Supreme Council lowered the voting age from 21 to 18 and, more importantly, introduced a 4 percent minimum vote required for any group to be elected to the Saeima.[38]

The Saeima elections, June 5–6, 1993

While, in 1990, the primary political contest had been between the Latvian People's Front and the Moscow-oriented Latvian Communist Party, the political fray in 1993 saw the participation of twenty-three groups distinguished mainly by their approaches to economic reform and to the question of citizenship. Traditional concepts of left and right did not apply. Rightist parties were categorized as such mostly on the basis of their exclusivity on the question of citizenship, their desire to "repatriate" postwar immigrants to their countries of origin, their toughness with respect to former Communists and the need for a strong military defense system. Fatherland and Freedom and the Latvian National Independence Movement were the two main right-wing parties, a designation based on self-identification and common perceptions. These two parties, however, were for a strong state role in the economy and for comprehensive state welfare programs. The former even held conditional views on the question of privatization, although both supported a market system. The main left-wing parties were seen to be Ravnopravie, Harmony for Latvia and the Latvian Democratic Work Party. On several economic issues they were more right-wing than Fatherland and Freedom. The centre parties such as Latvia's Way and the Democratic Centre Party were moderately nationalistic on the citizenship question and decidedly free-enterprisers in economics.[39]

One of the prominent features of this election was the widespread participation and role of Latvians from the West. The Western-based World Association of Free Latvians mobilized Latvians abroad to join political parties as candidates, solicited funding and pushed for registration of eligible voters within the Latvian diaspora. The organization also decided to actively support four of the more moderate parties and to push for a greater turnout by direct advertising within Latvia.[40]

The Latvian language section of Radio Liberty organized, hosted within Latvia and broadcast debates featuring spokesmen of different parties. These broadcasts helped familiarize many voters with the key differences in the political positions of parties.

One of the curious phenomena of this election was the avoidance of the term "party." In large part this came about because most of the electoral organizations incorporated several coalition partners. As well, there was still a negative reaction to the term because of its connotations with the former monolithic Communist Party. Indeed, the Communist Party had been declared illegal after the putsch of August 1991 and was not allowed to contest the election.

The group which garnered the most votes in the election was Latvia's Way. It was organized in January 1993 largely as a result of the initiative of Latvian activists from abroad who wanted to inject more stability into the Latvian political process. There was an implicit fear that the Latvian Democratic Work Party (composed mainly of former national Communists) could duplicate the success of its ideological counterpart in Lithuania, where the former Communist Party First Secretary Brazauskas had been elected with a majority. Ironically, these Western Latvians had attempted to unite the parties of the centre right, but having failed to do so, decided to organize the grouping which they named Latvia's Way. They hoped to attract individuals from diverse political origins who were above all dedicated to the strengthening and modernization of Latvia in all realms of life and who were willing to be pragmatic rather than ideological in this pursuit. They adopted the detailed economic program "Latvia 2000" which had been carefully worked out by a consortium of economists from Latvia and by those of Latvian origin from abroad. Carefully weighing public opinion polls, they decided to approach Gorbunovs, who as yet had not found a comfortable political niche in the new political spectrum.[41]

In the atmosphere of fractionalization and revelations of graft and corruption which had dominated Latvian politics during the previous year, Latvians from abroad were seen as dedicated and honest patriots by many sectors of the population. The momentum created by the blending of the widely popular Gorbunovs and the Western Latvians convinced many others to join the bandwagon.

The winning theme of Latvia's Way was simple but effective: "Only those who can unify themselves can unify others." Latvia's Way garnered the largest support of any electoral organization, receiving 32.4 percent of the total votes and thirty-six seats in the Saeima. Almost half of this group, or seventeen people, had previously been deputies and eight were imports from abroad. Most were young, with sixteen born in 1950 or later and another eleven between 1940 and 1949. Almost all came from professions requiring higher education, but only four were women and two were non-Latvians.[42]

The organization receiving the second highest support, or 12.4 percent of the vote and fifteen seats, was the Latvian National Independence Movement. Its members were disappointed with their relatively low standing. The Independence Movement had been a highly active political force since May 1988; however, polarization over policy in 1992 resulted in the breaking away of the ultra-nationalist wing, most of whose members joined the Fatherland and Freedom group. Internal strains were also created by the activities of a colorful and wealthy

German citizen, Joachim Siegerist (in Latvia renamed Zigerists). He did not speak Latvian, although his father had been born in Latvia. He helped bankroll a large part of the advertising and election expenses of the organization, but his uncompromising, non-indigenous right-wing views, populist approach and talent for publicity-seeking and self-promotion alienated many prominent members of the Movement. He was also characterized as an adventurer, an impostor (having no real ethnic Latvian ties), a liar and a shady businessman. In spite of his strong defenders, including the founder of the Movement, Eduards Berklavs, Zigerists was the reason why several prominent members left to join Latvia's Way. Zigerists himself was elected to the Saeima but within six months was forced to resign from the Movement. Among the others elected, seven had previous parliamentary experience, three had come from the West and three were women.[43]

The Latvian Farmers' Union was the party of Latvia's leading politician during the interwar period, Karlis Ulmanis. At a conference held on July 5, 1990, the participants decided to reinstate the party on the same basis as its original foundation. Nostalgia no doubt played a large role in the rebirth of this party, but the growth of private homesteads and the dire straits experienced by many farming cooperatives and shareholding organizations created a genuine constituency. The Farmers' Union was fourth in popularity with 10.7 percent of votes and twelve seats, but its decision to form a coalition with Latvia's Way assured it proportionately greater importance and power. Indeed, Guntis Ulmanis, one of its deputies, was also elected President of Latvia, creating another niche of power for this group.

Harmony for Latvia–Rebirth for the Economy, a union of several political movements and groups, received 12 percent of the vote and thirteen seats and was the most successful political organization of the left. It was led by the former Minister of Foreign Affairs, Janis Jurkans, who helped create the organization on March 15, 1993, only a few months before the elections. This electoral union incorporated several associations. Harmony was also the beneficiary of the transfer of many prominent personalities from the Latvian Democratic Work Party (the former national wing of the Communist Party) because they could not agree with the policies of its leader, Juris Bojars. Harmony received the bulk of its support from non-Latvians. It did very well in the south-eastern province of Latgale with its ethnically mixed population, receiving 22.7 percent of the vote there, but poorly in the homogeneous Latvian province of Kurzeme where it attracted only 3.9 percent.

Of the twenty-three contending organizations only eight were able to surpass the threshold of 4 percent. In addition to the four already described, the Ravnopravie movement received 5.8 percent, the un-compromising Latvian nationalist group Fatherland and Freedom received 5.4 percent, the Christian Democratic Union 5.0 percent, and the Democratic Centre Party 4.8 percent. It is noteworthy that Ravnopravie, which had originally been predominantly Russian, changed its strategy somewhat for this election and of its twenty-five candidates, fifteen were ethnic Latvians.[44]

Of the hundred deputies elected to the Fifth Saeima, thirty-three had been deputies in the earlier Latvian Supreme Council, eighteen were Western émigrés, fifteen were women and eighty-eight were Latvians.[45] Within a month, however, five deputies had resigned for various reasons of health or business and academic duties. The newly elected President, Guntis Ulmanis, also had to be replaced in parliament. These positions were filled by candidates next in rank on each of the parties' lists. Another deputy, former head of the Latvian Communist Party, Alfreds Rubiks, was unable to take his seat with Ravnopravie because he was being tried for sedition and held in jail.

Overall the elections were "fair and free" as attested by international observers and, officially, very little negative publicity was generated.[46] However, three parties suffered substantial losses as a result of the charges of corruption raised against their leading members by journal-ists. Thus, the leader of the People's Front, Godmanis, was accused of having deposited $160 million into secret bank accounts in Switzerland, the USA and Denmark. The journalist, who published his accusation five days before the election, claimed that the news had come from Interpol, and to lend credibility to his charge provided actual bank account numbers.[47] Similarly, Jurkans, of Harmony, suffered because of charges made three days before the election that he had personally spent $60,000 without any accounting, money which had been given to him in the United States by the Latvian embassy in 1991 for use in furthering Latvia's foreign policy.[48] One week before the elections, Zigerists, of the Latvian National Independence Movement, was accused by the German media of having appropriated humanitarian aid and of having been involved in contraband activities.[49] Godmanis cleared his name in court in the fall of 1993 when the accusing journalist was unable to substantiate his charges and was fined for defamation. The case of Jurkans was reviewed by the Latvian court in the spring of 1994. The court found no basis for bringing charges. In both cases the proof of innocence came after the damage had been done.

Financing for these elections was not controlled or publicly registered. The biggest spender was Latvia's Way with its disbursement of 12–14 million Latvian rubles (about $160,000).[50] Only voluntary financial reviews were offered by individual parties. There were some unorthodox donations that did receive wide publicity. One of these involved the donation of 1.5 million rubles for the right-wing organization Fatherland by the civic government of one of the boroughs of the city of Riga.

The Supreme Council of Latvia had also passed a resolution forbidding all former or current foreign intelligence operatives from sitting in the Saeima. Its most direct impact was to exclude the leader of the Latvian Democratic Work Party, Juris Bojars, who had been a high-ranking member of the KGB. Other potential candidates, no doubt, were deterred from running because of this.

The elections were a victory for the moderate centre forces, and both the nationalist right and the more cosmopolitan left were disturbed by their unimpressive performance. The Chairman of the People's Front considered it a clear "defeat of the national conservative forces" and the leader of the Latvian Democratic Workers' Party wrote an extensive post-mortem asking, "Why did the non-Communist left parties lose in the Saeima elections?"[51]

The elections, with their 89 percent turnout and 874 candidates, were a reaffirmation of the choice of democracy in spite of the pervasively pessimistic mood that had dominated Latvia for over two years. Indeed, the high turnout was surprising because many people had lost confidence in political leaders, feeling that many of them were corrupt and self-seeking. Indeed, one party decided to capitalize on this negative backlash against politics and at the same time provide some humor. The Latvian Fortune Party, which was forced to change from its original name of the Stupid Party, loudly proclaimed its message that it would "steal less" than the other parties. While its initial reception among Latvians had been enthusiastic, the seriousness of the electoral responsibilities prevailed and this group received less than 1 percent of the vote.

The Fifth Saeima

After the results of the elections were known there was much conjecture about the possible combinations of coalition partners. It was clear that Latvia's Way with its thirty-six seats and its moderate centrist policies had the initiative in determining which other political group it wanted to cooperate with. The Farmers' Union with twelve seats became the official coalition partner. Other groups were also approached but their exaggerated demands for top leadership appointments were deemed unacceptable. As a result the coalition was two votes short of a majority.

However, before this union was formalized (on July 21) the Saeima proceeded, at its first sitting on July 6, to accept the 1922 Latvian constitution in its entirety and then elect the President. There were three nominees for this very important position: Gunars Meierovics of Latvia's Way (born 1920); Aivars Jerumanis of the Christian Democrats (born 1938); and Guntis Ulmanis of the Farmers' Union (born 1939).

Only Ulmanis was a local Latvian whereas the other two had come from the West. After the inconclusive first ballot, the leading contender, Meierovics, stepped aside and endorsed Ulmanis. Ulmanis did not receive the required absolute majority on the second ballot, but after a brief recess when the coalition was allowed to roam the corridors and lobby for their candidate, he emerged a victor with fifty-three votes. Harmony for Latvia boycotted this vote because it wanted the President elected by all citizens rather than by the Saeima alone.[52] Many radical nationalists and the Independence Movement were opposed to Ulmanis for "moral reasons," because he had been a Communist Party member for over twenty years. On the other hand, this record was softened by the fact that in his youth he had been deported to Siberia.[53]

The presidency in Latvia is a powerful political position. The President appoints the Prime Minister, ratifies international treaties, appoints and receives diplomats. He can return laws for a second perusal and can initiate laws himself. He can also call for the dissolution of the Saeima. After such a declaration, however, a referendum must be held. If over half the electorate agrees with the dissolution, then the decision is ratified and new elections must be called within two months. If more than half are opposed, the President must resign.

After his election as President, Ulmanis nominated the former law professor Valdis Birkavs as Prime Minister. Birkavs (born 1942) in turn selected thirteen full ministers and nine ministers of state for his cabinet. Two ministers of state were nominated later. Ministers of state can only vote on issues of direct relevance to their portfolios. The appointments were all approved by a majority vote in the Saeima. In contrast to the previous cabinet almost all appointees were parliamentary deputies, although several were appointed from outside parliament. Ten of the thirteen full ministers were from Latvia's Way and only three from the Farmers' Union. One-third of the cabinet had been former ministers or deputy ministers and five were Western Latvians. All but one had completed studies at institutions of higher education and, as well, all were men and of Latvian ethnic origin. Nine cabinet members had been born during the 1950s and two in the 1960s. Only seven had been born prior to Latvia's occupation in 1940 and, of these, four were from the West. About one-half of the ministers were members of Club 21, with Birkavs being one of the founders of this club.[54]

A high degree of continuity prevailed in other posts as well. The top positions in the Presidium of the Saeima went to the same three individuals who had filled these posts in the previous parliament: Anatolijs Gorbunovs (Latvia's Way) was elected presiding officer of the Saeima, Andrejs Krastins (Independence Movement), deputy chair, and Imants Daudiss (Latvia's Way), secretary. Ironically, Gorbunovs and Daudiss had even been members of the Presidium of the Latvian SSR Supreme Soviet before May 1990.

In contrast to the practice in the transitional Latvian Supreme Council, the various parties in the Saeima tried to maintain strong voting discipline. This created some early defeats of desired legislation for the coalition. As a result, discipline in the coalition was tightened and all ministers were obligated to be back in Latvia to vote during plenary sessions on Thursdays regardless of their duties in other parts of the world. All members of the coalition were expected to be bound by their caucus decisions for both plenary and committee votes.[55]

The Saeima consciously attempted to counter some of the problems of the earlier Supreme Council. All deputies were provided funding to hire one or two assistants and each fraction had a car, a computer, a copying machine, a technical secretary and from one to seven additional assistants depending on its number of representatives. Each parliamentary committee, as well, was provided with a technical secretary and one to two consultants. In addition, limited funds were provided to fractions and committees for temporary hiring of experts.[56] Minutes of Saeima plenary sessions were also published in the official state newspaper *Latvijas Vestnesis*.

To avoid conflicts of interest all deputies were forbidden to receive state contracts either directly or indirectly and could not be employed in competitive profit-making organizations. Employment exceptions included higher education teaching, legal consultancy, scientific research and art. Deputies who were absent from plenary sessions without a valid reason would have 10 percent of their monthly base salary deducted for every absence. In 1995 the basic salary of deputies was raised from 150 to 206 lats (about US $407).

The Saeima had fifteen parliamentary commissions ranging in size from three to fourteen members. The chairmanship of these commissions was divided more equitably than in most Western parliaments with only seven going to Latvia's Way and two to the Farmers' Union, but four to the Independence Movement and one each to the Christian Democrats and Harmony for Latvia. Accommodation could also be seen in the fact that one of the deputies of the Christian Democrats was appointed minister and several legislative initiatives from other parties were passed.

Waning popularity of the Fifth Saeima

The high expectations placed on the Saeima, the populist-style wrangling and demands by pensioners and other groups for a larger slice of the limited state budget, the apparent bickering between and even within parties and the perceived high monthly incomes set by deputies, all helped create great disillusionment in the population. A poll published in March 1994 indicated that among the Baltic states the Latvian parliament received the least favourable assessment with only 16 percent giving it a positive rating compared to 20 percent for Lithuania and 38 percent for Estonia. The negative ratings were 75 percent, 57 percent and 51 percent respectively.[57] The Latvian Saeima, moreover, was elected in June 1993 compared to the fall of 1992 for the other two Baltic bodies. In contrast, the Latvian president, Ulmanis, received the highest rating of all three presidents with 75 percent; the Estonian president, L. Meri, had 57 percent and the Lithuanian, A. Brazauskas, had 52 percent. The Latvian prime minister, Birkavs, with a 38 percent positive rating, compared well with Lithuania's prime minister's 27 percent and Estonia's 39 percent.[58]

Within a year there were open rifts, resignations and expulsions in most parties, induced in large measure by personality clashes, refusal to abide by caucus discipline and the strains created in the tug-of-war between lofty principles and the large and small compromises required in the fashioning of Saeima policy within the context of a minority government. Aivars Berkis, the leader of the Farmers' Union fraction bluntly told his delegates on March 25, 1994 that the real reason he no longer desired to renew his leadership mandate was his inability "to stabilize discipline in either the fraction or the organization itself." Berkis was also bitter about the pervasive mood of "morbid distrust" within the Saeima, where the members of the coalition did not trust their own appointed ministers, where the Farmers' Union deputies did not trust Latvia's Way deputies, and where the rank-and-file deputies distrusted their own leadership when it was engaged in coalition discussions. "It is the same as in the Supreme Council, when the LPF fraction did not believe and distrusted its own appointed Prime Minister, Ivars Godmanis."[59]

Suspicion about which deputies had been involved with the KGB also affected the atmosphere. When the Saeima was convened in 1993 one of the first items on the agenda was the creation of a special committee to investigate available KGB records that had been seized by the Supreme Council in 1992 and to check whether any deputies had been implicated. The special committee reported back that it had found five such connections and provided their names on April 27, 1994. The apparent KGB-tainted individuals included: the Minister of Foreign Affairs, Georgs Andrejevs; the Minister Without Portfolio, Edvins Inkens; the chairman of a Saeima commission, Andrejs Silins; the leader of the Democratic Party, Aivars Kreituss; and the head of the special committee to investigate the Supreme Council's activities, and Fatherland and Freedom deputy, Roberts Milbergs. The first three were from Latvia's Way.[60] Andrejevs resigned voluntarily, stating that he had only provided scientific reports. The others refused to admit any guilt and hired lawyers to defend themselves in a special investigative court. By January 1995, three had been cleared of the charges because of inconclusive evidence, and the fourth case had not then been concluded. However, the prosecution was trying to appeal the decisions to higher courts.

Restructured cabinet, 1994

The rampant mood of suspicion, as well as discord over import tariffs and subsidy policies for farmers, led to the break-up of the ruling coalition in the Saeima. The Farmers' Union withdrew from the coalition on July 11, 1994. The Birkavs government resigned several days later although by law it had to continue to work until replaced by a new executive. The opposition forces were offered the option of building their own ruling coalition. The Latvian National Independence Movement together with several right-of-centre parties spent over a month trying to forge a credible alternative cabinet. This coalition led by Andrejs Krastins was not able to gain the support of the Saeima, however. Latvia's Way, meanwhile, had held meetings with other centre and left-of-centre parties and managed to construct a new government which received majority support in mid September. The apparently major political crisis did not create the expected popular discontent. Most people were more concerned with coping with the unprecedented heat wave than with politics. As well, many had already turned their backs on politics and no longer felt that political wrangling at the top concerned them or their lives.

The decision by the Birkavs government to step down rather than immediately try to work out a new coalition or to govern with a minority alone proved to be a good strategy if judged by Latvia's Way's relative improvement in the popularity polls. The low-profile and rather stiff Prime Minister, Valdis Birkavs, voluntarily stepped down and assumed the mantle of foreign affairs minister. He was replaced by one of the more popular ministers, Maris Gailis. This period of political hiatus in the party's rule allowed Gailis to initiate a major overhaul of the cabinet. Those most closely associated with economic reforms, known as the "Georgetown Gang" because of their studies at Georgetown University in Washington, were replaced. For the first time since May 1994, several women were appointed to the cabinet. Many of the cabinet members also decided to set aside their mandates as deputies in order to have more time to perform their duties, and, as well, many more people this time around were appointed from outside the Saeima. The cabinet, however, still remained entirely of Latvian ethnic origin.

The most serious changes occurred in policy. A new relatively stringent import tariff law was passed providing protection, especially for local farmers. In effect, this was the policy that had been desired by the Farmers' Union, but had not been acceptable to the Georgetown Gang nor supported by IMF advisors. It is noteworthy that high tariffs had on previous occasions been applied against grain and sugar, but the results had been disastrous because of the lack of proper control at the borders. It remains to be seen whether the quality of border controls has been upgraded sufficiently to provide real protection in this area.

Prime Minister Gailis is a communications specialist who has an amiable "teddy-bear" image. He is also a hard worker, an innovative administrator and a team-oriented leader. He has made himself accessible, writing a weekly column on government actions and problems. During his first six months in office he has been able to maintain a relatively favorable image in the media.

The nationalist forces in the opposition have also made changes. They strengthened cooperation in the fall of 1994 by creating the National Bloc, a loose coalition of several parties. They want to establish greater law and order, strengthen Latvia against greed and corruption and provide more open access to business competition, especially against the perceived criminally backed foreign oligopolies. If the National Bloc is able to maintain a common front, it may eventually evolve into a more permanent union and could win control of the Saeima after the next elections.

Latvia's Way carries the accumulated burden of rule during a period of great economic upheavals, social tensions and widespread criminality. As in all democracies it is blamed for all the negative conditions found in the country whether deservedly or not. Latvia's Way finally became an official political party in the fall of 1994, but it has decided to remain highly elitist. Only selected individuals are allowed to join and in December 1994 it had fewer than 400 members. Within the Saeima this party has demonstrated stability, inner discipline and solidarity in spite of general expectations to the contrary after its victory in the elections.

After all, it had been formed rather hastily by a motley collection of candidates from the former Communist *nomenklatura* on the one hand, and anti-communist Western diaspora Latvians on the other. The political struggle in the future will most probably be between the centre and the national conservative forces. The left in Latvia appears to have very little support, in contrast to many countries in Eastern Europe and the former Soviet Union.[61] The pervasiveness of low party loyalty and attachment among voters, however, may present problems of stability and continuity in future parliaments, especially if no party is able to gain a commanding lead, as did Latvia's Way in June 1993, and coalition governments will require the juggling of demands from four or five different parties. The glue of nationalism alone may be too weak to allow for strong coalitions of the national conservatives to remain united in the face of economic pressures.

Citizenship

The issue of citizenship has bedeviled Latvian politics for many years and has created tensions among Latvians themselves and between Latvians and Russophones. The issue has even generated tensions between Latvia and its eastern neighbors, the European Union and the USA. After August 1991, it was relatively easy to accept the continuity of Latvian citizenship for all those who could prove that they or at least one of their parents had held it or had claims to it prior to Latvia's occupation on June 17, 1940. This was passed by the Latvian Supreme Council on October 15, 1991. The problem, however, was how to deal with over 724,000 mostly Russophone non-citizens who had come to Latvia after 1944. According to international law this large mass of people were technically "illegal aliens."

On the same day that the restoration of citizenship rights was passed, guidelines were also introduced for naturalization. Three requirements in these guidelines created discontent: a knowledge of spoken Latvian; residence in Latvia for at least sixteen years; and the renouncement of citizenship of any other country. The vast majority of non-Latvians had been residents of Latvia for over sixteen years, hence this fact alone should not have been a particular cause of concern. It was also clear that because of the impending dissolution of the USSR, the renouncing of Soviet citizenship was not going to be very traumatic. The language requirements, however, appeared insurmountable to many who had never bothered to learn Latvian.[62] Charges of "apartheid" and "violations of human rights" were widely made by Russophones in Latvia and by Russia's politicians.[63] Nevertheless, these guidelines were never confirmed into law because of opposition by Latvians who felt that the Supreme Council, which had been elected by "Soviet citizens," did not have the legitimacy to act on constitutional matters and that only the Saeima, elected by Latvian citizens, could deal with such issues.

The Fifth Saeima had to resolve the issue and in June 1994 it passed a citizenship law which set very strict quotas for naturalization. Again there was widespread protest by local Russophones and by Russia's politicians. More important, Western Europe and the United States applied pressure to eliminate the quota provisions. This threat of being seen in a bad light by Western powers led to a decision by President Guntis Ulmanis, supported by Prime Minister Birkavs, not to sign the document but to send it back to the Saeima for reconsideration. On July 22, 1994 the Saeima passed a new bill without the numerical quotas which was signed into law by the President on August 11.

The citizenship law of Latvia follows guidelines found in most such laws of Western countries, yet Russia's politicians were still unhappy. Citizenship is to be granted to those who have been formally registered as residents and who can satisfy the following conditions:

(1) have permanently resided in Latvia for at least five years, counting from May 4, 1990 or from the date of a permanent residence permit
(2) have a command of the Latvian language
(3) know the basic principles of the Latvian constitution
(4) know the national anthem and the history of Latvia
(5) have a legal source of income
(6) have taken an oath of loyalty to Latvia
(7) have officially renounced any previous citizenship.

Some categories of residents, including those who served in foreign security services or those convicted of serious crimes, were disallowed from naturalization.[64]

The period of controversy over citizenship appears to be over although some Latvian nationalist parties are still opposed to the "watered down" law and are intent on changing it in the future in order to limit access to only several thousand a year. There is, however, little support for revising these laws among most Latvian citizens and a major hurdle towards full democratization has been overcome.

The media

It is a universal truism that a pluralistic system requires free media. In 1994 Latvia had a wide array of domestic newspapers and journals reflecting a broad spectrum of political views and had access to periodicals from the entire world. It had several independent radio and television stations. This is a prosaic statement, yet only a few years earlier under Communist rule, the media in Latvia had to stay within the narrow confines of Communist censorship and only a select few individuals had access to foreign periodicals with political content. Many foreign broadcasters, including Radio Liberty, were systematically jammed. Latvia did not have the benefits enjoyed by Estonians who could receive Finnish television programs in a closely similar language and thus become familiar with the cultural and political traditions of the Western world.

The media are important factors affecting the tone and orientation of the two principal language communities in Latvia. Two major newspapers are published regularly in both languages: *Diena* (Day) and *Rigas Balss* (Voice of Riga). These are predominantly staffed by Latvians and their stories are oriented to a Latvian audience. Indeed, their Russian-language circulation is relatively small, though significant.[65] Another two-language newspaper, *Labrit* (Good Morning), went bankrupt in June 1995.

There are two Russian-language dailies: *S. M. Segodnia* (Soviet Youth Today) and *Panorama Latvii* (Latvian Panorama). A sociological study published in December 1993 indicated that only 15 percent of the readers of the former and 11 percent of the latter were Latvians. The Latvian-language newspapers *Neatkariga Cina* (Independent Struggle) had 14 percent non-Latvian readers and *Latvijas Jaunatne* (Latvian Youth) 19 percent.[66] The latter ceased publication at the end of 1993, however.

Among Latvians, major access to the Russian world is provided by two Moscow television channels. Their main appeal for Latvians includes the various Western soap operas that can be followed on the Ostankino and Russia television stations. Ostankino is a serious source of discord among Latvians because of its negative treatment of the Baltic question. Efforts by nationalist politicians at ending this channel's access to Latvia have so far failed mainly because of the Latvian soap opera devotees and pressures from the Russian-speaking sector of the population. However, the difficulties experienced by Ostankino in paying rebroadcasting fees may achieve what politicians could not.

Several incidents concerning the media and the government have, however, created some controversy. In the fall of 1992, the weekly newspaper of the nationalist-oriented Latvian Citizens' Committee, *Pilsonis* (Citizen), was charged with violating the Latvian law forbidding the press from encouraging defiance of the laws of the republic and attempts to overthrow the government. The main thrust of the newspaper had been that the existing "regime" was "collaborationist" and that all true citizens had the duty to install a Latvian provisional government. Although *Pilsonis* was banned after a court trial, it reappeared almost immediately as *Pavalstnieks* (a synonym for citizen) and has since been coming out weekly without harassment.[67]

Several successful libel cases against the media have made them more cautious in their attacks on politicians and other individuals, a development applauded by many. Indeed, the lack of objectivity of newspapers has been a recurring theme of criticism in Latvia. Nevertheless, when asked to name the most objective newspaper in Latvia only 11 percent of those questioned in an October 1993 poll stated that none were objective. This group had a majority concentration of people with higher education and in the age category 30 to 39.[68]

The problems associated with the media do not differ substantially from those of long-standing democratic countries and the pressures for conformity are minimal. Ownership is still not concentrated in just a few hands. The absence of state subsidies for the press in Latvia prevents development of one possible avenue of undue political influence. A new law has also provided equal access for all parties to the media (if they can pay) before elections. There have been attempts by organized crime to influence the media, and secret listening devices in several press offices were discovered in April 1994. The dangers from the underworld were underscored by the murder of a leading journalist in Lithuania. Latvia is not immune to such dangers and overt security measures are being taken. In sum, however, most journalists in Latvia are relatively iconoclastic and several of the best ones have a feisty sense of independence that would react loudly against any threats of censorship or muzzling. The main dangers for the media in Latvia could come from the economic front and the world-wide trend to concentrated media ownership.

Civil society and rule of law

Intermediate groups and elites

One of the consequences of the totalitarian system was the extirpation of independent group activity. A network of independent groups is one of the major prerequisites for a civil society. A specialist on Eastern Europe, George Schopflin, has described some of the common elements expected in civil societies:

Civil society is one of those elusive concepts more widely used than defined, but it evidently involves an autonomous society and a self-limiting state: in other words, a state that recognizes that the rule of law applies as much to itself as it does to citizens.[69]

This self-limitation is to apply as well to society and throughout the political systems but as Schopflin notes, "self-limitation does not have strong roots in Central and Eastern Europe."[70] Ideally the constraints on state power have to be multifaceted and should include not only legal but political, economic, social and other counterforces in order to create a "dynamic but equilibrative order."[71]

No comprehensive studies have as yet been made of the extent and nature of independent group activities, the nature of elites and the striving towards equilibrium in Latvia. As a result, analysis can only be elementary and subjective. There is a relatively dense network of political organizations at the municipal and national level, but most of these are Latvian, because only citizens can vote and about three-quarters of citizens are Latvians. Secondly, many of the prewar organizations have been renewed, but these as well are mostly Latvian and include the various Latvian associations (*Latviesu biedribas*) in almost every locality. Religious organizations exist among most ethnic groups, but the Russian-oriented Orthodox and Old Believer networks, for example, are much less visible and have fewer organizations – including fewer Sunday schools and church-related social groups. Russian-speakers are also generally less religious than Latvians. The occupational associations are open to all regardless of ethnicity, but the language of communications is usually Latvian and this hinders participation by many Russophones. Even the network of local media is predominantly Latvian and much of Russian-language television is received from Russia.

The Russian-speaking society in Latvia in many respects can be described as a "mass society" with few linkages between the primary family and friendship levels and the elites. There is very little solidarity and only a vestigial ethnic consciousness among the various groups that make up this society whose main links are those of Russian language and of Soviet culture. Another important factor in the isolation of this group is its weak access to the republic's power elites. There are only a few non-Latvian representatives in the political and bureaucratic elites. The economic elites, on the other hand, many of whose members have arisen from the Russian-speaking milieu, have not yet fully taken on the mantle of intermediaries for local ethnic groups, although this appears to be in the process of changing. This Russophone isolation from elites and paucity of intermediary groups inevitably heightens alienation, discontent and a sense of unfair treatment by Latvian authorities, and could presage the availability of this population to populist mobilization, or more critically to outside interference and agitation.

In spite of the relative vigor of Latvian intermediate organizations in comparison to those of the Russophones, there are nevertheless serious problems that will have to be overcome on the road to a developed civil society. Latvian organizations differ in their characteristics, but many of them are insubstantial, poorly organized and do not appear to be acting as credible centres of interest aggregation. They have not yet mastered the functions of interest gate-keeping and the filtering out of unreasonable demands. Discontented groups without a trusted and mediating leadership are easy prey to the appeals of extremist politicians.

There are many examples of this lack of "self-limitation." The very active Pensioners' Association has been successful in lobbying for higher pensions. In 1994 pensioners already claimed over 30 percent of the state budget. Nevertheless, a large section of this Association decided to organize their own political party in 1994 in order to more than double their existing pensions. If they were successful their claim on the state budget would be over 60 percent. The relative absurdity of such claims, however, appears to have no impact on their pressing, loud and determined demands. Doctors and teachers also want larger incomes and have gone on strike to force the issue in their favor. Ironically, many among them were the greatest supporters of larger pensions. There appears to be a pervasive narrow sectarian view of interests, lacking a broader perspective on the interrelationships between the various elements of the population and the state. Such lack of integration and uncritical willingness to listen to unreasonable demands has already attracted the attention of radical political leaders and very definitely has had a negative impact on the popularity of governments trying to rule in conditions of material scarcity.

If the middle layers in Latvia are still frail it appears that the top layers are also not soundly established. There has been an extremely rapid turnover of political elites in the Latvian cabinets between 1990 and early 1995 and many of yesterday's heroes have turned into villains, at least in the eyes of the general population. Most of the leading politicians are young and inexperienced. There are, to be sure, individuals who have been in politics for many years and enjoy a broadly based authority and credibility, yet their numbers are few. With the rapid rotation of politicians, the reshuffling of leadership in state administrative organs and the weakly organized nature of economic elites, there is a widespread perception of a power vacuum at the top. There does not appear to be a permanent matrix within which elite accommodation and gate-keeping can occur. Indeed, there is no vigorous establishment within which functional power elites can meet and integrate. Club 21 was established for exactly such a purpose, but it is widely seen as an undemocratic base for conspiracies inimical to the best interests of Latvia. For this reason many in the political elites avoid joining it or have departed from its ranks.

One of the missing ingredients at the top is the almost wholesale disappearance of the cultural and moral leadership once provided by the Latvian cultural intelligentsia. After a most prominent role in the development of the period of "awakening" and of the Latvian People's Front, the creative intelligentsia has become demobilized on a massive scale. The state funding of their salaries has ceased. Moreover, there has been a dramatic decline in the consumption of cultural outputs, from poetry books to new musical compositions. The demands of daily existence have forced this creative intelligentsia into jobs not commensurate with their previous prestige and status. Very few of them have anything to say about the present period and most have simply disappeared from public view. The apparent power vacuum at the top and the absence of elites of integration have encouraged a proliferation of conspiracy theories and diffuse aimlessness in many parts of the population.

Rule of law

It is hard to disagree with Egils Levits, the former Minister of Justice in Latvia, who claimed in April 1994 that the republic had achieved "complete democracy." This same minister, however, pointed out that Latvia did not have a "juridical state at least at the level we would desire."[72] The "rule of law" has not yet permeated the thinking of all layers of society.

Latvia's General Procurator, Janis Skrastins, has well described four causes of this problem. In his view juridical "nihilism" is prevalent in Latvia. Many people do not defend or practice their rights largely because they are not interested or do not know the law. Secondly, the moral restraints which once existed have been weakened. Thirdly, juridical nihilism has been fostered by the growth in organized crime and violence. Finally, there is "patriotic pragmatism": people consciously overstep the law in the belief that they are doing it for the achievement of higher goals.[73]

Other specialists have noted additional factors creating disregard for the law. These include the populistic desire for vengeance, absolute poverty, radical changes in society and the lack of an infrastructure and procedures for the application of existing rights and laws. A legal specialist has detailed the latter state of affairs: "In many cases procedural questions have not been worked out. If they have been worked out then there are no institutions which can realize them. If there are institutions, then these have a dearth of workers, but if there are workers, then their level of knowledge is too low."[74]

Above all, the most invidious threat to the acceptance and implementation of laws lies in the prevalence of distrust. Rumors of corruption, KGB linkages, compromised judges and police officers, hidden agendas and secret societies, coupled with perceptions of increasingly worsening economic conditions and personal loss of status among a majority, have created a debilitatingly high degree of cynicism.

To be sure, no society, regardless of its maturity and pure pedigree of democracy, has been able to avoid problems of public and private corruption, immorality, tax evasion, organized crime and disregard for the law. One can only speak about the degree of lawlessness and corruption and such assessments by their very nature are extremely subjective and not amenable to statistical comparisons. Most Latvians acknowledge a serious problem in the rule of law but for the most part they also believe that the situation is worse in most other republics of the former Soviet Union. There is also a slow but steady growth in the application of the law at all levels and a general assessment that things are slowly improving. Even at the most mundane level of traffic violations there has been an increase in vigilance by police officers as witnessed by the author in the summer of 1994. General driving culture, while still abominable, has improved somewhat. Parking on the street and on sidewalks is being controlled by meters and by tickets. Tighter control over the collection of taxes has resulted in greater government revenues. The dockets of most courts are filled with people suing for unpaid loans and other perceived transgressions.

Certainly legislation is being passed in a systematic fashion to fill gaps in the criminal code, business and property laws and many other areas of civil conflict. Perhaps the growth in the prestige and remuneration of lawyers could be taken as an index of the growth of a legal culture and the greater orientation to courts rather than to illegal means.

State-building

After half a century of being directed by Muscovite bureaucrats and politicians Latvia had lost control of most of the institutions responsible for internal law and order. After the dissolution of empire ties Latvia had to begin strengthening these institutions or building them *de novo*.

The armed forces and other institutions of law and order are expected to protect the country and its borders against illegal activities and illegal entry and exit by people and goods. The Latvian defense forces in August 1994 contained only 5,383 regular military personnel (mostly inexperienced draftees aged eighteen or nineteen), 572 officers and 470 civilian administrators. Their equipment was limited to 20 small-sized ships and cutters, 4 airplanes and 6 helicopters.[75] It is obvious that Latvia could not defend itself very long against armed aggression by outside forces. Nevertheless, according to the Minister of Defense, their prime duty is to resist as long as possible, to demonstrate to the world that Latvia is being occupied and then to switch to partisan or guerilla warfare. Almost all Latvians appear to be in agreement with the view of the minister: "One thing is clear, 1940 will not be repeated and Latvia will not give up without a fight."[76] Internally the basic thrust is to provide security against riots or small-scale disasters and conflicts and to protect and control borders. Indeed, over half of the armed forces are deployed as border guards.

During the Soviet period, Latvia did not have controlled borders with neighboring Soviet republics. Only the sea frontier was heavily fortified, defended and controlled. After independence, Latvia had to begin the task of training border guards, constructing border crossings and marking actual state boundaries. By the end of 1994 controlled borders had been established but many problems remained. The illegal transportation of goods and people is a widespread and frequent occurrence. The corruption of many border guards and technical inadequacies have been endemic, limiting the options for many state policies, including the proper application of tariffs. No foolproof index of progress can be applied; nevertheless, there is a widespread perception that many of the inadequacies are slowly being surmounted. The revamping of border control and customs buildings or the construction of new ones, as well as the replacement of incompetent or compromised managers and lower personnel, have created a new mood of service in this area. Equipment, technical aid and advice from such organizations as PHARE (Poland and Hungary Assistance for Economic Reconstruction) have improved the impermeability of Latvia's borders. Deep ditches and new patrol roads have been constructed in remote forested and swampy areas. Sweden and other Baltic Sea countries have donated patrol boats and have trained personnel because of the increased smuggling of drugs and refugees (mostly Kurds and Afghans). According to Western European border control experts the situation of Baltic borders in January 1994 was similar to that of Hungary and Poland two years earlier.[77]

Crime is a major problem that could destabilize the rate of progress in almost all areas of reform. The murder rate has been among the highest in the world with 640 recorded slayings in 1993 (a rate of 24.7 per 100,000 population) or two-and-a-half times that found in the USA.[78] In 1993 there were 52,835 recorded crimes or a rate of 204 per 10,000 population. The recorded crime rate reached a peak in 1992 and dropped significantly during 1993 and 1994.[79] Organized criminal groups have found Latvia and the Baltic a useful base of operations. According to the Latvian General Procurator there are close to 300 known mobsters working in Latvia, most of whom are foreigners.[80] Almost all businesses must set aside about 10 percent of their profits to pay protection racketeers. Insurance companies, with few exceptions, no longer insure against car theft. Corruption is believed to be widespread. Bribery is one of the common forms of corruption with a long tradition during the Soviet period which has found fertile ground in which to develop after independence.

Most of the approximately 10,000 police officers in Latvia were trained and hired during the Soviet period, and most as well are non-Latvians with a weak knowledge of the state language. Equipment shortages, low wages, relatively low morale, high personnel turnover and low status in the eyes of the population have weakened the effectiveness of Latvia's police forces.

The volunteer paramilitary Home Guard, or Zemessardze, has provided a mostly Latvian-speaking addition in the fight against crime. Its contingent of about 20,000 people is composed only of Latvian citizens. Members of the Zemessardze have been successful in rural areas and are now beginning to establish their presence in larger urban areas. Their relationship to police forces has been strained. Some of these dedicated volunteers, unfortunately, are undisciplined and poorly trained and have been involved in incidents characterized by poor judgment, overreaction and even unwarranted killings by shooting.

In spite of the problems, slow changes are being made. A new police academy has been established. Better equipment, new leadership, increasing investigations of corruption, new bilingual recruits to police forces and Western advice and aid are improving the level of service. Obviously much more needs to be done before Latvian residents will feel secure.

Civil servants are responsible for the daily and routine functioning of the state. Their collective abilities, judgment, efficiency and fairness have a most important effect on the capacity of the state to thrive, respond to problems and receive general support and trust from the population. The Latvian SSR bureaucracy had a reputation for a Soviet Russian orientation, inefficiency and corruption. Since independence, efforts have been made to change these traits. In August 1994 the

10,383 individuals on the direct payroll of fifteen ministries became subject to the requirement of Latvian citizenship and a knowledge of the state language and another foreign language.[81] In effect, by 1994 a large majority of the civil service was composed of Latvians and the language of work was Latvian. Appointments to positions are now independent of political patronage, and civil service candidates must pass special qualification examinations. The quality of management personnel was being reviewed in 1994 and some upper-level directors did not receive attestation and were replaced.

There are many problems yet to be overcome. The rapid turnover of individuals, the relatively low pay, the initially haphazard hiring practices and the generally low esteem of governmental workers have created problems of morale and have hampered efficient service in most ministries. The widespread perception of corruption and the lack of coordination between departments have also created strains. A poll taken in the fall of 1994 by the State Reform Ministry found that 60 percent of people believed that state employees could be readily bought and were dishonest. Only 3 percent had a positive evaluation of them. Within the previous year 6–7 percent of respondents had provided private material compensation for services received whereas another 13 percent had refused to do so even after having received signals for "donations" from bureaucrats. Most of the bribery cases occurred during decisions involving size of living quarters and apartments, medical treatment and business deals. The Minister for State Reform believed that the situation could be improved with the creation of an "ethics council."[82]

Lax tax collection was one of the greatest weaknesses affecting policy-making by the state. The number of specialists to check and review tax payments was increased dramatically in 1993 so that the Ministry of Finance now accounts for 43 percent of all civil servants.[83] New incentives for more efficient tax collection include the right of departments to keep a share of taxes collected from tax evaders. A new comprehensive law of the state civil service was passed in May 1994. It outlines procedures for hiring, firing and promotions, conflicts of interest and disciplinary penalties. Specific positions are receiving job description and outlines of expected duties. Funds have been allotted for an elite academy of management to train future civil servants, a project initiated by Prime Minister Maris Gailis.

Suggestions for the creation of an ombudsman office have not been accepted, but residents have the right to take their grievances to court. The security of tenure and the growing problem of unemployment have made the civil service somewhat more attractive. The existence of clear

laws on institutional functions and responsibilities, as well as the
creation of a board to check and monitor its quality, should raise the
prestige of this underpinning of state power. According to Prime
Minister Gailis, "One will have to wait five or six years or even more
before our civil servant will be like the one in pre-war Latvia, [or] in
Germany and elsewhere, where an administrator is the representative of
a very prestigious profession."[84]

Conclusion

atvia became an independent state or "returned to independence" as a
result of many external and internal factors. The overall collapse of
communism, first in Eastern Europe and later in the USSR, was a
precondition for the emergence of an independent Latvia. Yet, in their
own way, Latvian activists were instrumental in extending the boundaries
of glasnost and in helping the collapse of communism within the Soviet
empire. As many treatises and theories will no doubt be published about
the collapse of the Soviet Union as have been published about the Russian
Revolution of 1917. Many revelations of hidden agendas and covert
connections will appear, as participants in the tumultuous years from
1985 reminisce and record their side of reality. Winners and losers will see
events from different perspectives. Whatever the verdict about the role of
Gorbachev, the KGB, foreign powers, internal contradictions, loss of
ideological faith, nationalist revival, economic collapse or divine providence, Latvia has been able to break the ties of empire and is an
independent actor recognized as a sovereign body by most countries of the
world.

Latvia has been able to establish a viable democracy and, in spite of
widespread discontent, popular preference is still given to centre or centre-
right parties. There are, to be sure, problems that need to be addressed but
none of these are of such dimensions that they could paralyze the pace of
progress towards westernization. Even the thorny issue of citizenship has
been resolved and debates on this have almost ceased.

The rule of law was badly shaken by the period of contested
jurisdiction and the wholesale reorientation of institutions from one set
of values to another. In this area, as well, one can see the slow
establishment of professionalism and routine administration. The
dramatic decline in crime figures may be a harbinger of the consolidation of state infrastructures. The forces of law and order, the military,
and the state administrative institutions are still in comparatively
"frayed" condition, but here also one can perceive innovative attempts
at improvement.

In sum, the direction of change is perceptibly positive. Latvia's leadership is eager to rejoin Europe and jettis n the communist, totalitarian and imperial burdens of the past. Unless unforeseen problems arise, especially from neighboring eastern states, Latvia will no doubt integrate into Europe and help in the building of a stronger European Union.

4   Economics and reform

Historical legacy

Of all the European post-Communist states, Latvia and the other two Baltic republics stand out with their unique economic history and legacy. They differ from other former Soviet republics because they have a living memory of a period of independence between 1920 and 1940, a period which is being used as a guide and a morale booster to overcome present problems. They differ from the Eastern European states because they were subject to a unified central economic plan directed from Moscow and had no economic autonomy or borders as did states such as Poland and Hungary.

During two decades of independence the three small Baltic states established economic stability and prosperity in spite of the tremendously wrenching dislocation of World War I and the equally debilitating impact of the Great Depression of the early 1930s. The Baltic states coped on their own without any foreign aid and managed to accumulate very little debt. The relatively large quantities of gold deposited in Western countries (as well as appropriated by the USSR immediately after its occupation of the Baltic states) is only one index of the success of economic policy during the independence period. This Western gold, moreover, has become the foundation for current Baltic monetary stability.

The period of independence has provided another reference point, especially for Estonia and Latvia. Neighboring Finland, which had much the same history as the Baltic states, had been a part of the Russian empire until 1917 and was, as well, at comparable levels of economic development in the 1930s, managed to avoid incorporation into the USSR. Its attainments in economics offer the Balts a perspective of what their standard of living could have been, but for their occupation by the Red Army.

Communist period

In common with most other communist states Latvia experienced the theft without compensation of almost all private property by the state and the dragooning of farmers into primitive farming collectives. It also went through periods when ideological purity and class background were far more important than expertise and ability. Under communism there was an inherent upgrading and even glorification of physical work at the expense of mental work. In particular, the value of the services sector as a legitimate sphere of economic activity was discounted and the sector was chronically underdeveloped. Central planning was a universal tool to determine prices, inputs, outputs, location of industries and the division of "profits." As a result of its gross inefficiencies, the black and grey markets flourished. People spent much time cultivating contacts with each other and especially with those in power positions for various exchanges based on bartering and favors. The process strengthened the bonding of individuals within society, but deformed rational economic relations.

No one is as yet certain why the Baltic republics were incorporated into the USSR and the Eastern European countries were not. Probably the Soviet-Russian empire felt it had a natural right to expand up to the former borders conquered by the czar. This decision not to incorporate the seven "satellite" countries into the USSR left these states with advantages that the Balts could only envy.

While the Eastern European countries were involved in a loose division of labor within Comecon, most of their economic planning was done and decisions made within the confines of their own state. Latvia and its sister republics were merely regional economic units within the central planning apparatus headquartered in Moscow. During the last two decades this planning was based almost entirely on the branch system with increasingly autonomous ministries determining development and production strategies within their own spheres of control and jurisdiction. Republics and their legal infrastructure were of little import in the determined realization of goals set by the powerful ministerial bureaucracies. These economic "fiefdoms" became more than production-oriented units. To maintain the loyalty of their workers under conditions of tremendous labor deficit they became involved in very extensive sidelines which specialized in building and maintaining apartments, providing scarce retail merchandise, organizing kindergartens, children's camps, old age homes, garden plots, cottage lots and vacation resorts. Even entertainment, sports and cultural endeavors were not forgotten. Most importantly, the huge production complexes in Latvia went out of their way to recruit labor in other republics with all kinds of enticements; as a result, non-Latvians eventually accounted for the bulk of industrial workers.

In effect, Latvia had very little control over its own economy, the rate of its development or its specialization profile. Later, especially after the purge of Eduards Berklavs and other national Communists who had argued for greater republic autonomy in many areas, but particularly in the economy, a wave of overt centralization occurred (see chapter 1). Thereafter, the theme of the "Soviet division of labor" became a key point of reference and pride for the Communist leadership in Latvia. The Party First Secretary in Latvia, Augusts Voss, was fully convinced in 1978 that "not even our enemies can assert that the separate nations of our land working in isolation could have achieved such significant gains in economic and cultural developments in the past decades."[1]

The overwhelming subordination of industry to central control from Moscow became one of the key elements that Latvians had to change in their struggle for independence. Their biggest inroad in 1990 was in the area of joint union/republic jurisdiction, a large part of which they were able to reclaim for exclusive republic control (table 4.1).

In August 1991, Latvia inherited all of the industries which had been under Moscow's jurisdiction either directly or jointly. Unfortunately, these Latvia-based industries had been constructed and organized to serve the entire Soviet Union. Latvian production was dependent on Soviet sources of raw materials and semi-processed component parts, and on energy which came from thousands of diverse sources scattered throughout the other fourteen Soviet republics. The recipients of finished products were equally dispersed. Latvian imports and exports from and to other Soviet republics accounted for 45 to 50 percent of gross domestic product (GDP) during the late 1980s, a level comparable to ten other Soviet republics, but not the Russian republic itself which, because of its size, had only a 15 percent export dependency.[2]

There are other important features of Latvian industrial structure inherited from the Soviet period which have created problems of adjustment on the road to a market-style economy. The average Latvian industrial enterprise had a larger number of employees than equivalent firms in Western countries. Thus the five electronics enterprises in Latvia had an average of about 8,000 workers, and the fifteen chemical firms employed about 1,300 people each.[3]

Several of the larger machine-building and electronics firms were the major or even exclusive sources of a number of items of production for the Soviet Union. Thus Latvia was the sole producer of passenger minibuses, milking equipment, chain belts for bicycles, motorcycles and

Table 4.1. *Jurisdiction over industries in Latvia, 1980–90 (percent)*

Type	1980	1987	1990
All union	37	40	37
Joint union/republic	46	50	21
Republic	17	10	42

Source: Latvia: An Economic Profile for the Foreign Investor (Riga: Council of Ministers of Latvia, September 1991), p. 8.

agricultural combines, electrical equipment for electric trains, automatic telephone switchboards and other items. In some areas of production Latvian firms made more than half of certain items in the USSR. Most significantly, a high share of production was engaged in supplying military needs. According to a World Bank estimate, "more than 15 percent of the labor force in Latvia in 1985 was employed in military production, higher than in Lithuania and three times higher than in Estonia."[4]

With the rupturing of the Soviet system of central planning and allocation, Latvia was left with the dilapidated and plundered remnants of an archaic industrial infrastructure constructed to serve the entire Soviet empire. Many of the specialized industries so dependent on former Soviet input and sales could no longer retain their production volume.

A country cannot jettison or convert all its industries overnight. Latvian decision-makers will have to work with the types of industry they have inherited from the Soviet period at least for several years. The industrial output profile of Latvia in 1990 indicated engineering in the lead with a 26.3 percent share. The next two largest sectors were food (24.9) and light industry (18.0), especially textiles. These were followed by chemicals (7.2) and wood and paper industries (5.6). These five areas accounted for about 80 percent of all industrial output in 1990.

The Latvian economy inherited other distortions from the socialist system which have required readjustments. In 1990 proportionately too many people in Latvia were employed in agriculture and industry (45.8 percent) and too few in the services sector (36.6 percent). In comparison, the same sectors in Finland in 1989 employed 31.5 percent and 53.2 percent respectively.[5]

The shock of reforms

With the regaining of control over its own economy after independence, Latvia very assiduously followed the economic advice of the International Monetary Fund (IMF). Reforms included many unpopular measures. The greatest political confrontations occurred over the issues of the ending of state subsidies to firms and for specific goods and services. There was a great outcry, as well, concerning the lifting of most price controls and the determined limitations of currency emissions. The Latvian government was under tremendous pressure to annul these measures. Political parties of different persuasions began to clamor for a slowing down of reform initiatives. Even the People's Front government appeared at times willing to heed these determined pleas. The government was limited in this desire, however, by the unflinching stand of the Bank of Latvia and its chairman, Einars Repse. Because of its institutional independence from the government, the Bank was able to resist demands for the emission of more money and the granting of more credits than it deemed appropriate for the control of inflation. Without money and credits the government was forced to pursue a program of austerity.

Bank of Latvia strategists also began a successful educational counter-offensive in the media against the populistic anti-reformers. They pointed out in detail the expected negative results if currency emissions were not correlated to existing economic outputs. They asked people to compare Latvia's inflation levels with those of Russia and the Ukraine where adequate controls had not been instituted. The IMF also proved to be a convenient reference point for government policy-makers, who pointed out that unless they adhered to IMF agreements they would not receive proposed aid from this organization as well as from other donor states.

The introduction of reforms created unexpectedly harsh results in production, wages, consumption, trade and inflation. The severity of decline in these areas even surprised IMF planners. The Latvian economy began to falter in 1991 with a decrease in GDP of 6.4 percent and deteriorated dramatically in 1992 when the drop was 32.9 percent.[6] Production in Latvian industry declined by 44.4 percent between October 1991 and October 1992.[7] Real wages decreased by 60 percent between September 1990 and September 1992 although consumer goods sales decreased by only 35 percent, cushioned in part by the utilization of previously accumulated savings and by unregistered economic transactions.[8] International trade also plummeted and the inflation rate rose from 10.5 percent in 1990 to 124.5 percent in 1991 and then to 951 percent in 1992.[9]

The economic decline in Latvia was exacerbated by the rupturing of ties with the USSR. Great problems were caused by the price reforms instituted by other republics. The drastic hike of export energy prices by Russia and the instability of the monetary systems of the former Soviet republics were especially disruptive. As well, Latvia was struck by a severe drought in 1992 which created great hardship in agriculture. Latvia experienced an economic crash which was worse than the one associated with the Great Depression of the 1930s. The slide in economic output had been arrested by mid 1993, however, and in that year the decrease in GDP was a less daunting 20 percent. During the fourth quarter there was even a modest growth of 0.5 percent.[10]

The pattern of decrease and stabilization is not unique to Latvia, and has been experienced by most other Communist states that have attempted serious reforms. Only the degree and steepness of decline have varied from state to state. The three Baltic republics experienced very similar declines in GDP between 1990 and 1992. However, their adherence to economic discipline and proposed reform measures has resulted in overall optimistic assessments about their future.

The scope of reforms in the Latvian economic system was, indeed, immense and included in its purview macroeconomic, structural and institutional-legal measures of change. Not surprisingly, all the areas requiring changes have not met with equal success. The most satisfactory progress has been achieved in the reform or management of currency, prices, inflation, taxation, budgets and financial institutions. Privatization of small businesses and farms made progress, but that of medium and large businesses, and of dwellings, had barely started by early 1995. Agricultural and industrial production is flagging and foreign trade is subject to the vagaries of external tariff policies and other barriers. The impact on people of belt-tightening policies has been acute. In the future, however, certain reserves of resources could help increase economic development.

Currency reforms

One of the first macroeconomic measures was the establishment of a strong national currency. This was achieved without creating any panic in prices or loss of credibility in the newly minted emissions by introducing changes gradually to allow people time to adjust. The Soviet ruble was accepted as legal tender for several months alongside the transitional Latvian currency, the Latvian ruble, which was first issued on May 7, 1992. The permanent currency, the lats, was introduced on March 5, 1993 but the Latvian ruble was allowed to remain in circulation until June 28, 1993.

One of the major criticisms of the Soviet ruble for many decades was its lack of convertibility. In Latvia this problem was solved at a practical level by the licensing of over 500 private money exchange booths which determined currency prices on the basis of supply and demand. A more official decision was made with effect from July 20, 1992 to let the value of the Latvian lats find its own level against other foreign currencies. Latvia decided to peg its currency to the IMF basket of currencies called Special Drawing Rights. Estonia, in contrast, decided to tie its currency to the Deutschmark and Lithuania to the US dollar. This convertibility and floating exchange rate allowed Latvia to stabilize import–export relationships and set the foundation for more rational planning for the future by individuals, firms and governments.[11] Rather than decreasing in value with respect to other Western currencies, the Latvian lats had significantly strengthened its value one year after its introduction, especially against the American dollar. A strong lats, however, has caused discontent among many producers and farmers because a high exchange rate makes imported goods more marketable, but Latvian-produced goods more expensive.

Prices and inflation

With state price controls lifted on all but 8 percent of goods and services in 1992, and the rise in import prices of energy and other goods, inflation was unavoidable.[12] After attaining a rate of 951.2 percent in 1992, inflation decreased significantly thereafter and the monthly rates for the most part remained between 1 and 3 percent. The overall inflation rate in 1993 was 34 percent and in 1994 26.3 percent.[13] This relative taming of galloping inflation by 1993 contrasts with the situation in the Ukraine where rates of over 1,000 percent were recorded in 1993 and in 1994.

A large part of the achievement in Latvia came about as a result of the strict control of monetary emissions by the Bank of Latvia. Other strategies were also utilized. The governmental budgets were kept within strict boundaries with very little leeway given to deficit financing and borrowing. Until new annual budgets are introduced (sometimes several months late into the fiscal year, which begins in January), expenditures are held by law at the levels of the average monthly rate of the previous year. In cases of revenue shortfalls, expenditures have to be adjusted quarterly or new sources of revenue have to be located. Credits from the Bank of Latvia are limited to a maximum of one-twelfth of budgetary revenues during the year. Finally, all municipal governments have to receive permission from the Ministry of Finance to borrow from the local banking system or from abroad.[14] In effect there was no budget deficit for 1993 and a small deficit within planned limits in 1994.[15]

Besides monetary emissions and budget controls the state has initiated strict wage policies. State enterprises are taxed at high and progressively increasing rates if they exceed the government's guidelines on wages. While wages did indeed go up, they did not keep pace with inflation until mid 1993. Thus, real wages for state enterprises and government ministries, as calculated by the IMF, decreased by 14.25 percent in 1991 and 17.5 percent in 1992. Starting with June 1993 and continuing to December, however, wages in the public sector increased faster than inflation, and real wages for the entire year of 1993 increased by 19.8 percent and for 1994 by 19 percent.[16]

Government revenue and taxation

Under the Soviet system Latvia's taxes and budget were integrated with those of the USSR and on these issues local administrators could change very little. As an independent state, Latvia had to introduce its own system of revenue generation to fulfill obligations in the budget.

In line with the shrinking role of the state, budgetary revenues as a proportion of total GDP declined significantly. In 1989 such governmental revenues accounted for 51.8 percent, but in 1993 for only 27.7 percent, of GDP. Of this 1993 total, 22.5 percent was retained by the central government and 5.2 percent was assigned to local budgets. Not surprisingly, the bulk or 92.1 percent of government revenue in 1993 came from taxes.[17]

Taxation policy is usually dynamic and changes with circumstances and experience. The two levels of government in Latvia, that is, the thirty-three municipalities and the central government, depend on distinct sources of revenue. As in most Western countries, property taxes are kept at the municipal level. However, in contrast to most other countries, personal income taxes based on a flat 25 percent rate form the major source of funding for local governments. In view of the differing levels of income in various parts of Latvia, a certain share of income taxes is placed into an equalization fund which is then used to supplement the budgets of weaker municipalities. There were three major sources of central government revenue projected for 1995: the social tax was expected to provide 30 percent of the total, the goods and services tax 30 percent and the profits tax 12 percent. In addition, excise tax was to yield another 4 percent and customs duties 4 percent. The bulk of personal income taxes, slated for municipal governments, was expected to provide 10 percent of total governmental tax revenue.[18] A small percentage of unusually high incomes are taxed differently.

The social tax is a payroll tax which for several years theoretically had to be diverted into a separate fund to provide pensions and disability payments, but which in reality was not distinguished from the rest of the budget until 1995. The overwhelming part of it is paid by the employer who deducts 37 percent from the organization's wage fund. In contrast, the worker pays only 1 percent from personal wages. According to the Ministry of Finance, employers avoid this tax on a "massive scale."[19] They officially record payments of minimal wages but then disburse additional but unregistered and untaxed pay. New controls and new patterns of payment are being seriously considered by the government.

Until November 1993, the Latvian goods and services sales tax had been significantly lower than in its Baltic neighbors. With IMF support and with the pressures of a budgetary revenue shortfall looming, a new rate of 18 percent was introduced, a rate which is also used in Estonia and Lithuania. Indeed, most Scandinavian countries have rates which are even higher. Nevertheless, this new tax hike precipitated broad discontent and a parliamentary crisis, and as a result temporarily lower rates for food items were allowed. In September 1993, the Minister of Finance estimated that only about 60 percent of the potential tax is collected.[20] This high proportion of untaxed sales will no doubt diminish, especially because government controls are becoming stricter and all establishments are required to have computerized cash registers.

Profit tax rates in 1993 for private firms were significantly lower than for state enterprises, that is, 25 percent and 35 percent respectively. Mixed ownership firms had to pay increased taxes with every increment of state ownership. However, banking, insurance and trade establishments were targeted with rates of 45 percent and gambling and casino operations with 65 percent.[21] Attempts to introduce one flat rate of 25 percent for all met resolute resistance but it was finally introduced in 1995. The major problem in this area, as well, is tax evasion which is facilitated by the lack of exchange records. According to former Prime Minister Godmanis, in early 1993 only 9 percent of accounts were settled through banks and the rest involved direct transfers of cash "in suitcases," thus avoiding any official records of transactions for government controllers.[22] As in other states of the former Soviet Union, the preferred manner of tax evasion is to transfer liquid assets to foreign banks. The Minister of Economics has claimed that large sums of several billion dollars are involved.[23]

Tax evasion by firms and claims of billions of diverted dollars abroad have created a populistic backlash from ordinary people who believe that all their demands for increased pensions, family allowances, farm subsidies and other services could be easily satisfied by more rigorous and determined tax collection practices. Indeed, in 1993 the government created a large new layer of bureaucracy, including 1,500 finance inspectors, to verify the accounts of enterprises. Much effort was also applied to collect arrears of taxes although many of the delinquents turned out to be state firms on the edge of bankruptcy. The discovery of tax transgressions by finance inspectors and others allows for the transfer of 20 percent of new funds into the coffers of the respective inspection organs as an incentive for more vigorous sleuthing. To preempt one of the largest single sources of tax evasion, the state has now taken full control of alcoholic beverage distribution and sales. Unregulated gasoline sales by tanker trucks on the side of the road have also been banned and only accredited businesses are allowed to operate.

Personal income tax collection has also received a new approach. Beginning in 1994, workers must hand in their work book to employers and by law no person without such a book can be legally employed in Latvia. Severe penalties are applied for evasion or for lateness in filing tax returns. Although the bulk of revenue derived from this means is allotted to municipal coffers, a small part derived from exceptionally high-income earners is kept by the central government.

Fair taxation of all is seen as a high priority by the Latvian government because those who avoid taxes become more competitive in their businesses, thus driving out the "fools" who diligently pay full taxes or play by the rules.

This differentiation between honest and dishonest merchandising was highlighted in the case of sugar tariffs. A foreign business agreed to buy Latvian sugar beets and process them in the country. For initial protection, however, this firm demanded and obtained the setting of a high tariff for imported refined sugar. To its dismay, it found that only a small portion of its locally refined sugar could be sold in Latvia because about 80 percent of the estimated annual consumption of 80,000 tonnes was crossing Latvia's porous borders without being registered or paying any duties.[24] The weakness of governmental control of import and export items accentuates the difference between theory and reality. At the same time, the realization of such problems over time forces new innovations in policy or changes of personnel. As well, the customs service is to receive, at least theoretically, 20 percent of the value of seized goods that have not been properly cleared or declared.

Governments have many options in determining sources of revenue. One of the guiding considerations in changing the tax system in Latvia has been the desire to conform more closely to the standard practices of OECD countries. Consequently, Latvia's policy favors increasing consumption taxes and encouraging savings and investments. Thus, between the 1993 and 1994 budgets, sales tax revenue increased by 133 percent, excise tax by 125 percent, but profit tax by only 11 percent and social security tax by 23 percent. The rate of sales tax went up from 10 percent to 12 percent in October 1992 and to 18 percent one year later.[25]

The budget and government spending

Latvia's budget differs from the average Western European budget in several important ways. Latvia started its economic reforms without a debt burden, hence it does not have to cope with servicing debt, one of the largest items in other budgets. This has been one of the debilitating legacies borne by Eastern European countries, especially Poland which, incidentally, managed to have some of its loans reduced. Russia also has to carry a large debt load. Latvia, in only a few years, has joined other countries in obtaining credits and by January 1, 1994 the total of all external debt had surpassed US $223 million.[26] There is also a growing internal debt. No doubt, a large part of this will be collected from secondary creditors, but, inevitably, future budgets will include a section for the repayment of debts.

The most onerous outlay in 1994 included old age and disability pensions, which claimed 31.6 percent, a proportionately larger share of the budget than was claimed in most other countries of the world. The proportion of pensioners to workers was two times higher than the average in Western Europe. Thus 660,000 individuals received pensions, while 970,000 workers paid the social tax.[27] Pensioners are also entitled to various welfare payments and heating allowances. Their benefit levels were increased by the Latvia's Way party and were fixed at 30 percent of the average income in the state sector, and were to be readjusted every three months. Pensioner organizations are still discontented and many parties, seeing the possibility of harnessing such a large block of votes, have been willing to engage in populist sloganeering about "the poor fate of our older people."

Latvia's proportion of elderly people, however, is not much different from that of other Western European countries. The real difference lies in the definition of pensionable age. Latvia inherited from the Soviet Union the practice of paying pensions to women at the age of fifty-five and men at sixty, in contrast to the common practice in the rest of the developed world to start pensions at age sixty-five for both sexes. In addition, in Latvia many jobs allow for still earlier retirement.

The Latvian government is fully aware of the problem and the drain this places on other areas of Latvian life. It also knows that this large contingent of pensioners reduces Latvia's economic competitive capabilities. The government has introduced a policy which raises the pensionable age for both sexes every year by one-half year until the final goal of sixty-five years. Over 40 percent of the old age pensioners in Latvia are younger than sixty-five, hence the two decades involved in reaching the new goal will produce a serious negative impact on Latvia's ability to compete.

Arguments for lifting the age limit more rapidly have been angrily opposed by many people in Latvia. Most often they claim that the much lower life span of Latvians requires earlier pensions. With this argument the women should start their pensions later than the men because they live on average eleven years longer. A more credible argument is that if pension ages are increased many will simply join the ranks of the unemployed. This change, however, would place the problem into its rightful category and allow for improvements once the economy expands. Such a change would also lessen the present problem of working pensioners.

The 1994 budget allotments for defense (2.6 percent), education (10.3 percent) and health (5.2 percent) were lower than in most other developed countries, and various Latvian groups which so adamantly supported the raising of pensions were soon found picketing and berating the government for the low levels of funding in their own professions.[28] There is as yet very little awareness that budgets cannot be expanded at will and that a larger slice for one sector necessarily entails greater restrictions in other sectors.

Financial institutions

Ironically Latvia is a major beneficiary of tax evasion practices within other former Soviet republics. Large sums are transferred to about sixty Latvian banks, in part because the political situation is seen to be more stable and money is safe from the tax collectors of the countries of origin. Moreover, the increase in the value of the lats against the US dollar and other Western currencies in 1992 and 1993 has meant that investors obtained the full benefits of extremely high interest rates and the added dollar value of the lat currency. At the end of 1992, one US dollar was worth 0.835 lats, but only one year later only 0.5919 lats; thus the value of one lats in dollar terms increased by 41 percent. Doubling one's funds within one year was a very attractive prospect. To be sure, such high interest rates decreased in 1994 and in January 1995 average annual commercial bank deposit earnings in Latvia had a modal rate of 18 percent while lending rates were still on a monthly average of 4.8 percent or an annual of 40–80 percent.[29] High lending rates, especially in comparison to Estonia's much lower 15–30 percent, have been a major source of frustration and discontent among businessmen, entrepreneurs and farmers. A president of one firm claimed in February 1994 that it was impossible to repay interest on loans through production alone; it was only possible if "one is engaged in another business on the side."[30]

Part of the problem of high rates derives from the lack of credible collateral and the regular threat of bankruptcies and non-repayment. It is widely believed that with the introduction in 1995 of the right of corporations as well as citizens to own and sell land, the rates will decline. Another problem is the almost exclusive focus on short-term deposits and credits. Sound business planning is difficult unless long-term loans are readily available. Changes in rates could also come from greater competition, especially by Western banks. Bank of Latvia President Repse is optimistic that the worst is over, noting that in February 1994 banks were offering credits to the government at annual rates of 24 percent.[31]

Until the start of 1995 the Latvian banking system was relatively stable. To be sure, a number of less formalized financial organizations promising extremely high rates of return collected money from depositors and disappeared. In spring 1995, however, several prominent banks including the largest one in the republic, Banka Baltija, were declared insolvent. Most of the failures were seen in the media as the result of intentional criminal theft and conspiracy to defraud by bank owners.[32] Another problem area concerns the approximately 600 Soviet-era savings banks. They diligently transferred all their surplus funds to Moscow. With independence all these transferred funds were no longer accessible and no compensation is forthcoming. The savings banks are in dire straits but the fact that most people are not aware of it and have not flocked to withdraw their deposits has provided some respite. More importantly, the low interest rates paid to depositors in these savings banks has allowed inflation to compensate for a large part of the losses to Moscow. The Latvian government is also stepping in to back up these savings banks with special bonds, and international auditors and the World Bank have been participants in recommending the best strategy for survival.

One of the major suggestions by the IMF was for the Bank of Latvia to disengage itself from commercial banking functions. This suggestion was carried out successfully when the central bank disposed of its commercially operating branches in 1993. Now the Bank of Latvia is free to operate solely as a regulating agency with similar functions to those of the Central Bundesbank of Germany.

The IMF has pointed out several other weak areas. It feels that the number of financial institutions is too large for the size of the local market and that they are undercapitalized, creating problems of adequate supervision by the central bank.[33] As of January 1, 1994 the minimum share capital required for new banks went up from half a million to three million lats (US $5.4 million). Only recently has the Bank of Latvia required proper certification of banks and annual reviews of accounting procedures and financial policies. The recognized Western auditing firm of Coopers & Lybrand is one firm which has been asked to perform audits.[34]

According to the president of the Bank of Latvia, Repse, Latvian banks had deposits equivalent to about US $650 million in February 1994. A large part of that was invested within Latvia. Stability is also provided by the 10.6 tonnes of gold deposited abroad before 1940 and returned to Latvian control after August 1991.[35]

Many people see Riga as a potential Hong Kong of banking and the most important East–West trade center and gateway to the CIS countries. Indeed, both the IMF and the World Bank have suggested that Riga could become a large-scale center for offshore banking, similar to Singapore or Luxembourg. Transactions in such banks would be limited to foreign citizens. There are absolutely no limitations placed on geographical origins of investments into banking and about fifteen banks have been formed with the aid of foreign capital, mostly from Russia.[36] While such a scenario is possible in the future, many standard bank services will have to be made available before the confidence of foreign operators is captured. At the same time, the rapid pace of changes in banking in the period 1993–5, including the introduction of the SWIFT system and debit cards, as well as credit cards, indicates a desire to reach Western levels of banking.

Privatization

One of the intriguing aspects of Latvian economic reform is the extremely slow pace of privatization of businesses and dwellings. The first law on enterprise privatization was passed in November 1991 and affected only small municipal ventures engaged in trade, services and catering. Indeed, all such establishments had been placed under municipal jurisdiction because it was felt that privatization from one centre would be impossible. The reluctance and defensiveness of law-makers concerning privatization was underlined by the initial restrictions placed on the size of establishments which could be sold. They could not be larger than 100 square meters, nor employ more than ten people. Restaurants could not have a seating capacity of over thirty customers.

Transactions had to involve cash, and bidders were restricted to those who had resided in Latvia for over sixteen years. Several of these restrictions, especially those concerning size, were lifted in 1992.[37]

Initially, municipal governments, which were entrusted with the responsibility for privatization, were reluctant to proceed in such a direction and desired to take everything over themselves. There was much discussion about how to equitably divide proposed privatization objects which had been built by "the joint efforts of so many." The deputy director of the State Department of Conversion saw the heavy legacy of fifty years of communism in the attitudes of many state administrators whose approach was "if not for me, then for nobody."[38]

Over 1,200 objects were identified for privatization by municipalities. The pace of privatization accelerated during the second half of 1992 and continued into 1993, so that by September of that year 644 small enterprises were no longer the responsibility of the state. A majority of these, however, were not sold outright but leased, usually for five years. Although the original wish of the State Department of Conversion had been that the businesses be publicly auctioned, only 7.5 percent of them were disposed of in this fashion. Over 18 percent were privatized by employees. Three-quarters of the firms were bought by legal entities and one-quarter by individuals. Just over half were sold for cash and the rest on credit.[39] By May 1994, privatization had been effected for 813 concerns.[40]

Privatization created many dissatisfied people and widespread claims of favoritism, of underpricing and underhanded collusion. Thus the sale of the right to lease one of the largest department stores in Riga, called the Minsk, involved widespread media discussions about the under-valuation of existing stock, of the clandestine involvement of family members of the Council of Ministers and other similar charges. A new twist to the squabbling was achieved when the City of Riga suddenly discovered after the contract had been signed that the district which had organized this sale had no jurisdictional right to do so.

The IMF report claimed in 1993 that significant progress had been made in the privatization of small enterprises, but not in the sale of medium and large businesses.[41] An accurate overview of the number of concerns to be privatized and already privatized is apparently not available because different government sources provide conflicting statistics. Part of the problem rests with the definition of privatization. Another problem has been the diversity of institutions, government ministries and departments having the right to privatize. As well, the legality of some of these transactions has been questioned. Nevertheless, according to the Ministry of Economics, by October 1993, a mere nineteen concerns and, by April 1994, only forty-two large enterprises or 6 percent of the total planned had been privatized.[42] These involved the sale of the most successful state firms, usually to large local corporate buyers. Of the total of 703 firms slated for sale, privatization commissions had been stuck for only 193 by October 1993 and, of these, two-thirds had not yet begun their duties and thirteen had already disbanded without achieving their task.[43]

After such disastrous progress it is not surprising that the Latvian government decided in the spring of 1994 to create a single privatization agency to allow for the hiring of talented personnel and the contracting of specialized help from private firms. This agency was organized as a joint-stock company. The status of the agency created very acerbic debates and charges of hidden interests. Nevertheless, bitterness has been allayed somewhat because oversight of this agency is the responsibility of an all-party advisory committee whose members were chosen by individual political fractions in the Saeima.[44]

A single, powerful agency no doubt will accelerate the pace of privatization, but many obstacles stand in its way. One of these is the unsettled nature of ownership claims for previously nationalized firms. To speed up the process of restitution, June 1, 1994 was set as a final deadline for claims.[45] Yet, many things have changed over fifty years and most firms and buildings have been reconstructed. There is a need for a satisfactory method of compensation in cases where restitution is not possible. Another problem until 1995 was the lack of ownership rights by legal entities and non-Latvian citizens in the land associated with purchased property in urban areas. While land can now be owned by corporations there are still some restrictions and conditions with regard to foreigners.

A particularly difficult and explosive issue will be the scope for use and role of privatization certificates which residents of Latvia were entitled to from May 1, 1993. The idea of certificates began in Eastern Europe and has been accepted widely within the former Soviet republics including Russia as a populist measure to placate local populations and allow everybody a claim on public property. Latvian citizens are entitled to a disproportionate share of certificates because of the special features involved in this law on vouchers. One certificate has been allowed for each year of residence in Latvia. In addition, those who can claim Latvian citizenship prior to the Soviet occupation in June 1940 are entitled to an additional fifteen certificates as compensation for "ancestral investments." Those forcibly deported from Latvia in the past will receive additional certificates. In many instances, certificates have been given in lieu of nationalized property. The certificates have a nominal value of about 28 lats or about US $50 and will be allowed to be used for the purchase of state apartments and for the privatization of some firms. Many certificates were being sold at deflated prices (4 to 6 lats in January 1995) and organizations are allowed to accumulate large numbers of these certificates for more effective leverage in purchases of state property.

The privatization agency will have to deal with a universal problem in former communist states – the debt load accumulated by state firms. Many firms, in fact, are worth significantly less than their assets. Either the new proprietor or the government could undertake responsibility for the existing debts. Another route is to allow firms to undergo real bankruptcy proceedings. No clear policy had been adopted on the debt question of enterprises by the start of 1995.

The privatization of state housing will be a major boon for the Latvian economy. It will create a much needed real estate market and will improve the mobility of workers who in a majority of cases are tied to their present locations because of the deficiency of housing elsewhere. The decades-long practice of exchanging apartments is archaic and cannot meet the needs of a large mobile labor pool. In Latvia very few state-owned apartments have been sold, in contrast to Lithuania where privatization in this realm has been particularly far-reaching and successful.

In Latvia, certificates will become important ingredients in the privatization of state-owned apartments. There is, however, a major ethnic-based political problem which has slowed down policy in this area. Under normal circumstances people could be expected to have first option on buying the apartments in which they live. In the larger cities, most of the newer apartments built in the suburbs are occupied preponderantly by non-Latvians, and the more centrally based old and dilapidated houses with few conveniences are disproportionately occupied by Latvians. As well, almost all of the private claims for nationalized houses concern these older buildings.

The greatest progress towards privatization has been made in agriculture where in the spring of 1994 over 58,000 farmsteads holding about a quarter of farmland had been given over to individual control, although not necessarily ownership. At the same time another 100,000 families were assigned private plots averaging 4.4 hectares as a significant support for their economic survival. Not all collective farms were dismembered – in some cases they became shareholder associations – but where they did split up, the leadership of these farms was able in many instances to buy out equipment and animals at pre-inflation rates. This apparent unfairness has left a legacy of bitterness and charges about "red barons."

Ownership concerns and foreign investment

There is a very important psychological aspect to the entire process of privatization. Many Latvian citizens are afraid of "selling off Latvia" for a pittance. There is a widely held belief, mostly among former Communists, that the IMF is trying to wreck the Latvian economy so that foreign firms can make purchases for minimal payment. Rightists, on the other hand, while also seeing the signs of a conspiracy, claim that the old *nomenklatura* and former Communist managers are purposely sabotaging production so as to lower the value of their firms and allow them and their Moscow-based mafia allies to once again dominate the Latvian economy. Of particular note is the widespread belief among ethnic Latvians that the main beneficiaries of privatization will be non-Latvians. There is a common perception that about 80 percent of actual private economy activity is in the hands of other ethnic groups.[46] The reasons given for such a state of affairs are many and include the following:
- other groups are younger, more active and willing to take risks
- they have better contacts in the old Party *nomenklatura*
- they also have more links with crime groups
- they live mostly in cities where economic action is concentrated
- business has not traditionally been highly regarded in Latvian culture.

The state bureaucracy which can affect the rate of privatization is predominantly Latvian and apparently afraid of losing its power and the concomitant benefits involved in the control of industries.

There have been foreign investors who have started up new firms or enterprises, but initial investments have been cautiously small, that is, in most cases well below US $1 million. Some of the most commonly known private or joint initiatives include Coca Cola, Shell, Kelloggs, Rank Xerox, Avis Rent-a-Car. Total investments by the fall of 1993 reached 65 million lats (US $107 million). Germany and the USA accounted for one half of all investments.[47] The problems which face investors are similar to those in all former Soviet republics. In Latvia there is, however, greater stability, both political and economic, and the changes towards Western European levels and standards of moderniza-tion are more rapid than in the CIS. The Latvia's Way-dominated government has shown a great determination to carry out privatization, and its actions in eliminating many of the barriers to this process have been remarkably successful. In 1994 newspapers were filled with advertisements asking for bids on state firms to be privatized. The example of more rapid Estonian privatization has also provided an impetus for Latvians who have traditionally had a sense of friendly competition with their neighbors to the north. There is a feeling as never before, in the general population and even among firm managers, that the key to the increase in production is private control and the investment of new capital for modernization.[48] The old fears of Russian control are being tempered by a genuine desire to end the economic decline and privations of the last four years and a growing confidence that Latvians can compete in the ownership and successful operation of enterprises.[49]

Industry

Almost all Latvian industries were built to serve the Soviet market. They were supplied with imported raw materials and energy and produced low quality goods which did not have to be marketed, but were distributed according to the directions of the Central Plan. Most factories built in the last three decades were dependent, as well, on imported Russian-speaking labor, hence only about 38 percent of the workforce in this sector is Latvian. As a result of this historical legacy, Latvian industry is saddled with abnormal problems which had not yet been resolved by the beginning of 1995.

There are serious constraints on competitiveness weighing down the Latvian industrial sector. During the Soviet period, industry could depend on extremely cheap energy; consequently, very few steps were taken for its conservation. Russia, the main supplier of energy, provided industry with its first major shock when it raised prices close to world levels after 1991. Russian industry, however, continued enjoying subsidized energy prices, thus being able to produce at significantly lower costs. Many Latvian enterprises had to be closed as a result. Other raw materials such as cotton and wool for textiles were also underpriced during the Soviet period and presently can be obtained only at world prices. While Latvian labor is less expensive than in the rest of Europe, textiles are mostly produced in low-wage countries including China.

Soviet-built equipment, except for space and military purposes, was never noted for its quality. An official estimate in 1991 was that 85 to 90 percent of industrial equipment in Latvia fell below modern technological standards.[50] During the period of turmoil and independence very little was invested in the upgrading of the industrial infrastructure. Indeed, in the years since 1989 much large-scale, organized pilfering has significantly debased the quality of even the old system. The craze for easy profits in the sale of "colored metals" attracted many illegal operators who gutted and exported factory equipment. Sometimes this was done with the connivance of factory managers.

For decades the quality of produced goods was sufficient for the non-discriminating Soviet buyer for whom Latvian products were usually sophisticated and scarce items. At present, most manufactured goods cannot compete in Western markets because of the lack of proper quality control. Indeed, one of the most important official programs introduced by the Latvian government in 1994 focuses on the improvement of product quality through testing, certification standardization and safety control.[51]

One of the most invidious relics of the old system is lack of competition. Factories became complacent because they had an assured market and hence issues of price, quality, variety and customer orientation did not receive much attention. Soviet factories often became centers for socializing and welfare with production and work taking on secondary importance. Questions of discipline and labor productivity could not be resolved under conditions of labor scarcity. As yet, the dominant orientation of managers is to protect their redundant workers by keeping them on the payroll. For example, during the first two months of 1993, 16 percent or 343,000 of the paid industrial workers had not worked a single day in their enterprises.[52] Such artificial maintenance of employees increases the costs of production and of products that, as a result, become less competitive and often cannot be sold. The working employees cannot receive increases in wages because of this burden of "hidden unemployment" and their productivity and work satisfaction decrease and they become demoralized. All this misplaced paternalism only increases the likelihood of a total shutdown of production.

As in most post-communist states, managers of enterprises were selected for their technical skills. Modern management in a market economy, however, requires individuals with talent in marketing, procurement, finance and people motivation. Managers should also be free to make decisions without the constant restrictions of workers' councils. Even privatization, if it is going to be done by merely allowing workers to claim an enterprise as their own, is going to create more rather than fewer problems.

Latvian industry has no alternative but to restructure. In the short term this is going to produce high levels of unemployment and tremendous stress and discontent. The paradox of Latvian progress is highlighted by the $1 billion communications modernization deal signed between the Latvian government and Tilts Communications (Cable & Wireless UK and Telecom Finland). The initial capital of US $160 million will be invested by Tilts to provide Latvia with a new optical cable telephone network. All equipment will be imported after work begins. International lines will be ready within six months and complete digital service throughout the country will be available by 2002. Latvia retains 51 percent control but only small orders are going to be placed with Latvia's failing electronic giant, VEF. In 1993 VEF produced 6.7 million lats worth of electronic goods, but sold items worth only 632,000 lats. They need the order and claim that they cannot compete against Alcatel, the main supplier of cables and other equipment, because loans cost incomparably more in Latvia than they do abroad.[53]

The Latvian Ministry of Finance claimed in August 1993 that the statistics on the decrease of industrial production are exaggerated and do not reflect the real situation. This occurs because reporting by enterprises, especially private enterprises, is incomplete. The high rates of taxation and the inefficient tax collection system have encouraged under-reporting of production. Within the private sector the unregistered output has been estimated to be as high as 50 to 80 percent of all production.[54] Given this caveat it may still be useful to know what is published about the dynamics of Latvian industry. The value of Latvian industrial production at constant prices decreased by about 33.5 percent in 1992 and 36 percent during 1993. Among the 125 important types of production in Latvia, decreases were registered in 117 of them in 1993. The situation appears to be improving and by the end of 1993 more types of production were claiming growth than were registering decreases.[55] Production in March 1994 was 7 percent higher than for the previous month.

A World Bank study has recommended that Latvia shift its orientation away from production based on high energy input and imported raw materials, towards the manufacture of skill-intensive goods with high value-added to allow for competition in international markets.[56] Such areas as pharmaceuticals, biotechnology, electronics and furniture are already important components of production and could lead the way in the rebirth of Latvian industry. To do this, however, industry requires capital for modern equipment, and intensive retraining of its workers and managers for the development of various skills required in a competitive market-based capitalist economy.

One of the new developments by the end of 1993 which may help Latvian industry was that the costs of manufactured products in Russia and Belarus had escalated and reached Latvian levels, in part because of rising energy costs. Latvian products were deemed to be of slightly better quality, hence there was a new surge of demand from the East. For many months in 1994 this opportunity appeared to be blocked by the extremely high tariffs placed against Baltic products by Russia (averaging 40 percent). In May 1994, however, Latvia received favored-nation trading status from Russia, joining over 120 other countries with such a designation. In practice, however, Russian customs officers have been quite arbitrary in levying higher tariffs against Latvian goods.

Agriculture

Agriculture was the mainstay of the Latvian economy in 1939 and there are many people in 1995 – especially within the more nationalist-oriented groups – who proclaim that agriculture should still be the main thrust of the economy and government policy for a long time into the future. While agriculture accounted for 24.3 percent of the GDP in 1992 its share had diminished to 10 percent in the first half of 1994.[57] Nevertheless, agriculture was still providing about 20 percent of total employment in 1995. Politically there was a divergence on how much support from government this sector should receive and this issue was the main cause of the dissolution of the coalition between Latvia's Way and the Farmers' Union in July 1994.

There is another important but rarely articulated component of conflict. Most industrial workers are non-Latvians; almost all farmers are Latvians. Russian-language publications have sometimes seen the support of agriculture and the apparent failure of support for industry as a clear case of governmental ethnic bias.

Agriculture has a very strongly defined private sector and a crumbling public sector. Even this public sector has different juridical distinctions and many of the old *kolkhozes* and *sovkhozes* continue working as *paju sabiedribas*, or share associations. These, in effect, function as coopera-tives whose state ownership claims are rather unclear.

Agricultural production between 1991 and 1994 has decreased for many reasons. The dismemberment of more than a third of large farming units into smallholdings averaging seventeen hectares increased the enthusiasm and dedication of those who started farming for themselves, but it also lost the efficiencies provided by large operations. It now takes many more tractors and equipment to service the previous collective territory when divided into numerous small individual farms. A study of over 17,000 private farmers in 1993 found serious gaps in the infrastructure and facilities of their homesteads. A surprisingly high number (42 percent) did not have electricity, 52 percent had no tractors and 85 percent had no telephones. A quarter did not even have a house, and a majority of those who did lived in buildings constructed before 1940. Another quarter did not have animal barns, about half had to build feed storage barns and two-thirds required new equipment shelters. One fifth of farmers still had to build access roads averaging one kilometer in length. Isolation for many is also guaranteed by the fact that only 42 percent had any form of private transportation. Public transportation as a result of cost-cutting has become very infrequent and sometimes irregular. This problem has also affected school attendance by farm children. Labor-saving devices normally expected on farms are almost non-existent.[58] To be sure, such serious deficits of farming essentials have forced usually independent and taciturn Latvian farmers to share equipment and buildings.

It is often pointed out by the media that equipment from the break-up of collective farms was distributed unevenly and irrationally, and credit for buying new equipment and supplies is difficult to obtain and the rates exorbitantly high. These farmers cannot offer their land as collateral because only a small percentage have fully registered ownership title to it. Most only have leasing rights. Some relief, however, has been obtained through international loans and through government subsidies.

Both private and collective farmers have had to endure many shocks. The extremely rapid rise of the price of energy, especially gasoline, created much consternation and forced farmers to limit the areas cultivated and in some cases to switch to horses, especially in south-eastern Latvia. Since 1993 some compensation for diesel fuel has been provided by government. Prices of other import items such as equipment, feed, agrochemicals and veterinary pharmaceuticals have also risen dramatically.

State food-processing enterprises were forced to accept grain from farmers at high government-dictated prices set in 1992. As a result, surreptitious food imports from neighboring countries were able to compete at much lower prices and Latvian enterprises were not able to repay farmers for long periods of time. Many frustrated farmers were forced to take out expensive loans to sow their fields. High grain prices, as well, created a shock of their own. Animal feed prices climbed so high that many farmers were forced to slaughter their animals. The former head of the Farmers' Union fraction, Aivars Berkis, pointed out in his farewell speech in March, 1994, that "it is especially hard to oppose decisions which please the people." The setting of overly high grain purchase prices by the Supreme Council, and by all members of his fraction, created many long-term problems: "The high grain prices later undermined hog and poultry farming; in its wake customs protection barriers were demolished and we are still suffering today from this erroneous decision."[59]

The sequel to this unusual price-setting by government has been the plummeting of grain prices in 1993. Without intervention average grain purchase prices declined by 63 percent in 1993. Many farmers were totally surprised and depressed by the steepness of decline and a high number did not even harvest their crops. On the other hand, this change in grain prices raised the viability of meat production. Hog farming rebounded as a major growth area in agriculture in 1993.

One extremely problematical inheritance from the Soviet period is the widespread incidence of animal diseases. According to one insurance official about 80–90 percent of the animals in state and collective farms were sick. Many of these animals were later allotted to individual farmers. Insurance companies have suffered losses by insuring animals and are now refusing to do so.[60]

Latvian agriculture also suffers from excessive precipitation. In order to allow earlier sowing and satisfactory harvesting, major efforts have traditionally been put into drainage. With new private systems, farmers have to worry about maintaining and renewing underground pipe systems and drainage ditches. As well, a certain proportion of their land has been reclaimed from formerly uncultivated scrubland where drainage infrastructure did not exist. High precipitation also results in frequent leaching of fertilizers. All these difficulties raise the price of agricultural production.

Statistics for agriculture are suspect for many of the same reasons as for industry. Farmers have a vested interest in claiming low productivity and low profits to avoid taxes and to receive more government benefits. The tendencies, however, are clear. An increasing share of production comes from private farms, although the bulk of grain crops are still produced on state farms. There has also been a dramatic decrease in farm output in 1993 and 1994. Annual agricultural production decreased by 16 percent in 1993 compared to 1992. The greatest decrease, or 22 percent, occurred in animal products, but there was also a 5 percent decrease in plant products. The production of vegetables and potatoes, however, went up by 12 and 7 percent respectively.[61] A comparison of the yields of animal products for the first nine months of 1993 and 1994 provides an overview of the pattern of decreases during this period (table 4.2).

Latvia maintains a relatively high tariff rate on agricultural products because it contends, and correctly, that Western Europe provides heavy subsidies to its farmers and limits access to exported Latvian food products. In the free-trade agreements of the three Baltic republics, which began to be implemented on April 1, 1994, agricultural products were not included, although negotiations were continuing.

Table 4.2. *Animal products of state and private farms, January–September, 1993 and 1994*

	1993 Jan.–Sept.	1994 Jan.–Sept.	% change
All farms			
Meat (thousand tonnes live weight)	219	136	−38
Milk (thousand tonnes)	932	786	−16
Eggs (millions)	298	265	−11
State farms (shareholder societies together with private plots)			
Meat	110	49	−56
Milk	327	188	−43
Eggs	219	182	−17
Private farms			
Meat	109	87	−20
Milk	605	598	−1
Eggs	79	83	+4

Source: Latvijas Vestnesis, November 1, 1994.

Foreign trade

Small countries are usually dependent on trade for their economic well-being. In Latvia, trade accounts for a large part of GDP. During 1993 exports were valued at 675.6 million lats (US $1.2 billion) and imports were slightly less at 639.2 million lats. In nominal terms (without allowing for inflation) exports grew by 17.9 percent and imports by 18 percent in comparison to 1992. In the first seven months of 1994 the CIS was the main destination for exports at 43.3 percent (Russia: 27.8 percent) and source of imports 31.7 percent (Russia: 25.3 percent). The European Union and European Free Trade Association received 38.6 percent of Latvian exports and provided 37.6 percent of imports. The main components of direct exports during these seven months were wood products (19.7 percent), machinery and vehicles (15.8 percent), textiles and clothing (10.8 percent), food products (10.3 percent) and metals (10.1 percent).[62]

One of the major reforms which facilitated trade was the ending of import and export licenses and a switch to import and export tariffs. This eliminated the many charges of favoritism and price fixing and allowed for free competition by anybody who could make a profit. The introduction of Baltic free trade and free-trade agreements with Nordic and other European countries should be a spur to growth in trade in the future.

Consumption patterns and unemployment

One of the major effects of the economic changes and dislocations from 1990 to 1995 has been a change in the pattern of consumption. The proportion of the family budget spent on food is commonly used as an index of poverty because this is the least flexible item in family purchases. According to budget studies in Latvia, food claimed only 29.4 percent of expenditure in 1990, but this item's share rose to 37.8 percent in 1991, 48.2 percent in 1992 and was 44.4 percent in 1993. In the USA an average of 15 percent of income goes to food purchases.[63]

Unemployment in Latvia has reached higher official levels than in Estonia and Lithuania. In December 1994, Latvia had an official rate of 6.4 percent. If hidden unemployment is added then the rate was about 9 percent. There are two features of particular concern about unemployment in Latvia. One is that the area suffering the greatest unemployment levels is Latgale, the ethnically mixed south-eastern province. In Latgale, in December 1994, Kraslavas region reached a rate of 25.1 percent, Preili 23.6, Rezekne 22.4, Balvi 19.7 and Daugavpils 13.5. Only after these Latgallian concentrations of unemployment come areas from different regions such as Madona and Kuldiga.[64] It is noteworthy that higher unemployment also prevailed in Latgale during the interwar period. Not surprisingly this area gave a high proportion of its votes in June 1993 to left-wing parties (Harmony and Equal Rights). The other feature is similar to most other former Communist countries: there is a higher proportion of women among the unemployed – about 56 percent.

Resource prospects

Every country in the world has features which can be exploited for greater economic growth. In Latvia, besides agricultural land, such major features are ports, shipping and fishing, forests, construction materials, tourism, geographical location, energy resources and an educated population.

All-season ports are among the natural advantages of Latvia and these should provide long-term benefits to trade. The two ports of Riga and Ventspils are already used but not yet to full capacity. The third port of Liepaja, which was only recently vacated as a military base, is being reconstructed and will no doubt become a major asset. In 1994 a joint Lithuanian–Latvian project was agreed for the creation of an oil terminal in this port to partly supply the Lithuanian refinery at Mazeikiai.[65] Riga has a container terminal with a capacity of about one million tonnes a year which during the Soviet period was a major transit point for goods coming from Japan and destined for Western Europe.[66] The trans-Siberian route from Nakhodka on the Pacific to Riga could be revived, and earlier volumes of transit trade could even be surpassed. One of the problems during the Soviet period was that about 90 percent of port transit went West but only 10 percent went East. This pattern has not improved. In 1993 cargo leaving Latvian ports was considerably higher at 23.2 million tonnes than incoming cargo at 1.4 million tonnes. To be sure, 16.4 million tonnes of outbound cargo was accounted for by oil and oil products.[67] There are some concerns on the horizon for Latvian ports. The more modern and recently constructed Tallinn deep water port could become a serious source of competition.[68] As well, Russia is planning to build a large new port close to St. Petersburg.

Shipping and ship repairs are an area of future potential. Latvia inherited more than 100 commercial ships after the break-up of the USSR. These ships, often leased to foreign countries and run by Latvian Shipping Lines, have provided a major boost for the Latvian balance of services and trade.[69] Fishing fleets could be another source of income if they were modernized. The Baltic Sea is an important fishing resource and Latvians have access to other seas of the world.

Forests cover about 42 percent of Latvian territory and have an estimated volume of 426 million cubic meters of wood.[70] Forest products were a major source of governmental revenue before 1940, and the term "green gold" has been historically applied to this resource. Presently, lumber and wood-based products such as furniture are among the main items of export to Western Europe. Much potential for growth remains, especially in areas of pulp production. The main producer of paper, the Sloka Pulp and Paper Mill was forced to shut down in 1993 because of its excessive consumption of energy and because of low paper prices. Several foreign firms have expressed interest in renovating the mill. The chances of this appear to have improved with the steep increases in paper prices in 1994.

For several years now the allowable cut of trees has not been harvested. Thus in 1993, 6.6 million cubic meters were slated for cutting, but only 4.7 million were actually cut. A large part of timber resources is exported but most of it is sent away without even minimal processing within Latvia. Out of the total of 1.5 million cubic meters exported in 1993, 1.02 million cubic meters went as unprocessed round timber.[71] The forest and wood products industry has also suffered from the slow pace of privatization, from the slow settlement of land claims and from lack of service organizations. The transport of logs to ports often has to be done by the same organization that harvests trees because of the dearth of specialized trucking services. This creates bottlenecks and lowers the rates of delivery.

A boom in construction is expected as soon as privatization and land ownership issues have been resolved. Latvia has ample domestic supplies of good-quality bricks, cement, gypsum, glass and lumber, and a rebirth in this moribund industry should have a positive impact on many other areas.

Tourism as yet has not found its footing. Latvian hotels accommodated 311,000 people in 1993 with 31 percent being Latvian residents, 41 percent coming to Latvia on business and 15 percent on holidays.[72] During the Soviet period Riga and the famous seaside resort of Jurmala attracted millions of visitors from the rest of the Soviet Union. With the rupture of relations and the economic doldrums experienced in the CIS, very few people from the East are returning to their traditional haunts. At the same time the quality of services and resort buildings is not adequate to attract sophisticated Western tourists. It appears probable that privatization will inject new capital for renovation in the tourist industry and that increased economic normalization in Russia will attract those who cannot afford the prices of Western European resorts.

Latvia has many attractive areas for future tourism. Its old and architecturally eclectic cities have not as yet been hidden under neon signs. There are several hundred miles of unspoiled, mostly sandy seashore with nothing but forests and a few fishing villages. There are three separate undulating upland areas with numerous lakes and streams yielding an abundance of fish. There are still many virgin salmon streams that have not been developed with modern conveniences. The Gauja National Park provides a wilderness experience for those wishing to paddle down the Gauja river. Latvia is also one of the most productive areas for wildlife. During the 1993/4 season, hunters registered the following bag count: 3,200 moose, 7,000 elk, 22,100 deer and 15,300 wild boar.[73] Unregistered hunting, however, is on the rise as more guns become available and the price of meat increases.

Latvia's location on the shores of the Baltic Sea and adjacent to relatively landlocked Russia and Belarus may create potential opportunities for becoming a trading bridge between Western Europe, the CIS, China and Japan. The Scandinavian countries and Germany are also finding a new interest in strengthening the Baltic Sea ring of countries. Several projects including the modern highway link from Helsinki to Warsaw called the Baltic Way appear feasible and could provide access to millions of motorists who today are discouraged by poor roads, lack of facilities and cantankerous border guards. There have been discussions about reviving the historical trade links of the Hanseatic League around the Baltic Sea.

Oil is a resource which may help the Latvian economy in the future. Joint Latvian–Danish studies have found deposits of about 35–40 million tonnes most of which are located under the sea near the port of Liepaja. A total of 28,000 square kilometers has already been divided into twenty-one exploration blocks to be sold to interested bidders.[74]

A part of the energy dependence on neighboring countries could be decreased by the proposed use of biomass and peat in the running of electric power stations. There are vast peat deposits which were used for fuel several decades ago and waste wood is a plentiful resource. The large gas collector at Incukalns has become an important point in energy distribution within the Baltic.

A major resource which will affect the Latvian economy more than all the other factors combined is the orientation of people, their levels of education and entrepreneurship. No doubt many of the professions created to service the Soviet economy will lose their marketability. Soviet economists, for example, are not necessarily suited to a capitalist system. One of the key benefits of higher education, however, is that people increase their flexibility and are better able to adjust to new circumstances. The highly educated and skilled labor force in Latvia should become an important foundation of innovation and competitiveness.

Even more, the spirit of entrepreneurship is an important ingredient in the success of many economies. About a quarter of those polled in Riga in 1993 indicated their overall willingness to become entrepreneurs, with another third willing to try "depending on circumstances." About 40 percent would never consider such an option.[75]

Conclusion

Latvia has made surprising progress in macroeconomic stabilization. It has established its own financial institutions albeit some banks have become insolvent. Inflation has been reduced to manageable proportions. The government has been able to confine its spending within the restrictions of a broadly accepted budget and to end almost all unproductive subsidies. Its taxation system is being rationalized and simplified although much more work will be required to discourage cheaters.

Privatization, with the exception of agriculture, however, has progressed very slowly and with great reluctance. By 1994, about 60,000 private farms were in operation and most small enterprises had been taken over by private or cooperative entrepreneurs. In both instances the question of actual ownership has generally not been resolved. The prospects of success and survival for small-scale farmers and small businesses under their present operators are not particularly high. The average life-span of small businesses in North America is less than seven years. Given the limited-term contracts of most small businesses in Latvia and a variety of other impinging negative factors such as protection money payments to organized criminals, extremely costly loans, widespread tax evasion by the less scrupulous and low purchasing capacity, there will probably be a higher rate of attrition than experienced elsewhere in the West.

Medium and large industries have only begun to be privatized. In 1994 there appeared to be a singular determination on the part of the government to accelerate the pace of privatization and to eliminate long-standing obstacles which had slowed down the process in previous years. The real problem, however, is how to dispose of a large part of the unduly large and antiquated leftovers of Soviet industry. Many factories will necessarily have to be closed because they cannot avoid bankruptcy. Most are already debt-ridden. There is as yet not enough foreign investment and local private economic activity which could absorb the excess workers coming from doomed state enterprises, as has been the case in Poland.

Indeed, the modernization and competitiveness of enterprises is one of the weakest links in economic recovery within Latvia. During the 1960s some economists claimed that the reason why Germany became so competitive and productive in comparison to Britain was that almost all German factories had been bombed and had to be rebuilt with the most modern systems and machinery. Most people in Latvia are still psychologically attached to their rusting machinery and crumbling industrial carcasses, many of which date from the days of the czar. They still want to set formidable conditions for anyone who will receive these gifts "built by so many."

The privatization of dwellings has also been very slow but once this process begins with the help of certificates, expected sometime in 1995, the economy should receive a considerable boost. The unencumbered sale and rental of houses and apartments should inject new demand for repairs and construction, as well as for household goods, and have a ripple effect in most areas of the economy because of released capital.

The desire to be like other countries in Western Europe is a most important influencing factor. In general the services sector of the economy has become the agent of modernization and growth in the Latvian economy. In the first half of 1994 the services sector claimed 61 percent of the GDP, with agriculture down to 10 percent and manufacturing to 18 percent.[76] Services in Latvia are now close to the proportional share in the GDP found in Finland (60 percent) and Sweden (62 percent). The psychological orientation of people is also changing. Within just a few years the widespread abacus has been replaced by digital cash registers. Sales people have learned that attitude to customers can affect sales. There is greater stress on maintaining schedules and appointments. Riga appears to be a boom town which is finally shedding its dour Communist greyness and rebuilding its crumbling facades and infrastructure. The pervasive pessimism of 1992 and part of 1993 seems to be dissipating, albeit very slowly. A solid majority now believe that their family economic prospects will improve.[77] The shocks associated with changes induced by reforms are not over and unemployment looms as a major threat. Some people will never adjust and will remain bitter and frustrated. A significant proportion, especially among the younger age categories, appear to be more enterprising and believe in the likelihood of their own success.

Economic success for Latvia is not necessarily assured, however. One of the greatest stumbling blocks is the lack of capital for renovation and investment. Western Europe was once the beneficiary of the Marshall Aid program which provided the seed money for a vigorous postwar economic recovery. The sums provided for Latvia and indeed for all of the former Communist countries are extremely skimpy and annually add up to less than several stealth bombers manufactured by the USA at a billion dollars each. More aid money is received annually by tiny Israel than by all the countries in former Eastern Europe.

In addition to minimal aid, Western Europe and North America have created a tariff and quota wall as well as non-tariff barriers against the products which the former Communist countries could best compete in, especially in agriculture.

Latvia is slowly coming out of its shattering economic decline. There are expectations that with the renewed economic growth in the Western world benefits, will also accrue to Latvia. With increased stability, a modern system of telecommunications, and an industrious and enlightened labor force, prospects for recovery and even rapid growth are good. A more pessimistic scenario could envisage instability created by a conservative and belligerent Russia. Dependence on Russian trade is still large and could be affected by political developments within Russia and within Latvia. The issue of ethnic tensions could become the inhibiting factor which paralyzes Latvian economic development. The high crime rate and the consolidation of organized crime groups could be another threat to economic peace and prosperity.

If it was once common to claim that the only certain things in life were death and taxes, it appears that economic readjustment is now becoming a third certainty throughout the world. It is difficult to estimate how Latvia will do in the future and how it will adjust to economic imperatives. Nevertheless, in the short term, Latvia and the other Baltic republics have been judged to be models of successful macroeconomic reform that other republics of the former USSR could emulate. The IMF managing director, Michael Camdessus, in an interview in Washington on February 1, 1994, underscored the importance of the Baltic experience. "You have also the demonstration effect of the success of policies. I am absolutely certain, for instance, that the remarkable way in which the Balts have established their new currencies, and developed their reform programs ... is certainly a very inspiring example."[78]

5   Demography, language and ethnic relations

For almost half a century after the end of World War II, ethnicity and ethnic group relations in Latvia were discussed only within the narrow confines of accepted ideology. This usually meant that only positive aspects of ethnic groups were ever mentioned while in practice the dominance of Russian-speaking groups was encouraged. Only with the advent of glasnost and a relatively open press and media did the existing tensions among the ethnic groups come to the fore. Indeed, since the beginning of the period of awakening and especially since the advent of independence, demographic patterns and ethnic group relations have been among the most important factors affecting policy-making and political behavior in Latvia; and, no doubt, these same factors will play a large role on the Latvian political stage for the foreseeable future.

A paradoxical and inherently unstable situation has developed in Latvia wherein *all* ethnic groups can be considered a minority in one situation or another and *all* feel insecure and threatened. The insecurity of the Russian-speaking group began only after the declaration of sovereignty in May 1990 and reached its apogee in September 1991 when the USSR recognized Latvian independence. Previously this group had considered itself to be an integral part of the Russian majority of the USSR. All of a sudden it found itself in the unfamiliar role of being a minority in a foreign land whose citizenship rights were left at the discretion of another ethnic group. This insecurity of Russian-speakers has been somewhat mitigated, however, by the knowledge that they form a clear majority in all urban areas and can claim a two-thirds dominance in the city of Riga.

The Latvians have been under stress and on the defensive since the 1940 occupation of their country. After the declaration of sovereignty in 1990 and especially after the establishment of independence in August 1991, Latvians were able to take measures to strengthen the political presence of their group and stop the uncontrolled in-migration of aliens. Nevertheless, they feel threatened by their minority status in urban areas, especially in the city of Riga. By 1989 they had also become a

142

minority in all age groups from 19 to 44 in the entire country. Hitherto, Latvian natural increase has been only a small fraction of that of the other groups. If this trend were to continue, Latvians would soon make up less than half the population of the country. Since 1990 there are signs of a change in the pattern of natural increase, favoring the Latvians; this pattern, however, may be reversed at any time.

There is also a perceived political threat by Latvians even before the crossing of the "demographic Rubicon" of 50 percent. With only a 54 percent majority in 1994 and with the potential naturalization of over half a million non-citizens within a decade, Latvians feel they could lose control of the development of their country because the normal processes of democracy do not guarantee that all Latvians will vote together or be able to elect a ruling party to defend their interests. The Latvian language could once again be at risk and newly created immigration restrictions could be lifted to allow the influx of great numbers of new settlers from the vast hinterlands of Russia and other neighboring republics, especially if calamitous circumstances bring about a flood of refugees. These concerns of a people who lost control over the development of their native country for half a century are not merely juridical-legal. They touch the deepest emotional chords of group existence and group self-defense, with fears of extinction weighing heavily in the calculations of many Latvian leaders and in the political orientations of many Latvian voters.

It is clear that the Soviet period has left a demographic legacy which will most probably be an intrinsic part of the Latvian social and political landscape for many centuries to come. At the same time it is important to note that since 1990 there have been new demographic trends which, while not expected to change substantially the basic configuration of ethnic groups, may ease the stress levels among Latvians. This in turn could result in more generous and tolerant attitudes towards the other ethnic groups which share the territory of the Republic of Latvia and also consider it their only home.

The Soviet demographic legacy

Until 1991 and the assumption of control over their own borders, Latvians faced a relentless influx of people from other republics. They were powerless to stop this migration of aliens and faced a precarious demographic future where minoritization of the indigenous group of the republic appeared to be imminent. Latvians constituted 77 percent of the total population during Latvia's independence period in 1935, 83 percent just before the final occupation of the country by the Red Army in 1945, but only 62 percent in 1959, 54 percent in 1979, and 52 percent in 1989.[1] The percentage of Latvians in the big cities was even smaller. In spite of the advent of independence and the halt and even reversal of net migration among non-Latvians, the fear of minoritization continues to be a most urgent concern among Latvians. The fears of minoritization were particularly accentuated in the Latvian population after the publication of the results of the 1989 census. Concern on this score was widely expressed in public speeches, declarations and the media. The imminent loss of majority status was perceived as a collective catastrophe leading inexorably to political emasculation and Latvian cultural extinction. An academic voiced this fear in a Riga newspaper in 1990: "Let us look reality in the eyes! The Latvian nation has come to the edge of the dark precipice of oblivion. Just a little bit more and only geographical names will testify that at one time a people called the Latvians lived here [and disappeared] in a manner similar to the ancient Prussians."[2] A Latvian People's Front official entitled his 1990 English language appeal to the world as "The Latvian Nation and the Genocide of Immigration."

The principal cause for the dwindling Latvian presence in their own republic was uncontrolled immigration from neighboring Soviet republics for over forty-five years prior to 1990.

The Latvians did not choose to become a diminishing proportion in their homeland. Soviet occupation brought with it policies that were worked out in Moscow with little regard for local input on matters such as immigration and language policy. Indeed, the change in ethnic balance within the republic most probably was one of deliberate purpose.

This demographic legacy, however, cannot be reversed by legislation or by expulsion as was done with the Germans in Sudetenland and other areas immediately after World War II. The presence of a still powerful Russian neighbor as well as Latvian public opinion would not tolerate such an emulation of history. A majority of Russians and large proportions of other minorities have been born in Latvia and have only minimal ties with the regional areas of departure of their parents (table 5.1).

At the same time the relatively large size and past history of dominance in Latvia of the Russian linguistic community have created a certain inertia and reluctance on the part of many to adapt to the Latvian cultural community. If in the previous half-century Latvians were the ones forced to accommodate to the language and mores of the occupiers, it can be readily understood that with independence regained they no longer have the need nor desire to continue this unilateral and

Table 5.1. *Major ethnic minorities in Latvia by place of birth, 1989 (percent)*

	Latvia	RSFSR	Belorussia	Ukraine	Lithuania
Russians	54.8	36.2	2.2	2.4	—
Belorussians	31.3	3.6	62.2	1.1	—
Ukrainians	19.4	8.5	1.6	65.7	—
Poles	65.8	3.1	22.3	—	—
Lithuanians	36.0	2.2	0.6	—	60.0
Jews	53.3	12.8	9.9	19.7	—

Source: Latvijas Republikas Valsts Statistikas Komiteja, mimeo., May 24, 1991.

demeaning relationship. Latvians are not about to forget their Russian language skills but they have begun to be more assertive in demanding that those living in their midst make a serious effort to adjust to the language and traditions of the native population. The dramatic change in power relationships brought about by independence is causing palpable strains within the non-Latvian population. Many in their midst are finding it difficult adjusting from being integral units of the empire and part of the Russian-speaking majority to being a minority whose multiple ties with Moscow are being attenuated and severed.

The comparatively high number of Russian-speakers has created its own dynamic of inter-ethnic relations. Because of their large numbers, Russophones in Latvia feel less threatened than similar groups in Estonia and Lithuania. At the same time Latvians have been forced to take into account their own minority presence in most urban areas and especially in the six largest cities of Latvia. It is noteworthy, however, that the relationship between Russians and Latvians within the republic has often been strained but reasonably peaceful over the years, with relatively high rates of intermarriage. Whether this social peace can be maintained will depend on the sophistication of the policies of the Latvian government, the adjustment of non-Latvians to a new reality of power, the attitude of the Latvian population and the actions of Russia, Latvia's unpredictable, unstable and turmoil-prone neighbor.

The postwar history of migration to Latvia

Latvians have had to accommodate to ethnic diversity for several hundred years because large numbers of Germans, Poles, Russians and others have long lived within their borders, and especially in their cities. Riga was once predominantly a German city and Latvians accounted for only 24 percent of its population in 1867 and 42 percent in 1913.[3] A

Latvian demographer recently noted: "It is doubtful whether many Latvians can be certain of their 'pure blood' after [having survived] German lords and Polish, Swedish, and Russian periods."[4] While Riga attained a Latvian plurality by the end of the nineteenth century, it also attracted many minority groups, including Jews, Poles, and Lithuanians. The city had the sophistication that would be associated with being the empire's third largest port.

In 1935 Latvia contained 1,905,000 people, of whom 77 percent, or 1,467,000, were Latvians. By 1945, however, Latvia had lost an estimated 600,000 people or 30 percent of its population as a result of the war, executions, deportations and the exodus of refugees.[5] Qualified and ideologically reliable personnel were in short supply, and direly needed housing left by those who had fled or had been killed was readily available. Large numbers of people were brought into Latvia to occupy the available space (table 5.2).

During the 1950s, attempts were made by Latvian "national Communists" to stop the flow of in-migration. However, in 1959 these mostly Latvian-born local leaders headed by Eduards Berklavs were purged by Moscow. Thereafter, all the floodgates were opened for further settlers from the East. The number of Russians, Ukrainians and Belorussians in Latvia rose sharply between 1959 and 1970 – 32 percent compared with a growth of 3 percent for the Latvians. Thereafter the three Slavic peoples grew more slowly – by 17 percent between 1970 and 1979 and by 11.8 percent between 1979 and 1989. However, the Latvians grew by only 0.2 percent in the former period and 3.3 percent in the latter, hence their proportion in the population continued to decline. In the 1989 census the three Slavic peoples accounted for 41.9 percent of the total population compared with 10.2 percent in 1935. Latvians, by contrast, were still 79,200 short of their number in 1935 as a result of the bloody actions initiated by Hitler and Stalin.

The urban–rural distribution of ethnic groups

According to the 1989 census, Latvians had become a minority in the eight largest cities in their own republic. Indeed, the minoritization of Latvians had grown rapidly during the previous two decades. In 1970, in all of Latvia, 32 percent of Latvians lived in cities or *raions* where they constituted a minority. By 1979 this had increased to 37 percent and ten years later to 41 percent.[6]

Riga, the capital city, contains over a third of the total population of Latvia and has been responsible for an overwhelming proportion of the output of publishing, higher education and culture. In 1935 Latvians

Table 5.2. *Population of Latvia by ethnic origin, 1935–94 (thousands)*

Ethnic origin	1935 census	%	1959 census	%	1970 census	%	1979 census	%	1989 census	%	1994 Jan. 1	%
Latvian	1,467.0	77.0	1,297.9	62.0	1,341.8	56.8	1,344.1	53.7	1,387.8	52.0	1,391.8	54.2
Russian	168.3	8.8	556.4	26.6	704.6	29.8	821.5	32.8	905.5	34.0	849.2	33.1
Belorussian	26.8	1.4	61.6	2.9	94.7	4.0	111.5	4.5	119.7	4.5	105.1	4.1
Polish	48.6	2.6	59.8	2.9	63.0	2.7	62.7	2.5	60.4	2.3	57.2	2.2
Ukrainian	1.8	0.1	29.4	1.4	53.5	2.3	66.7	2.7	92.1	3.4	78.2	3.1
Lithuanian	22.8	1.2	32.4	1.5	40.6	1.7	37.8	1.5	34.6	1.3	33.2	1.3
Jewish	93.4	4.9	36.6	1.7	36.7	1.6	28.3	1.1	22.9	0.9	13.3	0.5
German	62.1	3.3	1.6	0.1	5.4	0.2	3.3	0.1	3.8	0.1	2.3	0.1
Estonian	6.9	0.4	4.6	0.2	4.3	0.2	3.7	0.1	3.3	0.1	3.0	0.1
Gypsy	3.8	0.2	4.3	0.2	5.4	0.2	6.1	0.2	7.0	0.3	7.3	0.3
Other	4.4	0.2	8.9	0.5	14.1	0.6	17.1	0.8	29.5	1.0	25.4	1.0
Total	1,905.4	100	2,093.5	100	2,364.1	100	2,502.8	100	2,666.6	100	2,565.7	100

Sources: Elmars Vebers, ed., *The Ethnic Situation in Latvia* (Riga: Ethnic Studies Centre, 1994), p. 4; *Cina*, June 23, 1971; Latvijas Republikas Valsts Statistikas Komiteja, *Latvijas Demografijas Gadagramata 1993* (Riga: 1994), p. 47.

accounted for 63 percent of the population of this city. By 1989 Latvians had dwindled to 36.5 percent of the inhabitants of the capital although their share had again increased to 37.7 percent by 1994. The non-Latvians have not been concentrated in isolated ghettos, but have systematically blanketed all Riga districts. Since non-Latvians still have a minimal knowledge of the language of the republic, Latvians cannot claim a single area where they can publicly converse in their native language as a matter of course. Even with language legislation in place little progress in the spread of Latvian has been made. Except at home, in certain small businesses and in government institutions, the daily life of Latvians in Riga unfolds within a sea of Russian-speaking individuals. In the capital city in 1989, only 17 percent of Latvians used Latvian in opening conversations with strangers, but 96 percent of Russians and 85 percent of other groups used Russian.[7] To be sure, many non-Latvians have become more linguistically assertive after independence; nevertheless, many taxi-drivers and shopkeepers were still adamantly unilingual Russian in Riga in 1994 and had not bothered to learn even a minimal dozen words of Latvian. Ironically, many of those who knew Latvian refused to speak it.

In Estonia and Lithuania there are secondary cities (Tartu and Kaunas respectively) that can provide alternate cultural inputs or serve as a counterweight to the capital. Latvia has no such city. The second largest city in Latvia, Daugavpils, with 124,910 inhabitants in 1989, was also one of the cities with the lowest percentage of Latvians – only 13.8 percent in 1994. Rather than being a counterweight to the non-Latvian atmosphere of Riga, this city has become a demonstratively Russian-speaking fortress rather oblivious to the changes that have occurred in the country. During the period of awakening, Daugavpils became an alternative center for the empire-savers. The newspaper of the International Front, an organization formed to counter the demands of the Latvian-oriented People's Front, was published in Daugavpils, and the Daugavpils city soviet adopted a resolution which proclaimed the Latvian declaration of independence of May 4, 1990 inoperative within the city's boundaries. Liepaja, the port city by the sea with 114,486 inhabitants, has historically been an important regional centre for Latvian culture, but it too faces the same problems as Riga. Latvians accounted for only 38.8 percent of the total population in 1989 and 42.1 percent in 1994 (table 5.3).

The countryside is the only area in which Latvians have majority status, but only 31 percent of the population of Latvia was rural in 1994. Moreover, there is one rural area – the predominantly Catholic province of Latgale in the south-eastern part of the republic – where a great deal

Table 5.3. *Ethnic composition of largest cities in Latvia, 1989 census and January 1994 (percent)*

		Latv.	Russ.	Belo.	Ukr.	Pol.	Lith.	Other
Riga	1989	36.5	47.3	4.8	4.8	1.8	0.8	4.0
	1994	37.7	47.5	4.5	4.5	1.8	0.8	3.2
Daugavpils	1989	13.0	58.3	9.1	3.1	13.1	0.9	2.5
	1994	13.8	58.6	8.6	2.9	13.2	0.9	2.1
Liepaja	1989	38.8	43.1	4.9	7.5	1.1	2.3	2.3
	1994	42.1	41.3	4.3	6.8	1.1	2.4	2.0
Jelgava	1989	49.7	34.7	6.0	3.9	1.7	1.2	2.8
	1994	50.7	34.1	5.9	3.6	1.8	1.3	2.6
Jurmala	1989	44.2	42.1	4.9	3.4	1.5	0.9	3.0
	1994	45.1	41.9	4.6	3.3	1.5	0.9	2.7
Ventspils	1989	43.0	39.4	5.8	6.4	1.0	0.7	3.7
	1994	45.2	38.4	5.5	5.5	1.0	0.7	3.8
Rezekne	1989	37.3	55.0	2.0	1.6	2.7	0.2	1.2
	1994	38.4	54.7	1.8	1.5	2.6	0.2	0.8

Sources: Latvija Skaitlos 1989. gada, p. 27; 1989 Gada Vissavienibas Tautas Skaitisanas Rezultati Latvijas PSR, p. 46; Latvijas Republikas Valsts Statistikas Komiteja, Latvijas Demografijas Gadagramata 1993, pp. 50–1.

of assimilation has occurred. In 1994, this province had more Russians (43.4 percent) than Latvians (40.4 percent) with the other groups being mostly other Slavs: Belorussians (6.1 percent), Poles (6.5 percent) and Ukrainians (1.8 percent).[8] After the war, the Latgallians had been tapped by the Bolshevik regime for middle and lower tiers of the bureaucracy because they came from a poor region and had been living side by side with Russians, Belorussians, Poles and others, and were more familiar with the Russian way of doing things. As they moved into the cities and settled in more fertile areas of Latvia in large numbers, especially in the first decade after the war, their abandoned houses and farms attracted many settlers from other republics. It should be noted, however, that the Russian-speaking community in Latgale forms a historic and compact group which has little in common with the Russophones of Riga. A majority of the former group were registered as Latvian citizens in 1993–4.

The two major cities of the Latgale area are Daugavpils and Rezekne. Rezekne is another bastion of Russian-speakers where in 1994 only 38.4 percent of the population was Latvian. In 1994 rural Daugavpils district (excluding the city) had 37.2 percent Latvians and Kraslava district 44.2 percent. In the other districts Latvians held a majority: in Rezekne (excluding the city) 53.5 percent, in Ludza 54.5 percent, in Preili 64.9 percent and in Balvi 71.8 percent.[9] During the period of occupation, many Latvians in Latgale did not have access to Latvian schools or local newspapers. The situation has improved somewhat, but major problems of access still remain.

The distribution of ethnicity by age in the 1989 census

The age distribution in the 1989 census has several noteworthy patterns that bear directly on the future of Latvia. The most important item is the minority status of Latvians in all age groups between 19 and 44, with the smallest percentages found among those aged 30 to 34 and 35 to 39 – 44.6 percent and 43.0 percent of Latvian origin respectively (table 5.4). In part, this low Latvian representation results from the stunted birth rates in the decade after the war when Sovietization, collectivization, guerilla war and deportations all combined to suppress family growth. At a time when North Americans were experiencing a baby boom, Latvians were being traumatized and were not in a position to plan normal families. It surely is abnormal to find more Latvians aged 60–64 (born 1925–9) than aged 40–44 (born 1945–50). At the same time, Russians and others have their highest representation precisely in the latter age category. These data indicate that the Latvians are a minority

Table 5.4. *Ethnicity and age distribution of population in Latvia, 1989*

Age	Total	Latvian	%	Russ.	Belor.	Ukrn.	Pol.	Lith.	Jew.	Other
0–4	207,669	114,179	55.0	75,050	5,064	5,527	2,294	1,412	933	3,210
5–9	188,473	100,920	53.5	71,078	4,885	4,617	2,223	1,237	972	2,541
10–14	174,943	94,778	54.2	64,026	4,661	4,702	2,279	1,390	951	2,156
15–19	184,341	99,387	53.9	62,415	6,525	6,078	3,133	2,182	896	3,725
20–24	184,237	91,970	49.9	62,260	9,193	9,176	3,611	2,426	824	4,777
25–29	208,944	98,821	47.3	74,474	11,846	10,210	4,466	2,857	1,181	5,089
30–34	200,268	89,396	44.6	76,755	11,526	9,753	4,095	2,657	1,564	4,522
35–39	183,479	78,871	43.0	73,195	10,427	8,683	4,382	2,491	1,717	3,713
40–44	156,982	76,125	48.5	55,149	7,879	6,359	4,663	2,417	1,948	2,442
45–49	178,327	100,994	56.6	49,677	9,633	6,203	5,092	3,110	1,187	2,431
50–54	173,459	89,899	51.8	55,652	10,171	6,183	4,553	2,948	1,727	2,326
55–59	161,773	88,081	54.4	50,207	8,899	3,859	4,623	2,658	1,608	1,838
60–64	148,672	76,548	51.4	51,311	7,007	4,236	3,708	2,103	2,063	1,696
65–69	102,946	54,521	53.0	33,750	4,131	3,086	2,892	1,492	1,889	1,185
70+	212,339	133,034	62.7	50,465	7,753	4,055	8,374	3,249	3,437	1,972
Average age	—	35	—	32	37	33	42	39	44	32

Source: Unpublished 1989 Latvian census data.

among those who account for the bulk of the workforce. Overall, Latvians constituted 47.6 percent of those employed in the economy in 1987.[10]

Not surprisingly, Latvians held a commanding lead of 67.3 percent among those aged 75 and older in 1989, but this guarantees a higher number of deaths among Latvians than non-Latvians in the republic for at least a decade. This factor alone could have pushed the overall Latvian population in the republic below 50 percent if natural increase patterns had remained constant and other factors such as net in-migration had not changed. Indeed, the extremely low natural increase of Latvians in the period 1979–89 suggests that this factor was already at work. In absolute terms, the total number of Latvians who were born minus those who died was only 2,300 in ten years or 230 a year. The natural increase of Russians in Latvia during this same period was 42,700, of Belorussians 10,300, and of Ukrainians 9,300.[11]

New demographic patterns

There are, however, new patterns which may alleviate the Latvian demographic quandary. As a result of the 1989 law controlling in-migration and of Latvia's independence it is not surprising that the flow of new migrants to Latvia has almost stopped whereas the outflow of non-Latvians has increased significantly. In four years, between 1989 and 1993, there was a net outflow of almost 100,000 non-Latvians, more than half of whom were Russians. Among all ethnic groups but one there was a loss of population because of migration; Latvians were the only exception with a net increase of 4,689 (table 5.5).

The intensity of out-migration reached a peak in 1992 with a net outflow of 47,188 people, but then decreased by over a third in 1993.[12] The bulk of emigrants in 1993 left for Russia (19,291), Belarus (5,120), Ukraine (3,427), Israel (830), Germany (744), the USA (559) and the other Baltic republics (445). These people were on the whole younger and better educated than the remaining population, a common pattern in most international migration.[13]

While the net outflow of non-Latvians was predictable, the sudden downward shift in natural increase patterns among non-Latvians was unexpected. In 1987 Russian births reached the high level of 13,396, but by 1993 had decreased to 6,495. Deaths went up from 8,397 in 1987 to 11,894 in 1993. Thus as a result of the combined effect of these two demographic variables in 1993, Russians decreased by 5,399. Indeed, the decrease began in 1991 and was ten times larger two years later. Belorussians, as well, decreased by 975 while the Ukrainians diminished

Table 5.5. *Migration patterns, 1989–93*

	1989–92 Net migration	1993 Came to Latvia	1993 Left Latvia	1993 Net migration
All ethnic groups	−65,868	4,114	31,998	−27,884
Latvians	+4,307	1,386	1,004	+382
Russians	−33,367	1,932	19,694	−17,762
Belorussians	−10,434	214	3,895	−3,681
Ukrainians	−12,408	203	3,879	−3,676
Poles	−966	100	548	−448
Lithuanians	−1,092	53	258	−205
Jews	−6,814	63	1,224	−1,161
Germans	−1,186	16	252	−236
Estonians	−70	4	40	−36
Other groups	−3,838	143	1,204	−1,061

Sources: *Latvijas Vestnesis,* March 16, 1994; *Diena,* October 9, 1993.

by 220 in 1993. Poles and Jews, with a higher than average population in the older age groups, had a negative natural increase in almost all years since 1980 (table 5.6).

The causes of the sudden reversal of Slavic demographic patterns have not yet been fully investigated. It seems probable that the disintegration of Soviet and Russian hegemony in Latvia and the uncertainties associated with a reassertion of Latvian political control have diminished births and may in fact have induced more deaths (suicides, homicides, and deaths through alcoholism). Even in the largest seven cities the proportion of Latvian births in 1993 was higher than the Latvian share of the population. In Riga, for example, Latvians claimed 46.8 percent of all births, but Russians 39.8 percent. This was almost the reverse of the population proportions, which were 37.7 percent for Latvians and 47.5 percent for Russians.[14] Paradoxically, even with a decreasing birth rate the Latvians were able to increase their proportion of births because the decrease in all other groups was close to catastrophic. The Latvian share of all newborn babies in 1980 was only 50.4 percent. This share increased very slightly in the following years reaching a level of only 51.7 percent by 1988. After that, however, the Latvian share moved up very rapidly to 53.9 percent in 1989, 56.5 percent in 1990, 58.1 percent in 1991, 61.5 percent in 1992 and 64.5 percent in 1993. During this period the absolute number of Latvian births fell from 20,964 in 1989 to 17,256 in 1993.

Another possible trend that could affect ethnic proportions in the future is assimilation. One of the most surprising phenomena in the data

Table 5.6. *Births, deaths and natural increase by ethnic origin, 1980–93*

	Total	Latvian	Russian	Belor.	Ukrn.	Pol.	Lith.	Jewish	Other
1980									
Births	35,534	17,918	11,839	2,225	1,197	850	662	213	630
Deaths	32,100	20,107	7,978	1,202	472	1,046	515	453	327
Nat. inc.	3,434	-2,189	3,861	1,023	725	-196	147	-240	303
1985									
Births	39,751	20,354	12,840	2,367	1,580	972	677	206	755
Deaths	34,166	20,537	9,023	1,451	618	1,057	569	461	450
Nat. inc.	5,585	-183	3,817	916	962	-85	108	-255	305
1986									
Births	41,960	21,613	13,317	2,419	1,799	990	748	222	852
Deaths	31,328	18,682	8,340	1,331	642	1,002	559	422	350
Nat. inc.	10,632	2,931	4,977	1,088	1,157	-12	189	-200	502
1987									
Births	42,135	21,617	13,396	2,471	1,808	1,002	745	189	907
Deaths	32,150	19,448	8,397	1,313	651	988	530	454	369
Nat. inc.	9,985	2,169	4,999	1,158	1,157	14	215	-265	538
1988									
Births	41,275	21,354	13,012	2,410	1,825	911	643	187	933
Deaths	32,421	18,962	9,018	1,412	683	1,042	544	385	375
Nat. inc.	8,854	2,392	3,994	998	1,142	-131	99	-198	558
1989									
Births	38,922	20,964	11,698	2,037	1,679	907	635	132	870
Deaths	32,584	18,784	9,239	1,425	760	1,008	554	454	360
Nat. inc.	6,338	2,180	2,459	612	919	-101	81	-322	510

1990									
Births	37,918	21,438	10,910	1,840	1,443	827	601	108	751
Deaths	34,812	19,892	10,033	1,564	756	1,111	587	440	429
Nat. inc.	3,106	1,546	877	276	687	−284	14	−332	322
1991									
Births	34,633	20,107	9,716	1,537	1,254	736	583	73	627
Deaths	34,749	19,797	10,261	1,583	762	971	567	404	404
Nat. inc.	−116	310	−545	−46	492	−235	16	−331	223
1992									
Births	31,569	19,458	8,292	1,180	968	612	512	60	487
Deaths	35,420	20,002	10,825	1,503	694	1,069	560	367	400
Nat. inc.	−3,851	−544	−2,533	−323	274	−457	−48	−307	87
1993									
Births	26,759	17,256	6,495	901	647	503	426	48	483
Deaths	39,197	21,685	11,894	1,876	867	1,219	660	353	643
Nat. inc.	−12,438	−4,429	−5,399	−975	−220	−716	−234	−305	−160

Sources: Latvijas Republikas Valsts Statistikas Komiteja and LZA Filozofijas un Sociologijas Instituts, *Etnosituacija Latvija* (Riga: 1992), p. 8; Latvijas Republikas Valsts Statistikas Komiteja, *Latvijas Demografijas Gadagramata 1993* (Riga: 1994), p. 95 and p. 153; *Diena*, October 9, 1993.

on the age distribution of different ethnic groups in 1989 was the higher than average Latvian proportion of the population between the ages of 0 and 19: 54.2 percent, compared with 36.1 percent for the Russians and 9.7 percent for other groups.

One possible partial explanation may be the ethnic identification of the offspring of mixed marriages. It is known that 13.1 percent of those born to Latvian women in 1993 had non-Latvian fathers. Probably there was a similar proportion of Latvian fathers partnered with mothers of other nationalities.[15] Parents were the ones to determine the nationality of children up to the age of 16 for census purposes in 1989. In families where one parent was Latvian, 71.4 percent of the children were considered Latvian. (When one spouse was Russian, 62 percent of those under 16 were declared as Russian, while the comparable figures for other nationalities were: Jews 22.5 percent, Poles 21.2 percent, Ukrainians 18.8 percent, Lithuanians 15.8 percent and Belorussians 13.9 percent.) At the age of maturity, when the young people themselves can designate national origin on their internal passports, the gap in favor of Latvian identification diminished, at least prior to independence, but it was still high in the 15–19 age group.[16]

In this connection there is one other figure worthy of note. Between 1979 and 1989, over 40,000 new Latvians were discovered by census-takers who could not be accounted for either by natural increase or by migration of Latvians from other republics. A Latvian professor of demography, Peteris Zvidrins, has suggested that some of these people could be of mixed parentage or formerly assimilated Latvians who decided to identify with their Latvian roots, in part because of the resurgence of Latvian consciousness and political power. Others, he feels, could be individuals frightened by rumors of immigrant repatriation to their countries of origin who decided to play it safe by claiming Latvian origin. He also leaves a certain margin for "tallying" deficiencies.[17]

If assimilative processes are beginning to work somewhat in the Latvian direction, we are only seeing the first signs of such a development. During the period of independence between World War I and World War II, most linguistic assimilation, as one would expect, was toward the Latvian language, even though the ethnic minorities (including Russians, Jews, Poles and Germans) had state-supported schools in their respective languages. During the postwar decades, however, the Russians became the main beneficiaries of assimilation and denationalization.

In part, the change occurred simply because Latvia was in the Soviet Union, where Russian was the dominant language – the language of communication with the center and the language that was necessary if one left the republic. The language of communication in government and increasingly in most industries and businesses in the larger cities also became Russian. In addition, an important policy change in education created a qualitatively different situation for ethnic groups other than Latvians and Russians. The self-proclaimed internationalists closed all the ethnic schools of these groups, and converted most of them to Russian schools in the first years after World War II.

Language use

The 1989 census statistics on language knowledge in the republic are, indeed, very eloquent. According to this census, 227,783 non-Russians in Latvia considered Russian their first language, but only 34,429 non-Latvians indicated Latvian as a first language.[18] Almost two-thirds or 65.7 percent of Latvians (excluding those for whom Russian is a first language) knew Russian, the highest rate for indigenous nationalities in any republic. Even in Belarus, the republic often considered most Russified, only 60.4 percent of the Belorussians knew the Russian language. At the same time, only 21.1 percent of Russians living in Latvia knew Latvian. Among all non-Latvian nationalities the rate of Latvian language knowledge was 18.3 percent (Belorussians 15.5 percent, Ukrainians 8.9 percent).[19]

People, in general, learn a language when they find a need for it, and the stark imbalance of linguistic knowledge in Latvia during the Soviet period is probably one of the best indicators of power relationships. When Russians emigrated in large numbers to France, the United States, and other countries, they did not expect their host countries to learn Russian. Indeed, in one or two generations, the Russians lost their language and were effectively assimilated. In the "sovereign" Latvian SSR, however, more inhabitants spoke Russian in 1989 (81.6 percent) than Latvian (62.4 percent).[20]

The school system and language differentiation

It is evident that the school system in Latvia has been a major factor contributing to the difference in language skills between Latvians and Russians. If both the Latvian and the Russian schools offered the other language in their curricula, then why the incredibly large divergence? There are several factors that can account for this. One of the most important is need. If students feel that a language will not advance their well-being in life, and if they do not need to learn it, they will expend a minimal amount of energy toward its mastery. Conversely, if a language determines well-being, upward mobility and access to power and if it is made mandatory, then the motivation for learning is much greater. Russian youngsters, until the advent of the awakening and independence, did not need Latvian. Russians lived in an environment where every aspect of institutional life could be satisfied in Russian. Latvians, on the other hand, required Russian if they desired to advance in life. Even more, refusal to learn Russian was considered a clear sign of "nationalism."

Another contributing factor was the uneven assignment of hours for the study of the other language. The number of hours of Latvian language and literature provided in Russian schools was less than 40 percent of the hours provided in Latvian schools for the learning of Russian. Moreover, in many Russian schools the "Latvian Studies" time slot was filled by school projects, sports events or other secondary activities. In these schools Latvian language learning was expendable and in many instances symbolic. In March 1990 a deputy of the Latvian Supreme Soviet characterized the teaching of Latvian in Russian schools as "simply catastrophic."[21]

During the period of the awakening and after independence, changes were inevitable. With a Latvian Front-dominated parliament and cabinet at the helm in 1990, the number of Russian language and literature teaching hours in Latvian schools, for example, was decreased from four to three a week and these hours were to begin only with Grade Two. Soon thereafter, even this number was made flexible and could be lowered by each school's "collective of teachers" according to circumstances. In Russian schools the successful completion of a Latvian language examination became a mandatory requirement for a secondary school graduation diploma.[22]

Before independence most institutes of higher education were organized to accommodate two language streams. There were two institutes which were unilingual: the Latvian Academy of Art held its classes only in Latvian, the Riga Civil Aviation Engineering Institute only in Russian. There was also some polarization or differentiated ethnic appeal for the other eight higher education institutes in the republic. The Riga Technical University (formerly Riga Polytechnical Institute) and the Daugavpils Pedagogical Institute had a majority studying in the Russian language stream. In the other six institutions Latvians predominated.[23]

For many years higher education entrance exams, except for specialized subjects such as Latvian literature, did not require Latvian language knowledge. Only in the fall of 1992 did a knowledge of Latvian become mandatory, at least theoretically. By law, a graduation diploma could be attained only if a Latvian language exam had been passed. The amended language law also stipulated that the language of teaching in higher educational institutes was to be Latvian, except in the case of first-year students. By the fall of 1994, this requirement was still being ignored at the Riga Technical University and Russian classes were being held out of necessity in all years.

Specialization, employment and the economy

One of the major demarcation lines in Latvia between ethnic groups is the differing proportions of people with higher educational experience and the differentiation of ethnic groups according to professional training and employment.

A comparison of educational levels indicates a significant gap between Latvians and other groups. Per thousand people over age 15, in 1989 there were 96 Latvians with a completed higher education, but 407 Jews, 163 Ukrainians and 143 Russians. At the same time, Belorussians with 82, Poles with 70 and Lithuanians with 36 were somewhat lower than Latvians.[24] The higher educational achievement rate of Russians in particular has created psychological problems for most Latvians. There is a widely held belief among Latvians that Russians who came to Latvia were far less cultured and educated than the native population. In 1940, certainly, statistics indicate a much higher educational rate in Latvia than in the USSR.[25] Most Latvians do not accept the veracity of the 1989 data, and in the spring of 1992 the Minister of Education of Latvia explained the "anomaly" as arising from misreporting on census forms, especially by officers' wives who considered some "insignificant" diploma as the equivalent of a university degree.[26]

There is a widely held belief among Latvians that most managers in industry and elsewhere are non-Latvians. Latvians were indeed under-represented in 1989 as heads of production management (35.6 percent), as leaders of production units (46.4 percent) and as leaders of enterprises (47.3 percent), but they were over-represented as leaders in other fields, especially agriculture and state organs. Of all "managers" registered in the 1989 census, Latvians accounted for 50.8 percent.[27] One should, however, be careful to note that many of the seemingly ethnic Latvians in management positions were among those who themselves or whose parents came to Latvia from the USSR after World War II. Many of these did not speak Latvian and socialized only with Russian-speaking individuals. The replacement of about one-third of managers in industry after August 1991 has probably changed the ethnic balance, but no new data are available on their ethnic composition.

A new source of tension is increasingly being mentioned in Latvia. In the eyes of many Latvians, other ethnic groups have obtained control of the lion's share of private production units and of commerce. The statistics mentioned range from 75 to 90 percent with the most popular being 80 percent. To verify this popular perception the author initiated a study which was effected by the Latvian Social Research Center in July 1993. According to this research a total of 15.3 percent claimed to be owners, co-owners or shareholders in some enterprises. Of these, the largest proportion, or 7.0 percent of the population, was involved in rural shareholders' associations, 3.3 percent were involved in private farming enterprises, 2.3 percent in industry, 1.4 percent in commerce and 2.3 percent in other types of venture. As one would expect, Latvians were clearly dominant in the agricultural sphere but industry was preponderantly non-Latvian. A very small number of owners fell into more than one category (table 5.7).

The ownership numbers are so small that given the normal allowable margins of variation for public opinion polls no refined assessments are possible. Nevertheless, taking population proportions into account, the Latvian share within industrial enterprises is about 30 percent, and within the private commercial field about 48 percent. The results should not be surprising given the Latvians' minoritization in most urban areas (especially in Riga), their low numbers in the most active age groups spanning 19–44, their lower levels of higher education and the Latvians' propensity to put their energy into agriculture (especially in private farms). This imbalance may change in the future.

A poll taken in the fall of 1993 indicated that Latvian business aspirations were somewhat higher than those of other groups. About the same proportion of Latvians (6 percent) and others (5 percent) had started a business or shop "in the past year or two." Sixteen percent of Latvians but only 10 percent of others indicated that it was likely they would do such a thing "in the next year." Such a move was considered unlikely by 58 percent of Latvians and 80 percent of others.[28]

A concentration of ethnic groups into particular fields of employment could have important effects in the future, especially as the economy undergoes dramatic changes. One of the most important changes that could inject instability in the mosaic of ethnic group relations is privatization. In practice, Latvians and non-Latvians were not evenly distributed throughout the different branches of the economy in 1987 with non-Latvians heavily concentrated in industry (63 percent) and transportation (70 percent). These are precisely the areas where privatization will almost surely lead to unemployment as many of Latvia's large industries will be forced to trim excess labor in order to

Table 5.7. *Ownership of enterprises by ethnicity, 1993*

	Latvians (percent)	Others (percent)
Total	19.7	10.0
Commercial enterprise	1.3	1.6
Industrial enterprise	1.3	3.5
Farming enterprise	5.3	0.9
Rural shareholders' association	10.0	3.3
Other types of enterprise	2.7	1.8

Source: Unpublished public opinion survey conducted by LASOPEC (The Latvian Social Research Center) in Riga, July 1993.

produce competitive goods. The areas of high Latvian employment such as communications, education, bureaucracy, culture and art are the ones less likely to be affected by privatization, competition and labor reduction. Agriculture, another Latvian work ghetto, is undergoing privatization, and in the short run has attracted more people than before.

As the relative share of industry in the Latvian economy decreases in favor of services, the language question will become more sensitive. The present language law requires that workers in areas of public contact should speak Latvian. Thus far, Latvian language inroads have been very limited among Russophone sales persons. If the language law is applied with firmness and if privatized stores see it as a benefit to have bilingual personnel, then a wholesale replacement of non-Latvian ethnic groups could be in the offing, or Russian-speakers will be enrolling in Latvian language courses in unprecedented numbers.

Ethnic marriages

It is noteworthy that at the social level many Latvians interact with Russophones on a friendly basis, and indeed the political strains of the period of transition have not lowered the degree of intimacy between these groups. In 1993, for example, 19 percent of both Latvian men and women married outside their ethnic group, a proportion very similar to that in 1987. Expressed another way, of all new couples married in 1993 which included Latvians, 31.9 percent had spouses of another ethnicity (see table 5.8).[29] The 1989 census indicated that in 43.6 percent of families both parents were Latvian; in 23.8 percent both were Russian, in 5.1 percent both were of another single nationality, but in 27.5 percent they were of mixed ethnic origin (table 5.8).[30]

Table 5.8. *Marriages by ethnicity of spouses, 1993*

Eth. orig. of grooms	Total	Latvian	Russian	Belo.	Ukrn.	Lith.	Pol.	Jewish	Other
						Ethnic origin of brides			
Total	14,595	7,674	4,976	609	469	203	387	70	197
Latvian	7,678	6,219	940	139	88	110	105	8	69
Russian	4,860	925	3,025	326	259	47	182	27	69
Belo.	583	110	319	63	30	14	35	1	11
Ukrn.	477	110	261	24	46	9	14	4	9
Lith.	193	97	56	8	7	15	8	6	1
Pol.	328	93	152	22	14	2	40	1	4
Jewish	106	14	50	6	3	—	4	27	2
Other	370	106	173	21	22	6	9	1	32

Source: Latvijas Republikas Valsts Statistikas Komiteja, *Latvijas Demogrāfijas Gadagrāmata 1993* (Riga: 1994), p. 184.

The relatively high rate of mixed marriages among Latvians has been double that of Estonians and similar to that of Ukrainians and Belorussians in their respective home countries.[31] While this has caused a certain amount of concern among Latvians committed to the strengthening of the Latvian identity, there have also been unplanned benefits from this fact during the period of transition. The offspring of mixed marriages have had a vested interest in minimizing nationality conflicts. In addition, more and more people have inevitably found a relative, a friend, or an acquaintance involved in a marriage across ethnic lines, and those involved in mixed marriages have acted as bridges and interpreters of policies and actions of the "other" group, helping to lessen tensions and increase understanding within Latvia. This fact may explain the rapid adjustment by the Russian-speaking community to the dramatic changes they had to face.

To be sure, social barriers and the wish to maintain the continuity of the Latvian ethnic group have created selective attitudes to marriage partners. A study by the Latvian Social Research Center published in February 1994 indicated clearly that about half of polled Latvians would be discontented if their sons or daughters were to marry a Russian, Ukrainian or Jew. Among Russians in Latvia, the level of discontent over exogamy was extremely small.

The rate of divorces could be another possible indicator of ethnic relations. Latvian men and women have significantly lower rates of divorce than Russians, Belorussians and Ukrainians. While Latvian men accounted for 52.6 percent of all marriages in 1993, their share of divorces was 43.7 percent. Among Russians the respective proportions were 33.3 percent and 39.8 percent. Beyond that, however, there is no clearly evident pattern of divorces being related to the ethnicity of spouses.[32]

Ethnic accommodation

There are at least two very distinct communities of Russophones in Latvia. Most of the quarter million living in Latgale have much deeper roots in the republic than those who came after World War II and settled mainly in larger urban areas. For a majority of them their history in Latvia goes back several generations and even several centuries. On the whole they are rural, and in contrast to the other Russophones are decidedly less educated, more religious, and economically less well established. They are also ethnically more mixed and many have an admixture of Latvian, Polish, Belorussian, Lithuanian and Jewish ancestry. The Latvians and non-Latvians outside Daugavpils have to a large extent blended their cultures and often speak a fusion of several languages. Within Daugavpils, however, the predominance of Russophones has overwhelmed the tiny group of Latvians. To be sure, new efforts are being made by the government to Latvianize those of Latvian ethnic origin.

The largest group of Russophones who settled in Latvia during the period of occupation are located in the larger urban areas. They are far more imbued with Soviet culture and values and are also less conscious of ethnic roots and traditions. Their former sense of superiority over the natives has largely crumbled with the disintegration of the empire they represented. Their environment and behavior bears the stamp of their proletarian and peasant origins. To some extent the Russophones have been perceived as "lower class" by Latvians, who on the whole are much more attached to middle-class values including a greater sense of privacy, personal reserve and more subdued and less emotional behavior. Anatol Lieven has outlined this division within the Baltic of typical class orientations and also the potential for change that this holds for the acculturation of Russians, especially younger ones. "Most Russian immigrants to the Baltic came from the working class or the peasantry, whereas the local populations comprised a substantial middle class and intelligentsia, damaged but not destroyed by Stalinism. The discrediting of Communism led many Baltic Russians, especially younger ones, to look towards the West. This in turn led to support for independence, and hopes of a move towards Western standards."[33]

In addition, the lack of roots and traditions among these Russophones and their priority emphasis on economic questions may help in their adaption to a new political environment. Rasma Karklins has suggested that the postwar settlers in Latvia can be largely considered "economic migrants." In her view economic migrants are different from territorially based minority groups:

"Typically, economic migrants focus on their economic rights rather than on group rights involving culture or political representation; consequently they assimilate more quickly. In this situation the migrants are less a source of ethnic tension than are titular nationals who fear ethnic contamination by foreigners."[34]

A poll taken in the fall of 1993 indicated differences between the two groups in their perceptions of each other. Among Russian-speakers 64 percent felt that they had a "great deal" or "some things" in common with Latvians. Among Latvians 29 percent felt the same way about Russians. Only 14 percent of Russians claimed there was "not much" or "nothing" in common with Latvians but 46 percent of Latvians felt this way about Russians.[35]

In living and working together, the two major language groups have inevitably influenced each other. Many diaspora Latvians often note the "Russian ways" of their relatives in Latvia. Russians are also affected by Latvians and with the increased spread of Latvian language knowledge and Latvian education they no doubt will become even more familiar with and, in part, will probably integrate the Latvian world-view and approach to living. In this respect the perceptions of the Russian Ambassador to Latvia, Alexander Rannikh, are worth noting. When asked whether he saw differences between the Russians of Latvia and those in Russia, he replied, "undoubtedly": "Russians of Latvia have adopted several typical characteristics of the basic nation. They are not as emotional, they are more balanced and pragmatic."[36]

Dynamics of nationality relations

There has been a tide-like ebb and flow in the relationship between the two main language communities in Latvia. During the pre-glasnost period, in spite of the linguistic inequalities and the inability of the Latvians to control immigration, tension between ethnic groups in Latvia was much lower than could have been expected. Latvians had become very accommodating to foreigners. In 1989, only 36 percent of Latvians first used Latvian to address strangers in their own country, while 64 percent used Russian. In case the addressed person did not know Latvian, 64 percent always switched to Russian, but only 3 percent adamantly maintained Latvian. Among Russians, 90 percent initiated conversations in Russian, switching to Latvian when necessary in only 20 percent of the cases.[37]

The pre-glasnost phase of ethnic relations was followed by a second phase which began approximately with the founding of the Latvian People's Front in October 1988. The Russian-speaking community, in spite of the various intermarriage bridges, was surprised and shocked by the sudden appearance of the period of Latvian awakening. Polarization and discontent became endemic. The Russian-speakers were frustrated and baffled by the new upheaval in nationality relations; and the Latvians were finally articulating in public the pain and strain of the preceding forty-five years of both harsh and subtle forms of repression of Latvian national aspirations. For the Russian-speakers at this point, identity was supranational: it was not so much Russian as it was denationalized Soviet. Indeed, their support systems included thousands of hardline Communist Latvians who were avid defenders of the Soviet way of life, whose underpinning was the Russian language.

According to Latvian social scientist Ilga Apine, this period of maximum alienation was replaced within one year, that is in the fall of 1989, by a third period of growing normalization and accommodation, which ended in August 1991. The barricades and killings of January 1991 and the subsequent March referendum drew the two groups together to such an extent that Apine characterizes this period as a "honeymoon" in nationality relations. In this third period Latvians became the political leaders and evinced a "new calm and composed self confidence." In their struggles against Moscow, Latvians attempted to include the other ethnic groups within their fold.

In Apine's view the fourth period began after the August putsch and was marked by a new alienation. There was a tendency to excessive stereotyping, with an idealization of one's own group and an exaggerated negative view of the other. The Russians began to feel a sense of isolation and hopelessness, whereas Latvians, still traumatized by the shock of the putsch and its potential for reversing all their gains, were particularly outraged at the "center" and the regime. In the wake of such strong sentiments local Russians were increasingly seen as an extension of this center.[38]

Public opinion polls, in part, bear out Apine's analysis, although there are some interesting contrary indications from the polling data. A very clear indicator of the milder and more relaxed ethnic relations in the third period can be found in the changed responses to the question: "Have you personally been touched by nationality type conflicts in the recent past?" In November 1988, 48 percent of Latvians and 54 percent of other nationalities gave a positive answer. In May 1990, in response to the same question only 8 percent of Latvians and 24 percent of others indicated such an experience.[39]

Already in June 1991, before the putsch, more people in each group considered ethnic relations to be bad than good. In September 1991, or one month after the putsch, contrary to the analysis by Apine there was a marked *improvement* in the positive perception of ethnic group relations. Only by March and June 1992 was there a significant decrease in the levels of goodwill. Since that time, however, there is evidence that a new fifth period in relations has emerged. In spite of the various pronouncements from Moscow about the suppression of human rights in Latvia, 62 percent of Latvians and 62 percent of others indicated in a fall 1993 poll that nationality relations were good or very good. Only 22 percent in each group felt that they were "bad or not very good" (table 5.9).

One can only conjecture why this change has occurred. Perhaps the economic upturn was a factor. As well, the increasing share of Latvians in the total population, up from 52 percent in 1989 to 54.2 percent in

Table 5.9. *Public opinion concerning inter-ethnic relations in Latvia, 1991–3*

	June 91		Sept. 91		March 92		June 92		Fall 93	
	Latvians	Others	Latvians	Others	Latvians	Others	Latvians	Others	Latvians	Others
Good	31	28	46	39	42	27	31	24	62	62
Bad	33	36	16	21	34	43	30	48	22	22
Hard to say	35	35	37	40	24	31	37	27	15	16

Sources: Brigita Zepa, "Public Opinion in Latvia in the Stage of Transition. The Dynamics of Views of Latvians and Non-Latvians," *EMOR Reports* 2:3, July–September 1992, p. 25; Richard Rose and William Maley, *Nationalities in the Baltic States: A Survey Study* (Glasgow: University of Strathclyde, 1994), p. 56.

1994 as a result of net out-migration and natural decrease for non-Latvians, could be decreasing Latvian stress levels and mitigating overall tensions.

While there are tensions between ethnic groups in Latvia, these tensions appear to have been preempted to some degree by other concerns. Even among non-Latvians, nationality-related issues such as language and citizenship were relatively low priorities in the hierarchy of "most important problems" during 1992 and 1993.[40]

At the present juncture it appears that most non-Latvians are deeply attached to their republic of residence, in spite of perceived linguistic and other pressures. Even if offered a job and living accommodation in the CIS countries, 89 percent of Russophones expressed a preference to remain in Latvia in May 1994 and only 5 percent were willing to leave permanently. Surprisingly, when presented with the same conditions but the choice of moving to the West, 90 percent preferred to remain, but 4 percent were willing to move permanently. No doubt the proportions favoring these choices will change and will depend on the situation in Latvia as well as the levels of development in CIS countries. It is clear from existing polls, however, that about 80 percent have decided to remain in Latvia unconditionally.[41] After all, an increasingly large number of them were born there and know no other home.

Anatol Lieven has claimed that in contrast to the other two Baltic republics Latvia has attracted "a higher proportion of educated Russians" who have become the driving force in the private business sector and areas of technological development. This Russophone-educated middle class in his view could become a most valuable intermediary between the two groups because of its skills in maintaining strong linkages with the government and its overt loyalty to the state. Lieven concludes that the treatment of this business class could be of utmost importance in the maintenance of stability:

So long as the Latvian government remains friendly to business, some sort of basic ethnic co-existence is probably assured. The real danger would follow any future national populist government with a programme targeted against 'foreign speculators', Russian professionals ignorant of the language, and unemployed industrial workers. In this eventuality, Russian resistance in Latvia would be more formidable than in Estonia, not simply because they are more numerous, but because they would be better and more articulately led.[42]

As outlined in the beginning of the chapter, all groups in Latvia see themselves as minorities and feel insecure and somewhat threatened. The problem is that the strengthening of the security of one often means the growth of insecurity in the other. The wider application of Latvian language laws is positive for Latvians but negative for Russophones. The strength in business of Russophones is widely resented by Latvians as a potentially new form of control by "foreigners." The public support for Russians in Latvia by Moscow strengthens the security of one but the insecurity of the other. Even the normalization of birth rates and death rates among non-Latvians can trigger fears of minoritization among Latvians. It will take extremely wise statesmanship and leadership to navigate the ship of state so that there is not a mutiny by one or the other section of the crew.

Conclusion

The Soviet period was not kind to Latvia and its original citizens. They endured many hardships and suffered deep demographic wounds which will leave their scar on future Latvian developments. While the deportations and deaths will eventually become a historical memory and a cause for collective remembrance, the Soviet period left a demographic legacy that will be an everyday reality for all Latvians, in all probability for centuries to come. The acceptance of this reality will take some time to permeate the consciousness of all Latvians. Many still subliminally hope for a miracle of some kind and a return to prewar ethnic proportions. This, however, is highly improbable. If the Latvians are able to strengthen the consciousness of their own ethnic group and at the same time strengthen the community of Latvia by minimizing ethnic tensions where this is feasible, they could achieve their goals of cultural survival and at the same time strengthen their goals of an economic commonwealth. Instability could give rise to economic stagnation and this in turn could result in unpredictable demographic scenarios including the out-migration of the most gifted of Latvian specialists. While it is not popular for any people to compare themselves to those who have experienced even worse circumstances, Latvians could thank providence that independence arrived when it did and before they suffered the fate of indigenous peoples in North and South America.

Conclusion

Latvia and the other post-Soviet republics have been able to break the ties of empire and are independent state actors recognized as sovereign bodies by most countries of the world. However, independence, no matter how important, is still only one dimension of the new reality demanding readjustments by post-Soviet societies. All of these newly independent republics face enormous problems of stabilization and reform. Many are involved in armed conflicts and disputes over state boundaries and political leadership. There are conflicts over state languages and the political and economic rights of different ethnic and religious groups. Most of these states have only begun to come to terms with their own true history, their relative backwardness and the bankruptcy of their former guiding ideology. All these areas have the potential for creating significant changes in attitudes, loyalties and strategies of future development.

No two republics of the former Soviet Union are alike. They each carry different strengths and weaknesses; they inherited different historical, economic and demographic residues and hold their own views of an ideal future. Within this group of newly independent countries the Baltic republics appear to have taken the most rapid steps towards reform in areas that are considered important by Western countries as criteria of progress. To be sure, no one has calibrated the exact specifications of "Western norms"; however, there is a broad consensus among Western decision-makers that in order to join exclusive Western organizations the post-Communist states must rectify the problems left by communism, totalitarianism and empire. In effect, each of these states is being advised to establish a viable state, democracy, a market system, rule of law and a civil society.

These requirements are being taken very seriously indeed by Latvia where the number one goal of government is to rejoin Europe and satisfy the terms perceived to be keys of entry into the European Union and NATO. In October 1994, the Latvian cabinet voted to create a European integration bureau whose main functions, according to the Ministry of Foreign Affairs, were to "prepare laws, defense forces, trade standards and norms and all structures so that at any moment we would be ready to join the European Union."[1] The Minister of Defense in 1994 pointed out Latvia's desire to become a member of the North Atlantic alliance and receive Western security guarantees. In his view the process of reaching this goal will require adjustments by Latvia to Western norms: "Latvia needs to become a partner of equal worth to Western countries, it needs to actively participate in the international arena; its internal political, social and economic conditions must conform to the demands of Western democracies."[2]

What distance has Latvia travelled and how much further does it need to go in order to reach the final destination and become an integral part of Europe? Latvia has been largely successful in the realm of state-building, democratization and marketization although serious actual and potential problems still exist in these areas. The establishment of the rule of law and civil society is extremely difficult to evaluate because of contradictory information coming from Latvia and because of the indeterminate boundaries of the definitions of these ideals. A subjective and tentative judgment would indicate that Latvia has made major strides in these two areas but the full maturation of the rule of law and civil society will require time and nurture.

Within a context of overall reforms, however, there are still problem areas which could seriously derail progress or even reverse the gains already made. There are issues seen by Latvians as threatening state stability. Democracy appears well established, but the endemic instability of politics, enhanced by the electoral system of proportional representation might create a "gridlock" which in a time of upheaval could lead to demands for shortcuts and unified decision-making. The market system itself is creating severe strains between Latvians and Russophones, between young and old, between communalists and individualists and between winners and losers. The first few years of economic reform have created more losers than winners and, under the rules of democratic politics, majorities composed of losers could force the end of such reforms. The issue of Latvian and Baltic security is the most threatening one for the survival of independence. The race is on for Latvia to join European structures in order to attain more rapid economic growth but more importantly to acquire a security umbrella. Russian chauvinism is seen as a credible future threat to Latvian sovereignty.

Perceived threats to state stability

After August 1991 Latvian sovereignty was recognized by most states of the world. Its real sovereignty, however, could be established only after the departure of the unwanted and illegally stationed troops of the Russian armed forces at the end of August 1994. These foreign troops controlled about 850 military facilities including large areas of land and many buildings throughout Latvia and did not allow themselves to be subjected to the laws and demands of the republic or local municipalities. They acted as a state within a state and before abandoning their areas of control they seriously aggravated problems of pollution, sank ships in harbors, illegally sold military hardware and weapons to local residents and demolished or burned almost every unsold building to signal their spite and discontent.[3] Other buildings and property were sold to local entrepreneurs even though these belonged to the Latvian state. The Russian armed forces became a major front for organized criminal activities providing safe havens for illegal entrepreneurs, very much as they had in Eastern Germany before all Russian troops were pulled out.[4]

The Chairman of the Latvian People's Front, Uldis Augstkalns, in October 1994 listed some of the controversial issues of state security remaining after the formal exit of the Russian armed forces. These included the rights of former Soviet military pensioners, the threat of Russian armed personnel left to guard the large and expensive early warning radar station situated at Skrunda and the fate of the region of Abrene.[5]

The first two issues have created much controversy in Latvia. Nevertheless, in the process of reaching an accord with Russia over the departure of their troops, the Latvian government and parliament felt obliged to accede to Russian demands in these areas. The approximately 25,000 former Soviet officers have been allowed to remain in Latvia and claim the same rights as other residents, including legal ownership of state apartments. They form about 1 percent of Latvia's population and are four times as numerous as the total of Latvia's armed forces. There is a fear among many Latvians that these retirees, some as young as forty, could become a destabilizing force used by Russia in the future for direct military functions, sabotage and for agitation among the Russian-speaking population. Most of these retirees are bitter about the breakup of the USSR and the emergence of an independent Latvia.

The manning of the early warning radar station at Skrunda in western Latvia involves close to 1,000 specialized Russian military personnel together with their family members living in a protected and specially serviced enclave. In theory there are international guarantees for a timetable which will provide for the shutdown of the station within four years and its demolition no more than sixteen months later. Nevertheless, many Latvians are nervous about this Russian military presence in the heart of Latvia. They remember the 1939 demand by the USSR for military bases and the fatal results of these conce sions.

The third issue mentioned by Augstkalns has not received any diplomatic resolution and, indeed, Russia has so far refused even to acknowledge the existence of the problem. The district of Abrene (about 2 percent of Latvia's territory) located in eastern Latvia and contiguous with Russia was illegally added to the RSFSR after the Red Army had entered Latvia.[6] Russia also annexed territory from Estonia.

Most moderate Latvians are reluctant to fight for the retrieval of an area which today is overwhelmingly Russian and whose addition would only depress the Latvian ethnic proportion in the entire country. It might be more reasonable, however, to expect Russia to pay compensation to former property owners from this district now residing in Latvia. Moreover, this area could become an item of bargaining for other desired policies of the Latvian government. Nevertheless, there is a relatively articulate constituency of nationalist-oriented Latvians who want to reclaim these territories which by international law belong to Latvia. Future tensions on this issue may escalate.

The problems of non-citizens

Without a doubt, the greatest and most intractable problem for state-building has been the large group of non-citizens living within Latvia. The impact of over 724,000 stateless individuals within a citizen population of 1.7 million cannot be overestimated.[7] About two-thirds of these non-citizens are of Russian ethnic origin and almost all came to Latvia after the Soviet occupation or were born to postwar immigrant parents. These people have been registered and have received a personal code in their Soviet passports. They have also been provided rights in the Latvian law on stateless individuals. A majority of these people can apply for Latvian citizenship following a five-year residency in the republic counting from May 4, 1990. Naturalization requires a knowledge of the Latvian language, the oath of allegiance and a minimal knowledge of the constitution and the history of Latvia. These stateless individuals who lost their Soviet citizenship as a result of the breakup of the USSR have all been provided the option of registering for Russian citizenship. Those with ties to the Ukraine or to other CIS countries have been allowed to apply for citizenship in their respective "home" countries. In view of the requirements of Latvian citizenship these individuals will not be able to vote for the next Saeima in October 1995. As well, non-citizens are not allowed to vote for municipal governments, in contrast to the practice in Estonia where all permanent residents, regardless of citizenship, can vote.

Politicians and delegations from Western Europe and North America have offered advice on how best to integrate this large mass of stateless individuals, seeing it rightly as a major destabilizing force, especially in view of Russian political pressures and threats. One of the politicians most committed to Baltic independence, former Prime Minister of Sweden Carl Bildt, has noted the potential dangers inherent in such a situation if left unresolved:

The Baltic countries, for their part, must recognize the obvious relationship between their internal harmony and their external, long-term national security. They are wise to be substantially more inclusive and generous to their Russian inhabitants than a strict interpretation of international law dictates. The aim must be to encourage the Russian speakers of the Baltic countries to feel loyal to the states where they are now living rather than to Russia, which they for one reason or another left during the Soviet period.[8]

The need for accommodation is clear. The process of accommodating a group which represents more than 42 percent of the citizens of Latvia, however, entails many risks and potential sources of instability. Most of these stateless individuals or their children will probably acquire citizenship within a period of ten to fifteen years. It is doubtful whether many of them will become assimilated by the leading nationality of the republic. Citizenship translates into political power and it is probable that the new citizens will desire to rectify some of the perceived problems seriously impinging on their ethnic standing and well-being. One such problem is the status of Latvian as a state language required by law in government, in many jobs and in higher education. The concept of a formally bilingual two-nation state is unacceptable to most Latvians. Moreover, the record of state bilingualism in the world, especially where applied across the entire state, is generally not favorable. Language disputes are rarely settled at a rational level and conflicts are endemic in such circumstances. Language is but one of many potential flashpoints. In a situation where Latvians represented only 54 percent of the population in 1994, the fear by Latvians of losing their birthright might seriously escalate tensions. Moreover, as long as neighboring Russia feels that it has a custodial right to support the Russophone side, conflicts might extend beyond Latvia's borders, even if all people in Latvia managed to acquire local citizenship.

The question often raised by Latvians is why they alone should be responsible for the absorption and integration of so many stateless individuals. The short answer, of course, is that Latvia was occupied by the USSR for half a century and these people now reside in Latvia. In effect, the victims are the sole ones being penalized. The ability of tiny Latvia to absorb a population of 724,000 aliens into its basic community of citizens requires more than goodwill, and is fraught with great potential dangers. Many of these stateless individuals, if given the option to settle in various countries of Western Europe, would certainly not exceed the carrying capacity of their host countries and would be able to integrate without any major problems. In this respect, a particular responsibility should accrue to Germany because it is the recognized successor state to the Third Reich which signed the secret protocols of the Molotov–Ribbentrop Pact in August 1939. Germany could acknowledge its culpability in Latvia's occupation and subsequent settlement by aliens and open its borders to any stateless individuals in Latvia wishing to live in a more developed economy. In addition, many thousands of these stateless individuals desire to return to their native countries of Russia, Belarus, Ukraine and other republics, but have no resources to move or to acquire housing at the end of their journey. Financial and technical help would encourage many to leave. By 1995 the "generosity" expected of the Latvian nation in its dealings with an enormous alien migrant population had not been reciprocated by generous offers from European states to accept these stateless settlers or to provide substantial aid for their return to their republics of origin.

Democracy

In Latvia the key indicators of a democratic state have been put in place. Latvia has reintroduced its constitution of 1922. Elections to the Fifth Saeima in June 1993 were successful with a voting participation rate of over 90 percent. Viable political parties have emerged and the institutions and mechanisms of democratic politics appear to be working. The municipal elections of May 29, 1994 were an important test of democracy because economic and other discontents at the time appeared to be deep and widespread. In spite of pervasive pessimism, these elections demonstrated a high degree of commitment. There were about 12,000 candidates willing to run for 4,771 positions. Moreover, 58.5 percent of eligible voters participated at the polls – an impressive turnout for municipal elections when compared to normal Western levels. In this instance, discontent, as in any other democracy, was expressed through the ballot box by the election of the "opposition" parties which in Latvian municipalities were mostly centre-right, national conservative parties.[9]

One of the key elements of a working democracy is a free press. There are many good quality newspapers, as well as several radio and television stations. The media in Latvia are owned by different sources and cover a broad spectrum of opinion and support a wide range of philosophies. Reporters are often iconoclastic and vigorous in their pursuit of truth and are not intimidated by government officials. Even minor attempts to influence the free distribution of "seditious" publications have resulted in major debates and a retreat by government. Attempts by organized crime to receive special treatment in publications have been publicized in spite of potential threats to personal safety.

There is an overall commitment by people to adhere to democratic norms. Nevertheless, polling studies in the fall of 1993 revealed certain equivocations about democracy. Both major language groups acknowledged overwhelmingly that the current democratic system was better than the communist system in allowing for freedom of speech, group association, religion, travel and emigration abroad, and choice of political parties. At the same time, about a third of Latvians and two-thirds of Russian-speakers gave a positive rating to the system of government before independence when Latvia was a part of the Soviet Union. Balancing this is the very positive view by both groups of the expected system of government in five years: 81 percent of Latvians and 71 percent of Russophones felt that the presumably democratic systems of the future will be to their liking.[10]

There is a high degree of ambiguity in attitudes to democratic processes. When asked whether the president should have the power to suspend parliament and rule by decree if he thinks it necessary, 64 percent of Latvians and 55 percent of others agreed and only 18 percent of both groups disagreed. On the other hand, when asked how they would react if parliament were suspended and parties banned, 54 percent of Latvians and 44 percent of others said they would disapprove and only 14 percent and 11 percent respectively that they would approve. A clear majority also considered it unlikely that such an event could occur within the next few years.[11]

The real danger to democracy in Latvia may lie in the proportional representation electoral system, the brief three-year term of parliament and the tendency by voters to elect many small parties. Unless a single party achieves a significant lead, as did Latvia's Way in June 1993, future governments may have to be formed by a coalition of four or five parties. In view of the semi-populistic tendencies of the Latvian electorate under conditions of rapid social and economic change, all minority parties in their attempts to improve their future standing will be forced to make unreasonable or unworkable demands on the political system. This may result in hopeless gridlock or in an unstable bribe- and scandal-ridden government of rotating cabinet chairs. Such a situation of gridlock and rotating governments was the reason why Karlis Ulmanis dismissed the Saeima and set aside the constitution and took over power on May 15, 1934. He promised to work on a new, more viable constitution. No new one was created and today Latvia is still weighed down by the 1922 document as well as by the old electoral system alleviated only by minor changes. As well, the lack of clarity on the powers and functions of the President, Saeima and government, combined with the lack of a legitimate constitutional court may result in another form of gridlock and possibly a destabilizing crisis of conflicting claims to power and jurisdiction.

The market system

One of the most important economists to encourage Poland to discard quickly its socialist economic trappings and embrace the free-market system, Leszek Balcerowitz, has very laconically pointed out that "democracy is no substitute for capitalism," and that "there is no correlation whatsoever between democracy and economic progress, i.e. economic growth." He does, however, offer the hypothesis that "democracy without capitalism may be vulnerable," especially in the long term.[12]

In his view there are three crucial elements required to build a market economy. The first two must be introduced early during the period when populations are open to dramatic changes while the third element can follow within a few years. These three important underpinnings of economic change are macroeconomic stability, liberalization and deep institutional reform, especially privatization.[13]

Latvia has been among the leaders in achieving macroeconomic stability. Its currency is stable, inflation is less than 2 percent a month, its debt is manageable and the tendency to excessively high wages has been curbed by various regulations. Indeed, in 1994 Latvia and the Baltic were considered role models for other post-Soviet republics in macroeconomic stabilization by Michael Camdessus, the managing director of the IMF.[14]

Liberalization, or the freeing of prices and the move to minimal state interference with subsidies and bail-outs, has also made giant strides forward. The introduction of high tariffs in September 1994, however, to protect local manufacturers and farmers was a highly political move acceding to the pressures of local producers. This move is understandable in view of the policies of extensive subsidies provided for farm products in the European Union and high tariffs in the East.

The third area, of institutional reforms and privatization, has made progress but not as much as could have been expected. Small and medium-sized establishments and enterprises have been successfully privatized. The bulk of the large ones have remained in state hands. Banking has been removed from political influences and almost all banks in Latvia are privately owned but closely regulated by the Central Bank. The Central Bank has divested itself of any commercial banking functions. According to estimates by the European Bank for Reconstruction and Development, in only nine of the twenty-five post-communist countries in the fall of 1994 did the private sector account for more than half of the gross domestic product. The Czech Republic was in the lead with a rate of 65 percent, followed by a group of five countries, including Latvia with a rate of 55 percent (the others were Estonia, Hungary, Poland and the Slovak Republic).[15]

Theoretically the framework of a free-market economy has been constructed. The rapid decrease in production associated with the conversion from a socialist to a capitalist economy slowed down considerably in 1994 and there are expectations of growth in 1995. Nevertheless, the discomfiture and even pain of economic transition has been very real and widespread. Latvia's official unemployment rate is over 6 percent, but its unofficial rate is closer to 9 percent. The largest part of family budgets must still be allocated to food; older people, especially in the urban areas, have problems paying for minimal needs. Suicides are an important index of stress. In 1993 there were 1,100 officially acknowledged suicides in Latvia compared to 611 in 1987. The average life-span had decreased to 67.2 years, but for men to 61.6 years, or 3.9 years lower than in 1985–6.[16]

Foreign investments have not yet reached expected dimensions and one of Latvia's major assets, its ports, were not even close to being utilized to full capacity during 1994. Many entrepreneurs avoid paying taxes and smuggling has been practiced on a grand scale. The web of illegal activities and the dictates of foreign-organized crime groups have had an impact on every entrepreneur and investor as well as on government policy.

In sum, the infrastructure for a market system is in place and privatization is progressing rapidly. Most visitors to Latvia see a vast improvement in access to a wide variety of goods; buildings and stores are being refurbished, and there is a vibrant private sector. The number of private cars has never been as high. However, discontent over economic conditions, especially among the middle-aged and older groups, has not abated and many people have been worn down by the uncertainties and the buffeting of changes involved in the transition to a market economy. Economic battle fatigue has made many people more rigid and cantankerous and susceptible to the attractions of what Balcerowitz calls the "Parties of Discontent."[17] In Latvia the mainstream parties have not turned away from reforms but within the present national conservative opposition two of those now involved in the National Bloc coalition, the Farmers' Union and Fatherland and Freedom, want subsidies for traditional forms of production, especially in agriculture, and want the state to retain control in areas which appear to be potentially profitable. A larger role for the state is seen by the more radical Latvian nationalists as a way of protecting Latvian interests against what they perceive to be the dominance of non-Latvians in the private sector. The same rationale was used by Ulmanis after 1934 in his Latvianization of the economy.

There are, however, some positive considerations favoring the continuation of reforms. The pervasive gloom and distrust in the population is tempered with hope about the future. Anger is mediated somewhat by the realization that very similar processes have afflicted all post-communist societies. Even more, Latvians and Russians alike can easily compare their rate of progress to that of resource-rich Russia and the once so promising Ukraine – both undergoing more serious problems than Latvia. As well, the progress of countries such as Poland and the Czech Republic strengthens the hope that this period of confusion and economic decline can be followed by a new period of renewed growth and progress. The limitation of options is another factor forcing people to come to terms with existing structures. Very few indeed want to return to communism or to a union with Russia. During moments of reflection most people in Latvia realize that in other Western countries democracy appears to work and the market system does provide a functional approach to economic well-being. Relatives from abroad reinforce this perception during numerous visits. Television provides graphic evidence of the bounty of goods in Western countries and of the fact that other parliaments have their scandals and their long-winded debates. Increasingly more Latvians are exploring the "new" world of Western Europe and North America and bringing back ideas and knowledge to apply to Latvia's many problems. Similarly, consultants from Western countries are able to see first-hand the dimensions of local problems and suggest solutions.

Baltic security

Latvian state security is inextricably tied to the security of all of the Baltic states. To say that "they lived happily ever after" might be a tempting and positive summary to apply to Latvian and Baltic independence. Yet, security concerns still exist. The Baltic republics are still entirely at the mercy of their giant neighbor to the east whose progress to democracy and to stability may be reversed by many factors. There is a large constituency within Russia that has not yet come to terms with the dissolution of the empire and the relative success of *Pribaltika*. Indeed, there is widespread bitterness in military and other circles toward the Baltic republics for their apparent role in rupturing their previously comfortable world. Russia appeared reluctant to withdraw its troops from Latvia and Estonia, although this was achieved by August 31, 1994. In spite of this departure, however, the security concerns of Balts have not disappeared. In the process of transition between the former Russian-controlled empire and the European Community, the Baltic states have been placed in what can best be described as a political no-man's-land, or a zone of subtle and overt claims and counterclaims about spheres of influence.

Baltic independence has no military guarantees and without direct NATO protection it is hard to imagine any group of Western countries putting their own security at risk for the defence of three relatively non-strategic countries. In contrast, it should be noted that NATO was prepared to go to war with the USSR to defend West Germany, Denmark, Holland, Belgium and other countries seen to be clearly in the Western sphere of interest.

Baltic fears are reinforced by Russian actions in the other former Soviet republics. All of them have joined the CIS and many have done so under considerable pressure from Russia. Economic and diplomatic pressures are also being applied against the Baltic states with tariffs considered a prime weapon of manipulation.

Within Latvia the general population distrusts Russia, but also appears oblivious to the potential dangers from it and has accepted independence as a self-evident, non-reversible reality. Just as Latvian independence was seen as "unreal" by a majority of Latvians even as late as 1988, so the loss of independence is considered unreal in 1995. Within such a context, radical nationalism and chest-thumping bravado, especially within an influential and vocal minority on the right, is rarely tempered by considerations of *realpolitik*. For example, the arrest, unceremonious handcuffing and kidnapping of two Russian generals and their attempted deportation outside of Latvia by a municipal politician and his selected policemen on January 10, 1994 were widely and enthusiastically applauded by tens of thousands still bearing the scars of Russian occupation and humiliation.

At the political level, however, Baltic leaders are very aware of their fragile position. They have made every attempt to break their isolation and become participants in international organizations. Estonia and Lithuania were accepted as members of the European Council in 1994 and Latvia became a member in early 1995. All three are members of NATO's Partnership for Peace program. A special joint Baltic peace-keeping battalion of 650 men was being trained by Britain and the Nordic countries in 1994 to be deployed by the United Nations in world trouble spots.[18] The Baltic states were granted status as associate partners of the Western European Union, and concluded free-trade agreements with the European Union. Cooperation, especially in the environmental field, has become a major joint activity of the countries on the shores of the Baltic Sea.

There is a very tangible reorientation of the Nordic countries to considering the Baltic states a special responsibility for aid and international support. Part of this supportive relationship no doubt springs from a sense of guilt for having totally ignored the plight of such close neighbors for half a century. More importantly, however, there is a new realization of the potential for extending the somewhat confining scope of the Nordic region without subsuming it entirely in the European Union. As Danish political scientist Ole Waever has stated, "Nordic identity is stretched between Brussels and the Baltic; being Nordic is to be involved both in Brussels affairs and in the development of the new Baltic states."[19] As well, according to Waever, this recently created possibility of reestablishing historical linkages is a "new" and "interesting" direction in region-building reflective of the trends in the new Europe where several regions, embracing members previously cut off from each other by Cold War boundaries, are emerging: "The Baltic states are the East Germany of the Nordic countries, the Hungary of Austria."[20] Indeed, there is much excitement over a new Baltic Sea regionalism, with a variety of models being suggested, including one which envisages the revival of the linkages of the Hanseatic League of the Middle Ages.[21]

The Baltic states themselves have achieved unprecedented levels of cooperation and coordination, in contrast to their poor record of mutual help during the inter-war years. A Baltic Ministers' Council, with secretariat headquarters in Riga, was established in June 1994 to facilitate cooperation between high-level state administrators in fifteen different fields. The Baltic prime ministers and presidents meet on a regular basis and the Baltic legislatures have their own organizations for interaction.[22] Military coordination is now a reality and Baltic free-trade agreements in most non-agricultural goods have helped expand markets.

The strategy of the Baltic states to expand their ties with the West and to accept Western suggestions and criticisms is bearing some dividends, at least in rhetoric and in subtle diplomatic shifts. The visit to Riga of US President Clinton in July 1994 was seen as an important symbolic gesture by the Balts. Standing in front of the Monument of Freedom, Clinton stated: "As you return to Europe's fold, we will stand with you. We will help you. We will help you restore your land. And we will rejoice with you when the last of the foreign troops vanish from your homelands. We will be partners so that your nation can forever be free."[23]

The British Foreign Secretary, Douglas Hurd, on his visit to Latvia in February 1994 told the Baltic foreign ministers that their independence was considered to be irreversible by the West. In an interview with *The Times* he stated: "These are countries that used to belong to the European family. They were stolen or kidnapped from the European family and they are returning to that family. They are entitled to their freedom."[24] According to former Prime Minister of Sweden, Carl Bildt, the European Union "has committed itself to having Estonia, Latvia, and Lithuania eventually become members."[25]

Indeed, not only Balts are nervous about the intentions of their giant neighbor. Russian historian and former politician Yuri N. Afanasyev in early 1994 came to a pessimistic conclusion that in Russia the "strengthening of the military-industrial complex in union with the neo-Soviet *nomenklatura* will result in an authoritarian regime." Afanasyev suspects that Russia's involvements in the near abroad may reflect an interest "to restore the empire."[26]

Most Balts do not doubt that a new Russian occupation would create a slightly bigger international uproar than did the 1940 occupation. At the same time they realize that they do not as yet have the defense protection umbrella of Western countries that would mean true security. With the new membership of Finland in the European Union, the Baltic states find themselves once again outdistanced by their northern neighbor. Baltic security is as yet almost entirely dependent on the actions of Russia. If Russian reforms are successful and democracy is able to spread its roots, the future economic progress of the Baltic states could be significantly enhanced and their security assured. Indeed, it is widely believed that democracies do not attack or invade other democracies. The stability of Russia is a key to the stability of the Baltic and, indeed, the guarantee of relative peace in the world. Much more could be done in this area and a new vision similar to that allowing for the creation of the Marshall Plan following World War II needs to be realized if there is going to be a real hope for a changed world order underpinned by security for all.

Notes

INTRODUCTION

1 Kristian Gerner and Stefan Hedlund, *The Baltic States and the End of the Soviet Empire* (London: Routledge, 1993), p. ix and p. 7.

2 *Diena*, November 4, 1994.

3 See Uldis Germanis, "The Rise and Fall of the Latvian Bolsheviks," *Baltic Forum*, Spring 1988, and Andrew Ezergailis, *The Latvian Impact on the Bolshevik Revolution* (New York: Columbia University Press, 1983).

4 The Latvian ambassador to Russia, Janis Peters, who has been in Moscow since 1990 and has had extensive contacts with the general Russian population and especially its intelligentsia, has observed that there are many currents in Russian attitudes to Latvia:

> For some Latvia is a matter of deep indifference, others react against us with suspicion, a third group regrets from the heart but the fourth group from pure schematic calculation the separation of Latvia and other republics from the Union, a fifth group thirsts for revenge and a new subjugation, a sixth group [expects] that Latvia and others will still beg to be 'taken back', a seventh group is enthusiastic about Latvia's freedom. *Neatkariga Cina*, October 31, 1994.

5 Carl Bildt, "The Baltic Litmus Test," *Foreign Affairs*, September–October 1994, p. 182; *Labrit*, April 16, 1994 (a translation of an interview in the German *Die Welt*).

6 For example, see the review in the *New York Times*, August 29, 1993, by Leah Greenfeld of Anatol Lieven's *The Baltic Revolution* (New Haven, Conn.: Yale University Press, 1993).

7 *Globe and Mail* [Toronto], November 29, 1994.

8 In his televised address to the Second Congress of USSR People's Deputies on December 23, 1989, Alexander Yakovlev, the CPSU Central Committee Politburo member and chairman of the committee investigating the protocols of the Nazi–Soviet Pact, claimed that it was "one of the most dangerous delayed action mines" from the minefield left by Stalin. *Foreign Broadcast Information Service (FBIS): Soviet Union*, December 28, 1989. His words on this score were indeed very prophetic.

9 In his outline of the "injustices committed by Stalin," Yakovlev in his address on December 23, 1989 gave the following summary using iconoclastic perceptions but Soviet terminology, especially with respect to the "restoration of Soviet power in the Baltic":

> Having embarked upon the path of dividing the loot with the predators, Stalin began

183

to speak with the neighbouring, especially small countries, in the language of ultimatums and threats. He did not consider it shameful to resort to force. This happened in the argument with Finland. With great power arrogance he brought Bessarabia back within the borders of the Union and restored Soviet power in the Baltic republics. All this deformed Soviet policy and state morality. *FBIS: Soviet Union*, December 28, 1989.

The idea of "restoration" is tied to the fact that the Bolsheviks were in control of these countries for different periods of time before 1920.

10 Richard Rose and William Maley, *Nationalities in the Baltic States: A Survey Study* (Glasgow: University of Strathclyde, 1994), p. 64; Richard Rose *et al.*, *How Russians Are Coping With Transition: New Russia Barometer II* (Glasgow: University of Strathclyde, 1993), p. 50.

11 Paul Goble, "The Baltics: Three States, Three Fates," *Current History*, October 1994, pp. 332–6.

12 Elmars Vebers, ed., *The Ethnic Situation in Latvia* (Riga: Ethnic Studies Centre, 1994), p. 4.

13 Surprisingly, 59 percent of Latvians and 75 percent of Russophones in Latvia in the fall of 1993 judged the economic system of "five years ago" as positive and only 27 percent and 16 percent respectively judged it as negative. The new economic system of independent Latvia was seen as positive by only 21 percent of Latvians (62 percent negative) and 24 percent of non-Latvians (62 percent negative). Rose and Maley, *Nationalities in the Baltic States*, pp. 27–8.

14 Ibid., pp. 34–5.

15 Ibid., pp. 1–31.

16 Alexander J. Motyl, *Dilemmas of Independence: Ukraine After Totalitarianism* (New York: Council on Foreign Relations Press, 1993), p. xi.

17 Robert Conquest, ed., *The Last Empire: Nationality and the Soviet Future* (Stanford, Calif.: Hoover Institute Press, 1966); Hélène Carrere d'Encausse, *Decline of an Empire: The Soviet Socialist Republics in Revolt* (New York: Newsweek Books, 1979).

18 The concept of "empire" has, for example, now been used in analyzing the present post-Soviet situation by the American political scientist Jerry F. Hough: "The trick is getting the post-Soviet states into a strategic partnership – and in most cases, into an economic common market of former republics – without rousing alarm about a new Russian empire, let alone, actually helping create one, in a world where many worry about the rebirth of Russian nationalism." "America's Russia Policy: The Triumph of Neglect," *Current History*, October 1994, p. 310.

19 Geoffrey Hosking, *The Awakening of the Soviet Union* (Cambridge, Mass.: Harvard University Press, 1991), p. 7.

20 T. H. Rigby, "Reconceptualizing the Soviet System," in Stephen White *et al.*, eds., *Developments in Soviet and Post-Soviet Politics*, 2nd edn. (London: Macmillan, 1992), pp. 318–19. Rigby does note that the "class" and "bureaucratic" approaches have also gained "additional weight."

21 Alexander J. Motyl, "The End of Sovereignty: From Soviet Studies to Post-Soviet Studies," in his edited *The Post-Soviet Nation: Perspectives on the Demise of the USSR* (New York: Columbia University Press, 1992), p. 309.

22 Motyl, *Dilemmas of Independence*, pp. 51–2.
23 *Elpa*, October 28, 1994, as translated from the original in *S. M. Segodnya*.
24 Steven L. Burg, "Nationalism *Redux*: Through the Glass of the Post-Communist States Darkly," in Minton F. Goldman, ed., *Russia, The Eurasian Republics, and Central/Eastern Europe* (Guilford, Conn.: Dushkin, 1994), p. 267.
25 W. Raymond Duncan and G. Paul Holman, Jr., "Introduction: Ethnic Nationalism in the Post-Cold War Era," in their edited *Ethnic Nationalism and Regional Conflict* (Boulder, Colo.: Westview Press, 1994), p. 1.
26 Rasma Karklins, *Ethnopolitics and Transition to Democracy: The Collapse of the USSR and Latvia* (Baltimore: Johns Hopkins University Press, 1994). See chapter 1 and Conclusion.
27 Anatol Lieven, *The Baltic Revolution: Estonia, Latvia, Lithuania and the Path to Independence* (New Haven, Conn.: Yale University Press, 1993), p. xxiv.
28 Motyl, *Dilemmas of Independence*, pp. 72–4.

1 HISTORICAL RESIDUES AND IMPACT ON PRESENT-DAY POLITICS

1 "Soviet Latvia," *Baltic Forum*, Fall 1984, p. 98.
2 The Libiesi had dwindled to only 844 in 1935 and to 135 in 1989. Only a handful still speak the language. Latvijas Republikas Valsts Statistikas Komiteja, *1989.gada Tautas Skaitisanas Rezultati Latvija* (Riga, 1992), p. 83. At the time of the first German incursions into east Latvia the Libiesi controlled north Latvia (Vidzeme) and were scattered along the coast of Kurzeme.
3 Traces of human habitation in Latvia have been found dating back to 9000 B.C. The ancestors of modern-day Latvians settled in Latvian territory before 2000 B.C. Edgars Dunsdorfs, *Latvijas Vesture* (Lincoln, Nebr.: Augstums Press, 1980), pp. 17–27. For a more detailed anthropological history see Marija Gimbutas, *The Balts* (New York: Praeger, 1964).
4 For an English language overview of Latvian history see Alfreds Bilmanis, *A History of Latvia* (Princeton, N.J.: Princeton University Press, 1951), and Arnolds Spekke, *History of Latvia: An Outline* (Stockholm: M. Goppers, 1957).
5 Bilmanis, *History of Latvia*, ch. 13.
6 Nicholas Balabkins and Arnolds Aizsilnieks, *Entrepreneur in a Small Country: A Case Study Against the Background of the Latvian Economy, 1919–1940* (Hicksville, N.Y.: Exposition Press, 1975), p. 21.
7 Stanley W. Page, *The Formation of the Baltic States* (New York: Howard Fertig, 1970), pp. 17–21.
8 Andrejs Plakans, "The Latvians," in Edward C. Thaden, ed., *Russification in the Baltic Provinces and Finland, 1855–1914* (Princeton, N.J.: Princeton University Press, 1981), p. 287.
9 Andrew Ezergailis, *The Latvian Impact on the Bolshevik Revolution* (New York: Columbia University Press, 1983), p. 24. A more detailed description of the political turbulence of the war period can be found in Andrew

Ezergailis, *The 1917 Revolution in Latvia* (New York: Columbia University Press, 1974).

10 Ezergailis, *The Latvian Impact*, pp. 34–9 and pp. 68–90.

11 Dunsdorfs, *Latvijas Vesture*, p. 243.

12 Page, *Formation of the Baltic States*, ch. 5 and 6. According to Page, Soviet Latvia occupied a "warm spot in the hearts of the founding fathers of Bolshevism" because it opened the gates to the Scandinavian countries and provided a springboard from which the Red forces could aid the revolution in Germany. He concludes that of equal importance was the fact that Latvia, the only non-Russian part of the former Russian Empire which showed a Bolshevik trend, proved to the world that Bolshevism was not merely a Russian, but an instrumental phenomenon, suitable for non-Russians as well as for Russians, for the West as well as for the East (p. 135).

A Russian who personally experienced the "Bolshevik experiment" in Riga, George Popoff, wrote a book in 1932 warning the West what could happen if they allowed the Reds to take over. In his *City of the Red Plague* he pointed out that in Latvia "conditions of life more nearly resembled those of Western Europe than those of Russia . . . For a Western European, therefore, the 'case of Riga' should be no less instructive than the history of Russian Bolshevism itself." (p. 11.) Originally published by E. P. Dutton Co., New York. Reprinted by Hyperion Press Inc., Westport, Conn., 1978.

13 *Literatura un Maksla*, December 16, 1988 (Ilgonis Bersons, "Atklati – ari par 1919, gadu").

14 A sample listing of Latvian Bolshevik luminaries killed in the Great Terror can be found in Uldis Germanis, "The Rise and Fall of the Latvian Bolsheviks," *Baltic Forum*, Spring 1988, pp. 21–5.

15 Jukums Vacietis, *Latviesu Strelnieku Vesturiska Nozime* (Pskov, USSR: Spartaks, 1922), 1:101, as quoted in Germanis, "Rise and Fall," p. 11.

16 Germanis, "Rise and Fall," pp. 19–20. Janis Peters, a poet and member of the Latvian Party Central Committee, provides the figure of 75,000 Latvian deaths in the USSR during the purges. *Literatura un Maksla*, March 18, 1988.

17 This information has been provided by the former executive assistant of Kalnberzins, Janis Liepins. *Jurmala*, January 5, 1989.

18 Joint Baltic American National Committee, *A Legal and Political History of the Baltic Peace Treaties of 1920* (Washington, D.C.: 1990).

19 Krystyna Marek, *Identity and Continuity of States in Public International Law* (Geneva: Librairie E. Droz, 1954), pp. 369–70.

20 Royal Institute of International Affairs, Information Department, *The Baltic States* (London: Oxford University Press, 1938).

21 Georg von Rauch, *The Baltic States: The Years of Independence 1917–1940* (Berkeley: University of California Press, 1974), pp. 87–91; Royal Institute of International Affairs, *Baltic States*, pp. 29–30.

22 Bilmanis, *History of Latvia*, p. 366.

23 See comparisons in Juris Dreifelds, "Belorussia and Baltics," in I. S. Koropeckyi and Gertrude E. Schroeder, eds., *Economics of Soviet Regions* (New York: Praeger, 1981), pp. 363–9.

24 von Rauch, *Baltic States*, p. 126.

25 Royal Institute of International Affairs, *Baltic States*, p. 189. Also see Balabkins and Aizsilnieks, *Entrepreneur in a Small Country*, pp. 81–3.
26 *Skolotaju Avize*, March 1, 1989 (H. Strods).
27 *Lauku Avize*, April 26, 1994.
28 *Padomju Jaunatne*, June 13, 1973. Average monthly unemployment in Latvia was: 1927: 3,100, 1931: 8,700, 1932: 14,600, 1933: 8,200, 1934: 5,000, 1936: 3,900, 1937: 3,000. Karlis Kalnins, *Vai Jus Zinat, ka Latvija?* (Ludwigsburg, W. Germany: 1946), p. 11.
29 For negative comments about Latvia's economy see Latvijas PSR Vestures Instituts, *Latvijas PSR Vesture* (Riga: Zinatne, 1986), vol. II, pp. 82–7. The Soviet Latvian annual statistical yearbooks almost always compared 1940 to 1913 or 1914. See, for example, Latvijas PSR Statistikas Parvalde, *Latvijas PSR Tautas Saimnieciba 1975.Gada* (Riga: Liesma, 1976), pp. 21–2.
30 Royal Institute of International Affairs, *Baltic States*, p. 33.
31 Ibid., pp. 33–4.
32 Ibid., p. 35.
33 Dz. Viksna, *Latviesu Kulturas un Izglitibas Iestades Padomju Savieniba 20–30 Gados* (Riga: Zinatne, 1972).
34 Osvalds Freivalds, *Latviesu Politiskas Partijas 60 Gados* (Copenhagen: Imanta, 1961), pp. 84–96.
35 Bilmanis, *History of Latvia*, pp. 357–62. *Padomju Jaunatne*, April 6, 1988.
36 The initial organizer of this campaign to locate Ulmanis's remains was the grand-nephew of Ulmanis, Guntis Ulmanis, who in 1993 became the President of Latvia.
37 *Diena*, July 21, 1992. Lithuania has copied the West German model, that is, one-half of deputies are elected through a proportional system and the other half using a majoritarian area-based system.
38 R. J. Sontag and J. S. Beddie, eds., *Nazi–Soviet Relations 1931–1941* (Washington, D.C.: US Department of State, 1948), p. 107.
39 William J. H. Hough III, "The Annexation of the Baltic States and Its Effect on the Development of Law Prohibiting Forcible Seizure of Territory," *New York Law School Journal of International and Comparative Law*, 6:2, Winter 1985, pp. 349–51.
40 Dunsdorfs, *Latvijas Vesture*, p. 296; Arnold Toynbee and Veronica M. Toynbee, eds., *Survey of International Affairs 1939–1946*, vol. XI, *The Initial Triumph of the Axis* (London: Oxford University Press, 1958), pp. 50–2. The detailed program, participants and fate of those who attempted to offer an alternative to the Communist candidate list may be found in Janis Jurmalnieks, *Latvijas Ieklausana Padomju Savieniba* (Stockholm: Memento, 1973), pp. 34–5.
41 Romuald J. Misiunas and Rein Taagepera, *The Baltic States: Years of Dependence, 1940–1990* (Berkeley, University of California Press, 1993), p. 27.
42 During the independence period there was a widely held belief that the Communists had changed since their excesses in 1919. The Latvian media, moreover, tended to ignore events in the USSR, in part because information was scarce and in part because Latvia did not want to antagonize its giant neighbor.

43 Bilmanis, *History of Latvia*, p. 402.
44 Janis Riekstins, "Stalinisko Represiju Aizsakums Latvija," *Latvijas Vesture*, no. 1, 1991, pp. 28–9.
45 *Latvijas PSR Vesture*, vol. 2, pp. 149–63. See also Lyubova Zile, "Socialistiska Sabiedriba; Visparejais Un Atseviškais Tas Tapsana Un Attistiba," *Padomju Latvijas Kommunists*, December 1984, pp. 19–24.
46 *Literatura un Maksla*, September 2, 1989.
47 Verbatim translation of Yakovlev's speech to the Second Congress of USSR People's Deputies on December 23, 1989, published in *FBIS: Soviet Union*, December 28, 1989, p. 248.
48 The secret documents were located in the Koblenz Federal Archives. They had originally been in only five copies. The translated Latvian version was published in *Latvijas Vesture*, no. 1, 1992, pp. 35–8.
49 Misiunas and Taagepera, *Baltic States*, pp. 67–8.
50 Frank Gordon, *Latvians and Jews Between Germany and Russia*, (Stockholm: Memento, 1990), p. 2. He provides the following assessment: "If anything can be called 'the Latvian ethnic bible' and the mirror of Latvian philosophy and attitudes through the centuries, it is the short, laconic folk songs, called *dainas*. There are more than one million of these four-line verses ... there are a good number about Jews. Most, one must say, are friendly and warmhearted, and those that poke fun at Jews do so in a well-meaning way" ...
51 Gertrude Schneider, "The Riga Ghetto, 1941–1943," Ph.D. thesis, The City University of New York, 1973, p. 25. The thesis was subsequently published as *Journey into Terror: Story of the Riga Ghetto* (New York: Ark House, 1979). The book left out the two pages of historical introduction.
52 Gordon, *Latvians and Jews*, p. 15.
53 Mendel Bobe, "Four Hundred Years of the Jews in Latvia," in M. Bobe *et al.*, eds., *The Jews in Latvia* (Tel Aviv: D. Ben-Nun Press, 1971), p. 71.
54 J. Lejins, *Latvian–Jewish Relations* (Toronto: Latvian National Federation in Canada, 1975), p. 18.
55 Dov Levin, "The Jews and the Sovietization of Latvia, 1940–41," *Soviet Jewish Affairs*, 5:1, 1975, p. 40.
56 Gordon, *Latvians and Jews*, p. 19.
57 Levin, "Jews and the Sovietization of Latvia," p. 53. The People's Commissar for State Security in Latvia, Semion Shustin was a Russian Jew. According to Gordon, "... many of his assistants, especially in the KGB, were local Jews, who knew both Russian and Latvian." Gordon, *Latvians and Jews*, p. 26.
58 Max Kaufman, "The War Years in Latvia Revisited," in Bobe *et al.*, *The Jews in Latvia*, p. 352.
59 Ibid., p. 366.
60 Gordon, *Latvians and Jews*, pp. 37–40.
61 Ibid., p. 61.
62 *Diena*, February 9, 1991.
63 Interview with a Riga Jewish representative, M. Mendels, in December 1992 in Riga.
64 The exact number of refugees is not known. The registration by the International Red Cross tallied about 110,000.

65 Misiunas and Taagepera, *Baltic States*, pp. 55–6. Latvian draftees also had the option of joining German units, but few did.

66 Ibid., p. 56.

67 Ibid., p. 57. Another source claims that between March 1943 and August 1944 the total who appeared at draft points included 128,866 Latvians, while 44,543 had ignored the order. Another 14,561 were classified as unfit for duty. *Padomju Jaunatne*, April 13, 1989 (Visvaldis Lacis). In *Skolotaju Avize*, March 29, 1989, Voldemars Steins provides data indicating that 36,000 Latvian soldiers were taken as prisoners of war by the Red Army, 22,000 by Western armies, 3,000 fled to Sweden and 80,000 died in the German army.

68 One particularly bloody encounter of this type occurred at Dzukste, in Kurzeme, several months before the end of the war.

69 An interesting book on intrigues involving the Latvian KGB and British Intelligence, based on conversations with former spies on both sides, has been written by Tom Bower in *Red Web* (London: Anrum Press, 1989). A book review in *The Times* provides the following introduction: "Between 1944 and 1955, MI6 sent dozens of agents into the Soviet Union to join anti-Communist partisans in the Baltic states of Latvia, Estonia and Lithuania and send back intelligence. But the entire operation became the victim of a masterpiece of deception by the KGB who had infiltrated the spy ring almost from the start." The book reveals the extent of deception and the creation of fake partisans. See also Adolfs Silde, *Resistance Movement in Latvia* (Stockholm: Latvian National Foundation, 1985).

70 *Cina*, October 20, 1974.

71 *Latvijas Vesture*, no. 1, 1992, p. 40.

72 Janis Riekstins, "Genocids," *Latvijas Vesture*, no. 2, 1991, p. 37.

73 *Cina*, March 18, 1988. According to original plans 38,662 were to be deported, but in actual fact 40,334 people were sent to Siberia in this action. Among them were 10,983 men, 18,801 women and 10,590 children under the age of sixteen. Latvian State Archives information request number 1–10.3 of May 26, 1992.

74 The author's grandmother was absent on the day of the deportations and her sister was taken instead.

75 *Skola un Gimene*, no. 1, 1989, pp. 5, 40, etc.

76 Misiunas and Taagepera, *Baltic States*, pp. 96–100.

77 *Latvijas Vesture*, no. 1, 1992, p. 40.

78 *Cina*, July 20, 1988.

79 *Lauka Avize*, August 20, 1988.

80 I. Apine, "Stalinisma Recidivs," *Horizonts*, no. 4, 1989, p. 29.

81 Personal interview, August 28, 1987, in Chauttauqua, New York.

82 The long letter can be found in Silde, *Resistance Movement in Latvia*, pp. 35–51. Its authorship is revealed in *Briviba*, no. 2, 1991, p. 1.

83 Personal interview in Toronto.

84 Gunars Rode, "Disidentu Kustiba Latvija, Baltija un PSRS," *Latvija Sodien*, 1979, p. 6.

85 Viktors Kalnins, "Neredzama Fronte," *Latvija Sodien*, 1980, p. 10.

86 Uldis Blukis, "Baltijas Pretestibas Kustiba," *Latvija Sodien*, 1982, p. 119.

87 *Neatkariga Cina*, January 29, 1991.

88 Information based on interview with Catholic clergy in May 1992 in Riga.
89 The latest revelations about the role of the KGB in the period of awakening have been provided by former KGB Colonel Juris Bojars in *Rigas Balss*, May 9, 1994. Bojars implicates Ivars Godmanis, the first premier of independent Latvia, as a KGB worker.
90 Melvin C. Wren, *The Course of Russian History*, 4th edn. (New York: Macmillan, 1979), p. 359 and p. 379.
91 *Literatura un Maksla*, March 18 and June 10, 1988.

2   THE LATVIAN NATIONAL REBIRTH

1 Interview with the first leader of the Latvian People's Front, Dainis Ivans; Nils R. Muiznieks, "The Influence of the Baltic Popular Movements on the Process of Soviet Disintegration," *Europe-Asia Studies* 47:1, 1995, pp. 3–25.
2 Helmi Stalts, "Cels Kopa ar Tautas Dziesmu," *Padomju Latvijas Sieviete*, April 1989, p. 2.
3 Ibid.
4 Interview with Arvids Ulme in *Briviba*, English edn., no. 5, 1988.
5 *Jurmala*, October 20, 1988.
6 Dzintra Bungs, "After the Jurmala Conference: Imperfect Glasnost," *Radio Free Europe Research*, Baltic Area Situation Report, no. 8, December 9, 1986.
7 More detail provided in Juris Dreifelds, "Two Latvian Dams: Two Confrontations," *Baltic Forum*, Spring 1989, pp. 11–24.
8 For interviews with the Latvian and Estonian organizers of the demonstrations and the Ideological Secretary of the Latvian Communist Party, see *Baltic Forum*, Fall 1987, pp. 1–29 and 42–53. For an overview of the critical response in the Russian-language press to the demonstrations, see *Current Digest of the Soviet Press* (Columbus, Oh.), September 23, 1987, pp. 1–8. A good overview of the November event is provided by Dzintra Bungs in "A Survey of the Demonstrations on November 18," *Radio Free Europe Research*, Baltic Area Situation Report, no. 9, December 18, 1987.
      It is interesting to note that, before the November 18 event, British double agent Kim Philby was summoned out of retirement to speak on Latvian television and discredit Latvian nationalism. *Globe and Mail* [Toronto], November 19, 1987.
9 *Christian Science Monitor*, June 27, 1988; *Literatura un Maksla*, November 25, 1988.
10 *Literatura un Maksla*, March 18, 1988.
11 *Baltic Bulletin*, nos. 2 and 3, 1988.
12 The plenum speeches and photographs of the speakers were published in the June 10 and 17, and July 1 and 8, 1988, editions of *Literatura un Maksla*.
13 *Jurmala*, October 20, 1988.
14 Ibid.
15 Personal communication from professor of law, Ilmars Bisers of Riga.
16 This euphoria was described in somewhat rudimentary English in an official publication of the Riga Video Centre, *Ars*, English edn., no. 12, 1988: "The energy of people was like dough: yes, God bless Latvia and be with us. It was

only trust in the Almighty in this desperate outcry of the last hope. It was togetherness – a power of one is suddenly aware of, Latvia's power. Power for Latvia. You cannot ask for love. You can ask for freedom."

17 The idea of holding a church service in the Domas Cathedral and broadcasting its proceedings was initiated by Rev. Juris Rubenis, who was also elected to the leadership of the People's Front (personal communication from Rubenis).

18 Ojars J. Rozitis, "The Rise of Latvian Nationalism," *Swiss Review of World Affairs*, February 1989, pp. 24–6; *Literatura un Maksla*, October 14, 1988; *Cina*, October 9, 1988; and *Padomju Jaunatne*, October 11, 1988.

19 *Padomju Jaunatne*, October 19, 1988.

20 Ibid.

21 *Cina*, October 30, 1988.

22 *Atmoda*, January 16, 1989.

23 Of the fifty-two delegates from Latvia, about three-quarters were reformists, and only five reactionary hardline Communists were elected. Personal communications with delegates.

24 *Padomju Jaunatne*, May 16, 1989.

25 *Cina*, May 16, 1989.

26 *Padomju Jaunatne*, May 25, 1988.

27 Ibid.

28 *Pravda*, May 22, 1989.

29 *Cina*, June 13, 1989.

30 The abridged transcript of this fractious plenum has been published in *Baltic Forum*, Fall 1988.

31 See *Latvijas PSR Vienpadsmita Sasaukuma Augstakas Padomes Sedes: Stenografisks Parskats* (Riga: Avots, 1988–9). These minutes of the Latvian SSR Supreme Soviet published in Latvian and Russian show a dramatic change of approach between the seventh session (November 13, 1987), with its denunciations of Radio Liberty and Helsinki '86, and the eighth session (April 14–15, 1988). The dam really began to break during the ninth session (October 6, 1988) when Anatolijs Gorbunovs was elected Chairman of the Latvian SSR Supreme Soviet Presidium. For the first time ever in such proceedings one person voted against his candidacy.

32 Personal communication from Dainis Ivans, summer 1992, New York State.

33 This appeal to Latvian Communists was reprinted, for example, on the front page of the largest-circulation newspaper, *Lauku Avize*, December 1, 1989.

34 Ibid.

35 *Latvijas Jaunatne*, February 1, 1990.

36 *Lauku Avize*, March 2, 1990.

37 Ibid., March 23, 1990.

38 Ibid., March 30, 1990.

39 Ibid., April 13 and 20, 1990.

40 Ibid., April 20, 1990.

41 *Atmoda*, March 16, 1990.

42 *Cina*, May 8, 1990; *Tevzemes Avize*, May 24, 1990.

43 *Latvijas Jaunatne*, December 29, 1990.

3 REGAINING INDEPENDENCE – ESTABLISHING
   DEMOCRACY

1 Brigita Zepa, "Public Opinion in Latvia in the Stage of Transition: The Dynamics of Views of Latvians and Non-Latvians," *EMOR Reports*, 2:3 July–September 1992, p. 11.
2 Ibid.
3 Western involvement was especially noticeable after the January 1991 shootings in Lithuania and Latvia. Riina Kionka, "Baltic Report," *Report on the USSR*, February 8, 1991. The European Parliament blocked a $1 billion food aid package for the Soviet Union in response to the January violence in the Baltics. *New York Times*, January 23, 1991. In general, various Western parliaments were more responsive to Baltic hopes for independence than their respective presidents or prime ministers. Nevertheless, the issue of greatest concern, reiterated by almost all Western leaders communicating with Gorbachev, was to stop any violence in the Baltic by Moscow. *New York Times*, March 27, 1990, January 15, 1991, January 18, 1991, January 22, 1991, January 23, 1991, March 6, 1991, March 17, 1991.
4 On March 25, 1989 over half a million people came out in Riga to commemorate the deportations of 1949. *Literatura un Maksla*, August 29, 1989. On January 13, 1991 over 700,000 people joined together on the banks of the Daugava River to show solidarity and support for Latvia's government. Dzintra Bungs, "Latvia in an Impasse?," *Report on the USSR*, February 1, 1991. The LPF-organized petition against the Union Treaty had garnered 1,002,829 signatures in Latvia by mid December 1990. *Baltic Chronology*, January 1991, p. 29.
5 *Baltic Chronology*, 1989–90, p. 8; American Latvian Association (ALA), *A Summary of Current Events in Latvia: January–September 1990* (Rockville, Md.: ALA, 1990), p. 9.
6 A good overview of the January crisis, especially its diplomatic aspects, including a full text of Boris Yeltsin's "Appeal to Russian Soldiers," is given in Jan Arveds Trapans, "Averting Moscow's Baltic Coup," *Orbis*, Summer 1991, pp. 427–39. For the nature and content of the treaty signed, see Dzintra Bungs, "The Latvian–Russian Treaty or the Vicissitudes of Interstate Relations," *RFE/RL Research Report*, February 28, 1992.
7 *Latvijas Jaunatne*, July 5, 1993.
8 Rein Taagepera, *Estonia: Return to Independence* (San Francisco: Westview Press, 1993), pp. 158–60 and ch. 7.
9 *Literatura un Maksla*, May 12, 1993.
10 Ibid.
11 Ibid.
12 ALA, *Summary of Current Events in Latvia: January–September 1990*, p. 5.
13 Ibid., pp. 8–9.
14 *New York Times*, January 19, 1991.
15 *This Week in the Baltic States* (RFE/RL Research Institute), October 25, 1990.
16 Karlis Streips, *Republic of Latvia: Crisis Chronology, January 20, 1991* (Rockville, Md.: ALA, 1991).

17 Ibid.; *New York Times*, January 21, 1991.

18 *Literatura un Maksla*, January 26, 1991.

19 According to the *New York Times*, January 19, 1991, Gorbachev's crackdown "has kindled long smouldering discontent into a blaze of censure by Soviet journalists, intellectuals and reform-minded bureaucrats who once were his main supporters."

20 Karlis Streips, *Republic of Latvia: Crisis Chronology, March 1991*, pp. 1–4 (Rockville, Md.: ALA, 1991); *New York Times*, March 5, 1991; Eric Rudenshiold, "Ethnic Dimensions in Contemporary Latvian Politics: Focusing Forces for Change," *Soviet Studies*, 44:4, 1992, p. 627.

21 *Baltic Chronology*, July 1991, p. 1.

22 Ibid., August 1991, p. 3.

23 Ibid., pp. 4–6.

24 Saulius Girnius, "Independence of Baltic States Accepted by World Community," *Report on the USSR*, September 27, 1991.

25 *Latvijas Jaunatne*, April 20, 1990; *Atmoda*, June 26, 1990.

26 Ibid.

27 Ibid.

28 Ibid.

29 Dzintra Bungs, "Political Realignments in Latvia After the Congress of the People's Front," *Report on the USSR*, December 20, 1991.

30 *This Week in the Baltic States*, October 30, 1992, p. 4.

31 *Diena*, December 9, 1992.

32 Ibid.

33 See, for example, the analysis by Ojars Kalnins, *The Government of the Republic of Latvia in Midsummer 1990* (Rockville, Md.: ALA, 1990).

34 *Lauku Avize*, September 20, 1991.

35 *Baltic Observer*, March 23–9, 1993.

36 *Tev*, June 7, 1993.

37 *Diena*, October 30, 1993.

38 *Lauku Avize*, May 18, 1993.

39 *Diena*, May 18 to June 1, 1993. This newspaper analyzed and weighted different economic aspects of the major political parties using their programs. The analyzed variables included attitudes to privatization, market philosophy, welfare, state role in the economy, openness to the world and monetary policy.

40 *Jurmala*, February 25, 1993. The four parties supported by the World Association included Latvia's Way, the Farmers' Union, the Independence Movement and the LPF. According to *Latvijas Jaunatne*, June 7, 1993, 18,413 votes were registered abroad. The pattern of party preferences was similar to the one in Latvia. Only Harmony and Ravnopravie received negligible support.

41 *Neatkariga Cina*, November 3, 1993.

42 Mimeographed document prepared by the Saeima.

43 Ibid.

44 *Baltic Observer*, June 11–17, 1993.

45 *Latvijas Vestnesis*, July 6, 1993.

46 These elections were monitored by fifty-five international observers from

sixteen countries and eight international organizations. *Neatkariga Cina*, June 8, 1993.

47 *Latvijas Jaunatne*, June 5, 1993; *Baltic Observer*, June 11–17, 1993.
48 *Baltic Observer*, June 11–17, 1993.
49 *Latvijas Jaunatne*, June 5, 1993.
50 *Tev*, June 7, 1993. About one-half of Latvia's Way finances came from forty businessmen. The Farmers' Union spent only 10 million rubles, one third of which had been donated by Latvians in the diaspora.
51 *Diena*, September 28, 1993.
52 Dzintra Bungs, "The New Latvian Government," *RFE/RL Research Report*, August 20, 1993.
53 *Lauku Avize*, October 15, 1993.
54 *Diena*, August 3, 1993; *Latvijas Jaunatne*, July 21, 1993; Bungs, "New Latvian Government."
55 *Diena*, October 8, 1993.
56 *Lauku Avize*, August 20, 1993.
57 *Vakara Zinas*, March 7, 1994.
58 Ibid.
59 *Latvijas Vestnesis*, March 26, 1994.
60 *Rigas Balss*, April 29, 1994.
61 *Diena*, November 22, 1994. All four "left"-inclined parties together received only 13.1 percent of support in public opinion polls in the fall of 1994.
62 Dzintra Bungs, "Latvia Adopts Guidelines for Citizenship," *Report on the USSR*, November 1, 1991.
63 Ibid., p. 18.
64 The full English language text of this citizenship law has been published in *Latvijas Vestnesis*, August 11, 1994.
65 At November 11, 1994, the Latvian version of *Diena* had a circulation of 62,000, the Russian 17,250; the Latvian *Rigas Balss* 36,170, its Russian edition 19,130; the Latvian *Labrit* 33,207, its Russian edition 12,003. *Vakara Zinas*, November 22, 1994.
66 *Diena*, December 4, 1993. The circulation of *S. M. Segodnya* in November 1994 was 66,328 and of *Panorama Latvii*, 25,104. Ibid.
67 *Christian Science Monitor*, November 23, 1992.
68 *Diena*, December 8, 1993.
69 George Schopflin, "Central and Eastern Europe Over the Last Year: New Trends, Old Structures," *Report on Eastern Europe*, February 15, 1991, p. 26.
70 Ibid.
71 Ibid, p. 27.
72 *Diena*, April 14, 1994.
73 Ibid.
74 Ibid.
75 *Labrit*, October 25, 1994.
76 Valdis Pavlovskis, "Pardomas par Latvijas Drosibas un Aizsardzibas Jautajumiem," *Militarais Apskats*, no.1, 1994, p. 7.
77 *Diena*, January 25, 1994.
78 *Latvijas Vestnesis*, September 1, 1994.

79 Latvijas Republikas Valsts Statistikas Komiteja, *Latvija Skaitlos 1993* (Riga: 1994), p. 49. The 1992 crime rate was 235 per 10,000 population and that for 1991, 157.
80 *Diena*, April 13, 1994.
81 *Lauku Avize*, August 16, 1994.
82 *Neatkariga Cina*, December 2, 1994.
83 Ibid.
84 *Latvijas Vestnesis*, November 17, 1994.

4 ECONOMICS AND REFORM

1 A. Voss, "Vienotaja Tautsaimnieciska Kompleksa," *Padomju Latvijas Komunists*, November 1978, p. 21.
2 *The Economist*, October 20, 1990.
3 The World Bank, *Latvia: The Transition to a Market Economy* (Washington, D.C.: The World Bank, 1993), p. 102.
4 Ibid.
5 *Latvia: An Economic Profile* (Washington, D.C.: National Technical Information Service, 1992), p. 5.
6 International Monetary Fund, *IMF Economic Review 1993: Latvia* (Washington, D.C.: IMF, 1993), p. 51. (Subsequently *IMF 1993*.)
7 Latvijas Valsts Statistikas Komiteja, *Zinojums Par Latvijas Republikas Tautas Saimniecibas Darba Rezultatiem 1992.g. janvari–oktobri* (Riga: Latvijas Valsts Statistikas Komiteja, 1992), p. 8.
8 *Diena*, September 25, 1992.
9 *IMF 1993*, p. 51.
10 *Labrit*, March 5, 1994. The GDP in 1993 was only 48.7 percent of that in 1990. *Latvijas Vestnesis*, April 16, 1994.
11 John M. Starrels, *The Baltic States in Transition* (Washington, D.C.: IMF, 1993), p. 13.
12 World Bank, *Latvia*, p. xv.
13 *Labrit*, March 11, 1994; Latvijas Banka, *1993 gada Parskats* (Riga: Jana Seta, 1994), p. 4; *Baltic Observer*, January 12–18, 1995. The inflation rate for Estonia was 41.7 percent and for Lithuania 45.1 percent.
14 *IMF 1993*, p. 13; Latvijas Banka, *1993 gada Parskats*, p. 15.
15 *Neatkariga Cina*, January 7, 1995.
16 Ibid., p. 10; *Latvijas Vestnesis*, January 18, 1994; Latvijas Banka, *1993 gada Parskats*, p. 4; *Neatkariga Cina*, January 20, 1995. The average monthly salary in the state sector in December 1994 was 103.8 lats, representing 45.3 percent growth in 1994.
17 World Bank, *Latvia*, p. 251; *IMF 1993*, pp. 60–1; Latvijas Banka, *1993 gada Parskats*, p. 15.
18 *Neatkariga Cina*, September 9, 1994.
19 *Latvijas Vestnesis*, April 6, 1994.
20 *Neatkariga Cina*, September 24, 1993.
21 *IMF 1993*, pp. 77–8.
22 *Diena*, February 11, 1993.

23 Ibid., June 2, 1993. The claim of over 10 billion dollars in foreign banks seems highly unlikely, however.
24 *Tev*, February 21, 1994.
25 *Diena*, March 7, 1994.
26 Ibid., February 7, 1994; Latvijas Banka, *1993 gada Parskats*, p. 19.
27 *Diena*, January 3, 1994, December 3, 1993.
28 *Tev*, February 21, 1994.
29 *Baltic Observer*, April 14–20, 1994; Latvijas Banka, *1993 gada Parskats*, p. 16; *Diena*, March 28, 1994; *Diena*, January 16, 1995.
30 *Diena*, February 17, 1994.
31 Ibid.
32 *Diena*, June 1, 5, 1995; *Labrit*, June 1, 1995.
33 *IMF 1993*, pp. 19–20.
34 *Baltic Independent*, April 15–21, 1994; January 14–20, 1994.
35 *Diena*, February 17, 1994; *Lauku Avize*, April 26, 1994.
36 *Dienas Bizness*, May 2, 1994; Latvijas Banka, *1993 gada Parskats*, p. 21.
37 *Diena*, September 21, 1991; World Bank, *Latvia*, p. 36.
38 *Diena*, September 21, 1991.
39 *Latvijas Vestnesis*, December 1, 1993.
40 *Diena*, May 2, 1994.
41 *IMF 1993*, pp. 26–7.
42 *Rigas Balss*, October 12, 1993.
43 Ibid.; *Diena*, April 5, 1994.
44 *Diena*, April 5, 1994.
45 Ibid.
46 *Dienas Bizness*, May 6, 1994; *Latvijas Jaunatne*, July 24, 1992.
47 *Diena*, October 11, 1993.
48 Richard Rose and William Maley, *Nationalities in the Baltic States: A Survey Study* (Glasgow: University of Strathclyde, 1994). In the fall of 1993, 75 percent of Latvians and 59 percent of other ethnic groups in Latvia felt that "an enterprise is best run by private owners," and only 19 percent of Latvians and 15 percent of others believed that "state ownership is the best way to run an enterprise." (pp. 2–3.)
49 Ibid. This survey also found that among Latvians 22 percent already had or were likely to start a business or shop, compared to 15 percent of others (p. 20).
50 World Bank, *Latvia*, p. 106.
51 *Labrit*, April 9, 1994. The Latvian government adopted ten "national programs" which will receive priority attention. These comprise macroeconomic stabilization, transport development, energy development, foreign trade development, quality control, agriculture development, Baltic Sea environment protection, health and social security, education and science, and national thriftiness.
52 *Neatkariga Cina*, August 6, 1993.
53 *Baltic Independent*, March 11–17, 1994.
54 *Neatkariga Cina*, August 6, 1993.
55 *Latvijas Vestnesis*, January 18, 1994.
56 World Bank, *Latvia*, p. 108.

57 *IMF 1993*, p. 54; *Dienas Bizness*, August 26, 1994.
58 *Lauku Avize*, May 21, 1993.
59 *Latvijas Vestnesis*, March 26, 1994.
60 *Neatkariga Cina*, October 15, 1993.
61 *Latvijas Vestnesis*, January 18, 1994.
62 *Diena*, March 1, 1994; *Monthly Bulletin of Latvian Statistics* no. 8, 1994, pp. 64–9.
63 *Latvijas Vestnesis*, April 20, 1994.
64 Ibid., December 21, 1994.
65 *Baltic Independent*, January 14–20, 1994.
66 Ibid., April 29–May 5, 1994; Juris Dreifelds, "Belorussia and Baltics," in I. S. Koropeckyj and Gertrude E. Schroeder, eds., *Economics of Soviet Regions* (New York: Praeger, 1981), p. 345.
67 *Latvijas Vestnesis*, January 27, 1994.
68 *Baltic Independent*, April 29–May 5, 1994. The Estonian port (Muugu) is deeper and bigger and large grain ships can be accommodated.
69 *IMF 1993*, p. 33.
70 *Baltic Independent*, April 8–14, 1994.
71 Ibid.
72 Ibid, April 29–May 5, 1994.
73 *Lauku Avize*, April 19, 1994.
74 *Baltic Independent*, March 4–10, 1994.
75 *Rigas Balss*, February 17, 1993.
76 *Dienas Bizness*, August 26, 1994.
77 Rose and Maley, *Nationalities in the Baltic States*, p. 26.
78 *IMF Survey*, February 7, 1994.

5 DEMOGRAPHY, LANGUAGE AND ETHNIC RELATIONS

1 The 77 percent in 1935 refers to the present territory of Latvia without the district of Abrene which was added to the RSFSR in 1944. Latvijas PSR Valsts Statistikas Komiteja, *Latvija Sodien* (Riga: 1990), p. 13. The 1945 estimate is found in Romuald J. Misiunas and Rein Taagepera, *The Baltic States: Years of Dependence 1940–1980* (Berkeley: University of California Press, 1983), p. 272. During World War II, the German minority in Latvia was evacuated to Germany and large numbers of Jews and Gypsies were executed by the Nazis.
2 *Rigas Balss*, July 6, 1990.
3 Georg von Rauch, *The Baltic States: The Years of Independence 1917–1940* (Berkeley: University of California Press, 1974), p. 10.
4 *Cina*, June 30, 1990.
5 Misiunas and Taagepera, *The Baltic States*, p. 275.
6 Ilmars Mezs, *Latviesi Latvija: Etnodemografisks Apskats* (Kalamazoo, Mich.: LSC Apgads, 1992), p. 11.
7 *Jurmala*, January 12, 1989.
8 Latvijas Republikas Valsts Statistikas Komiteja, *Latvijas Demografijas Gadagramata 1993* (Riga: 1994), pp. 48–9.

198   Notes to pp. 150–66

9 *1989. Gada Vissavienibas Tautas Skaitisanas Rezultati Latvijas PSR* (Riga: 1990), p. 133. Hereafter cited as *Census Latvia 1989*.
10 Latvijas PSR Valsts Statistikas Komiteja, *Latvijas PSR Tautu Forums: Iss Statistisko Datu Krajums* (Riga: 1988), p. 23.
11 *Atmoda*, September 4, 1990; *Cina*, September 7, 1989.
12 *Latvijas Vestnesis*, March 16, 1994.
13 Ibid.
14 *Latvijas Demografijas Gadagramata 1993*, p. 95.
15 Ibid., p. 87; *Diena*, October 9, 1993.
16 *Cina*, June 30, 1990.
17 Peteris Zvidrins, "Changes in the Ethnic Composition in Latvia," *Journal of Baltic Studies*, 23:4, Winter 1992, p. 361.
18 *Census Latvia 1989*, p. 20.
19 Latvijas Valsts Statistikas Komiteja, *Latvijas Tautas Saimnieciba: Statistikas Gadagramata '89* (Riga: Avots, 1990), p. 24.
20 Ibid.
21 *Cina*, March 3, 1990.
22 *Lauku Avize*, April 6, 1990.
23 Latvijas Republikas Statistikas Komiteja, *Etnosituacija Latvija: Fakti un Komentari* (Riga: 1992), p. 18.
24 *Census Latvia 1989*, p. 114.
25 In 1940/1 the number of students enrolled in higher education institutes per 10,000 population in the USSR was 41, in Russia 43, but in Latvia 52. Tsentralnoe statisticheskoe upravlenie Latviiskoi SSR, *Narodnoe khoziaistvo Latviiskoi SSR v 1978 godu* (Riga: Liesma, 1979), p. 221.
26 Private communication from A. Piebalgs in Toronto, Ontario.
27 Soviet Latvian census printouts described in detail in Juris Dreifelds, "Immigration and Ethnicity in Latvia," *Journal of Soviet Nationalities*, 1:4, Winter 1990–1, p. 72.
28 Richard Rose and William Maley, *Nationalities in the Baltic States: A Survey Study* (Glasgow: University of Strathclyde, 1994), p. 20.
29 *Latvijas Demografijas Gadagramata 1993*, pp. 184–5.
30 *Labrit*, March 30, 1994.
31 "Data on Ethnic Intermarriages," *Journal of Soviet Nationalities*, 1:2, Summer 1990, p. 170. Original in *Naselenie SSSR 1988: statisticheskii ezhegodnik* (Moscow: Finansy i statistika, 1989), pp. 204–321 (Latvian data, pp. 286–87).
32 *Latvijas Demografijas Gadagramata 1993*, p. 185 and p. 191.
33 Anatol Lieven, *The Baltic Revolution: Estonia, Latvia, Lithuania and the Path to Independence* (New Haven, Conn.: Yale University Press, 1993), p. 177.
34 Rasma Karklins, *Ethnopolitics and Transition to Democracy: The Collapse of the USSR and Latvia* (Washington, D.C.: The Woodrow Wilson Center Press, 1994), p. 149.
35 Rose and Maley, *Nationalities in the Baltic States*, p. 55.
36 *Elpa*, October 28, 1994. Translated from *S. M. Segodnya*.
37 *Jurmala*, January 12, 1989.
38 I. Apine, "Nacionala Pasapzina Cela uz Demokratiju," *Latvijas Zinatnu Akademijas Vestis-A*, no. 10, 1992, pp. 20–2.

39 *Atmoda*, June 26, 1990.
40 *Diena*, February 3, 1993. In December 1992 the three most worrying items for non-Latvians were price hikes for electricity, gasoline and heating (28.3 percent), then price hikes for food products (24.7 percent), and unemployment problems (14.3 percent). Only then do they express concern about citizenship and registration problems (7.4 percent), inter-nationality relations problems (5.8 percent) and crime (5.1 percent). The question was "What provided you the greatest anxiety in the past year?" Mimeographed poll results compiled by Latvian Social Research Center, December 1992.
41 Brigita Zepa and Aldis Paulins, "Choice of Residence – The Indicators of State Identity," unpublished paper summarizing data from the Latvian Social Research Center in Riga, obtained from their main office in September 1994.
42 Lieven, *The Baltic Revolution*, p. 188.

CONCLUSION

1 *Labrit*, October 25, 1994.
2 Valdis Pavlovskis, "Pardomas par Latvijas Drosibas un Aizsardzibas Jautajumiem," *Militarais Apskats*, no. 1, 1994, p. 6.
3 *Washington Post*, July 22, 1994; *Rigas Balss*, November 3, 1994.
4 In November 1994, Admiral V. Stalev was arrested in Kaliningrad because of his link with "massive corruption" perpetrated in Latvia while he was commander of the Liepaja war-port. The North West Army Corps has also been involved in widescale corruption and is being investigated. *Diena*, November 11, 1994.
5 *Labrit*, October 27, 1994.
6 *Labrit*, October 21, 1994.
7 *Diena*, October 27, 1994.
8 Carl Bildt, "The Baltic Litmus Test," *Foreign Affairs*, September–October 1994, pp. 80–1.
9 Dzintra Bungs, "Local Elections in Latvia: The Opposition Wins," *RFE/RL Research Report*, vol. 3, no. 28, July 15, 1994.
10 Richard Rose and William Maley, *Nationalities in the Baltic States: A Survey Study* (Glasgow: University of Strathclyde, 1994), pp. 35–40.
11 Ibid., pp. 43–4.
12 Leszek Balcerowitz, "Democracy is No Substitute for Capitalism," *Eastern European Economics*, March–April, 1994, p. 40.
13 Ibid. pp. 43–4.
14 *IMF Survey*, February 7, 1994.
15 *Globe and Mail* [Toronto], October 24, 1994.
16 *Latvijas Vestnesis*, September 1, 1994.
17 Balcerowitz, "Democracy is No Substitute," p. 49.
18 *The Times*, February 17, 1994.
19 Ole Waever, "Between Balts and Brussels: The Nordic Countries After the Cold War", *Current History*, November 1994, p. 394.
20 Ibid., p. 392.

21 Darrell Delamaide, *The New Superregions of Europe* (New York: Dutton, 1994), especially ch. 5, "Baltic League: Trading Places."
22 The fifth session of the Baltic Assembly in Vilnius in November 1994 passed seventeen resolutions on cooperation. Its work is coordinated by six commissions. *Labrit*, November 15, 1994.
23 *New York Times*, July 7, 1994.
24 *The Times*, February 17, 1994.
25 Bildt, "The Baltic Litmus Test," p. 82.
26 Yuri N. Afanasyev, "Russian Reform is Dead: Back to Central Planning," *Foreign Affairs*, March–April 1994, p. 22 and p. 24.

Select bibliography

BOOKS AND ARTICLES

Allworth, Edward (ed.). *Nationality Group Survival in Multi-Ethnic States: Shifting Support Patterns in the Soviet Baltic Region.* New York: Praeger, 1977.

Andersons, Edgars (ed.). *Cross Road Country Latvia.* Waverly, Ia.: Latvju Gramata, 1953.

Balabkins, Nicholas, and Arnolds Aizsilnieks. *Entrepreneur in a Small Country: A Case Study Against the Background of the Latvian Economy, 1919–1940.* Hicksville, N.Y.: Exposition Press, 1975.

The Baltic Review Publishers. *The Soviet Occupation and Incorporation of Latvia June 17 to August 5, 1940.* New York: Vilis Stals Inc., 1957.

The Baltic States: A Reference Book. Tallinn, Riga and Vilnius: Estonian, Latvian, Lithuanian Encyclopaedia Publishers, 1991.

Barnowe, T. J., G. J. King, and E. Berniker. "Personal Values and Economic Transition in the Baltic States." *Journal of Baltic Studies* 23:2, Summer 1992, 179–90.

Benton, Peggie. *Baltic Countdown: A Nation Vanishes.* London: Centaur Press, 1984.

Bildt, Carl. "The Baltic Litmus Test." *Foreign Affairs* 73:5 September–October 1994, 72–85.

Bilmanis, Alfreds. *A History of Latvia.* Princeton, N.J.: Princeton University Press, 1951.

Baltic Essays. Washington, D.C.: Latvian Legation, 1945.

Bobe, M., S. Levenberg, I. Maor, and Z. Michaeli (eds.). *The Jews in Latvia.* Tel Aviv: D. Ben-Nun Press, 1971.

Bower, Tom. *Red Web.* London: Anrum Press, 1989.

Brenner, Ian, and Ray Taras (eds.). *Nations and Politics in the Soviet Successor States.* Cambridge: Cambridge University Press, 1993.

Brikse, Inta. "Mass Media and Society During Perestroika, National Awakening, and Market Reforms." *Humanities and Social Sciences Latvia* 1:2, 1994, 68–82.

Bro, Carl. *Pre-Feasibility Study of the Gulf of Riga and the Daugava River Basin.* Stockholm: 1992.

Bungs, Dzintra. "Joint Political Initiatives by Estonians, Latvians and Lithuanians as Reflected in Samizdat Materials 1969–1987." *Journal of Baltic Studies* 19:3, Fall 1988, 267–71.

"Latvian Communist Party Splits." *Report on the USSR*, April 27, 1990.

"Latvia in an Impasse?" *Report on the USSR*, February 1, 1991.

"Political Realignments in Latvia After the Congress of the People's Front." *Report on the USSR*, December 20, 1991.

Carson, George B. (ed.) *Latvia: An Area Study*. New Haven, Conn.: Human Relations Area Files, no. 41, 1956.

Chicherina, N. G. (ed.) *Grazhdanskie dvizheniia v Latvii 1989*. Moscow: Tsimo, 1990.

Clemens, Walter C., Jr. *Baltic Independence and Russian Empire*. New York: St. Martin's, 1991.

Crowe, David M. *The Baltic States and the Great Powers. Foreign Relations: 1938–1940*. Boulder, Colo.: Westview Press, 1993.

Dellenbrant, Jan Ake. "The Emergence of Multipartism in the Baltic States," in S. Berglund and Jan Ake Dellenbrant (eds.), *The New Democracies in Eastern Europe: Party Systems and Political Cleavages*. Cheltenham: Edward Elgar, 1991.

Dreifelds, Juris. "Latvian National Demands and Group Consciousness Since 1959," in George W. Simmonds (ed.), *Nationalism in the USSR and Eastern Europe in the Era of Brezhnev and Kosygin*. Detroit: University of Detroit Press, 1977.

"Belorussia and Baltics," in I. S. Koropeckij and Gertrude E. Schroeder (eds.), *Economics of Soviet Regions*. New York: Praeger, 1981.

"Latvian National Rebirth." *Problems of Communism* 38:4, July–August 1988, 77–95.

"Two Latvian Dams: Two Confrontations." *Baltic Forum* 6:1, Spring 1989, 11–24.

"Immigration and Ethnicity in Latvia." *Journal of Soviet Nationalities* 1:4, Winter 1990–1, 41–81.

"Latvia: Chronicle of an Independence Movement," in Miron Rezun (ed.), *Nationalism and the Breakup of an Empire: Russia and Its Periphery*. Westport, Conn.: Praeger, 1992.

"The Natural, Economic and Demographic Environment in Latvia," in Philip R. Pryde (ed.), *Environmental Resources and Constraints in the Former Soviet Republics*. Boulder, Colo.: Westview Press, 1995.

"The Environmental Impact of Estonia, Latvia and Lithuania," in Joan DeBardeleben (ed.), *Environmental Security and Quality After Communism*. Boulder, Colo.: Westview Press, 1995.

Duhanovs, M., I. Feldmanis, and A. Stranga. *1939. Latvia and the Year of Fateful Decisions*. Riga: The Latvian University, 1995.

Dunsdorf, Edgars. *The Baltic Dilemma: The Case of the De Jure Recognition of Incorporation of the Baltic States Into the Soviet Union by Australia*. New York: Robert Speller & Sons, 1975.

Latvijas Vesture. Lincoln, Nebr.: Augstums Press, 1980.

Ezergailis, Andrew. *The 1917 Revolution in Latvia*. New York: Columbia University Press, 1974.

The Latvian Impact on the Bolshevik Revolution. New York: Columbia University Press, 1983.

Fitzmaurice, John. *The Baltic: A Regional Future?* New York: St. Martin's Press, 1992.

Germanis, Uldis. "The Rise and Fall of the Latvian Bolsheviks." *Baltic Forum* 3:1, Spring 1988, 21–5.

Gerner, Kristian, and Stefan Hedlund. *The Baltic States and the End of the Soviet Empire*. London: Routledge, 1993.

Gimbutas, Marija. *The Balts*. New York: Praeger, 1964.

Goble, Paul. "The Baltics: Three States, Three Fates." *Current History*, 93:585, October 1994, 332–6.

Gordon, Frank. *Latvians and Jews Between Germany and Russia*. Stockholm: Memento, 1990.

Grahm, Leif, and Lennart Königson. *Baltic Industry: A Survey of Potentials and Constraints*. Sweden: Swedish Development Consulting Partners AB, 1991.

Gross, Imants. "Getting on the International Agenda: Legal Status and Political Action." *Baltic Forum* 2:2, Fall 1985, 1–15.

Hiden, John, and Thomas Lane (eds.). *The Baltic and the Outbreak of the Second World War*. Cambridge: Cambridge University Press, 1992.

Hiden, John, and Patrick Salmon. *The Baltic Nations and Europe: Estonia, Latvia and Lithuania in the Twentieth Century*. London: Longman, 1991.

Himmer, Susan. "The Achievement of Independence in the Baltic States and Its Justifications." *Emory International Law Review* 6:1, 1992, 253–91.

Hough, William J. H., III. "The Annexation of the Baltic States and Its Effect on the Development of Law Prohibiting Forcible Seizure of Territory." *New York Law School Journal of International and Comparative Law* 6:2, Winter 1985, 301–533.

Hoyer, Svennick, Epp Lauk, and Peeter Vihalemm (eds.). *Towards a Civic Society: The Baltic Media's Long Road to Freedom*. Tartu, Estonia: Nota Baltica, 1993.

International Monetary Fund. *Economic Review: Latvia*. Washington, D.C.: IMF, 1992.

"Latvia: Review of the Stand-By Arrangement." Unpublished manuscript, November 1992.

IMF Economic Review 1993: Latvia. Washington, D.C.: IMF, 1993.

Joenniemi, Pertti, and Peeter Vares (eds.). *New Actors on the International Arena: The Foreign Policies of the Baltic Countries*. Tampere, Finland: Tampere Peace Research Institute, 1993.

Johnston, Hank. "The Comparative Study of Nationalisms: Six Pivotal Themes From the Baltic States." *Journal of Baltic Studies* 23:2, Summer 1992, 95–104.

"Religion and Nationalist Subcultures in the Baltics." *Journal of Baltic Studies* 23:2, Summer 1992, 133–48.

Kalnins, Ojars. "Fostering Baltic Freedom." *The World and I*. January 1989, 142–5.

Karklins, Rasma. *Ethnic Relations in the USSR: The Perspective From Below*. Boston: Allen and Unwin, 1986.

"Nationalities and Ethnic Issues," in Anthony Jones and David E. Powell (eds.), *Soviet Update 1989–1990*. Boulder, Colo.: Westview Press, 1991.

Ethnopolitics and Transition to Democracy: The Collapse of the USSR and Latvia. Washington, D.C.: The Woodrow Wilson Center Press, 1994.

Kaslas, Bronis J. *The Baltic Nations: The Quest for Regional Integration and Political Liberty*. Pittstown, Pa.: Euramexica Press, 1976.

Kavass, Igor I., and Adolfs Sprudzs (eds.). *Baltic States: A Study of Their Origin and National Development; Their Seizure and Incorporation Into the USSR*. Buffalo, N.Y.: William S. Hein and Co., 1972. Reprint edition of *The Third Interim Report of the Select Committee on Communist Aggression*, US House of Representatives, Eighty-Third Congress, Second Session. Washington, D.C.: 1954.

Kennedy Grimsted, Patricia. *Archives and Manuscript Repositories in the USSR: Estonia, Latvia, Lithuania and Belorussia*. Princeton, N.J.: Princeton University Press, 1981.

King, G. J. and D. O. Porter. "Moving to Markets: A Review Essay." *Journal of Baltic Studies* 24:4, Winter 1993, 395–402.

Kionka, Riina. "Are the Baltic Laws Discriminatory?" *Report on the USSR*, April 12, 1991.

Kirch, Aksel, Marika, Kirch and Tarmo Tuisk. "Russians in the Baltic States: To Be or Not To Be?" *Journal of Baltic Studies* 24:2, Summer 1993, 173–88.

Kolsto, Pal. "Minority Rights Protection in the Baltic States: A Least Destabilizing Solution to the Russian Diaspora Problem." *Latvijas Zinatnu Akademijas Vestis* no. 5, 1993, 25–30.

Krasts, V. "Cardinal Julijans Vaivods and the Catholic Church in Latvia." *Radio Liberty Report*, February 8, 1983.

Krumins, J. "Suicide Mortality in Latvia: Current Trends and Differentiation." *Latvijas Zinatnu Akademijas Vestis* no. 1, 1993, 9–12.

Kung, Andres. *A Dream of Freedom: Four Decades of National Survival Versus Russian Imperialism in Estonia, Latvia and Lithuania, 1940–1980*. Cardiff: Boreas, 1980.

Lapidus, Gail W., Victor Zaslavsky, and Philip Goldman (eds.). *From Union to Commonwealth: Nationalism and Separatism in the Soviet Republics*. Cambridge: Cambridge University Press, 1992.

Latvia: An Economic Profile. Washington, D.C.: National Technical Information Service, 1992.

Latvia, Republic of. Environmental Protection Committee. *National Report of Latvia to UNCED 1992*. Helsinki: Government Printing Centre, 1992.

Latvia, Republic of. Supreme Council Standing Commission on Human Rights and National Questions. *About the Republic of Latvia*. Riga: Rotaprint, 1992.

Levin, Dov. "The Jews and the Sovietization of Latvia, 1940–41." *Soviet Jewish Affairs* 5:1, 1975, 39–56.

Liepins, Valdis. "Baltic Attitudes to Economic Recovery: A Survey of Public Opinion in the Baltic Countries." *Journal of Baltic Studies* 24:2, Summer 1993, 189–200.

Lieven, Anatol. *The Baltic Revolution: Estonia, Latvia, Lithuania and the Path to Independence*. New Haven, Conn.: Yale University Press, 1993.

Loeber, Dietrich A., V. Stanley Vardys, and Laurence P. A. Kitching (eds.). *Regional Identity Under Soviet Rule: The Case of the Baltic States*. Hackettstown, N.J.: Association for the Advancement of Baltic Studies and Institute for the Study of Law, Politics and Society of Socialist States, University of Kiel, 1990.

Marek, Krystyna. *Identity and Continuity of States in Public International Law.* Geneva: Librairie E. Droz, 1954.

McAuley, Alastair (ed.). *Soviet Federalism, Nationalism and Economic Decentralization.* New York: St. Martin's Press, 1991.

Mezs, Ilmars, Edmunds Bunkse, and Kaspars Raga. "The Ethno-Demographic Status of the Baltic States." *Geojournal* 33:1, 1994, 9–25.

Misiunas, Romuald J., and Rein Taagepera. *The Baltic States: Years of Dependence, 1940–1990.* Berkeley: University of California Press, 1993.

Motyl, Alexander J. (ed.) *The Post-Soviet Nations: Perspectives on the Demise of the USSR.* New York: Columbia University Press, 1992.

   Dilemmas of Independence: Ukraine After Totalitarianism. New York: Council on Foreign Relations Press, 1993.

Muiznieks, Nils. "The Pro-Soviet Movement in Latvia." *Report on the USSR,* August 24, 1990.

   "Latvia: Origins, Evolution and Triumph," in Ian Bremmer and Ray Taras (eds.), *Nations and Politics in the Soviet Successor States.* Cambridge: Cambridge University Press, 1993.

   "The Influence of the Baltic Popular Movements on the Process of Soviet Disintegration," *Europe-Asia Studies,* 47:1, 1995, 3–25.

Nordic Investment Bank, *A Survey of Investment Plans and Needs in the Three Baltic Countries.* Copenhagen: Nordic Council of Ministers, 1991.

Nordic Project Fund. *Study of Environmental Protection: Estonia and Partly Latvia and Lithuania.* Helsinki: Nordic Council, 1989.

   Environmental Situation and Project Identification in Latvia. Helsinki: Nordic Council, 1991.

Norgaard, Ole. "The Political Economy of Transition in Post-Socialist Systems: The Case of the Baltic States." *Scandinavian Political Studies* 15:1, 1992, 41–60.

Page, Stanley W. *The Formation of the Baltic States.* New York: Howard Fertig, 1970.

Parming, T., and E. Jarvesoo (eds.). *A Case Study of a Soviet Republic: The Estonian SSR.* Boulder, Colo.: Westview Press, 1978.

Penikis, Janis J. "Soviet Views of the Baltic Emigration: From Reactionaries to Fellow Countrymen," in Jan Arveds Trapans (ed.), *Toward Independence: The Baltic Popular Movements.* Boulder, Colo.: Westview Press, 1991.

Petersen, Nikolay (ed.). *The Baltic States in International Politics.* Copenhagen: DJOF Publishing, 1993.

Petersen, Philip. "Security Policy in the Post-Soviet Baltic States." *European Security* 1:1, Spring 1992, 13–49.

Plakans, Andrejs. "The Latvians," in Eduard C. Thaden (ed.), *Russification in the Baltic Provinces and Finland, 1855–1914.* Princeton, N.J.: Princeton University Press, 1981.

Popoff, George. *City of the Red Plague.* New York: E. P. Dutton Co., 1932. Reprinted by Hyperion Press Inc., Westport, Conn., 1978.

Powell, David. *Antireligious Propaganda in the Soviet Union.* Cambridge, Mass.: MIT Press, 1975.

Rakowska-Harmstone, Teresa. "Baltic Nationalism and the Soviet Armed Forces." *Journal of Baltic Studies* 17:3, Fall 1986, 179–93.

Resis, Albert. "The Baltic States in Soviet–German Relations, 1939." *National-ities Papers* 17:2, Fall 1989, 116–54.

Rogers, Hugh I. *Search for Security: A Study in Baltic Diplomacy, 1920–1934.* Hamden, Conn.: Archon Books, 1975.

Rose, Richard, and William Maley. *Nationalities in the Baltic States: A Survey Study.* Glasgow: University of Strathclyde, 1994.

Royal Institute of International Affairs, Information Department. *The Baltic States: A Survey of the Political and Economic Structure and the Foreign Relations of Estonia, Latvia and Lithuania.* Westport, Conn.: Greenwoud Press, 1970. Originally published in London by Oxford University Press, 1938.

Rozanov, G. L. *Stalin–Gitler.* Moscow: Mezhdunarodnye otnosheniia, 1991.

Rudenshiold, Eric. "Ethnic Dimensions in Contemporary Latvian Politics: Focusing Forces for Change." *Soviet Studies* 44:4, 1992, 609–39.

Rutkis, J. *Latvia: Country and People.* Stockholm: Latvian National Foundation, 1967.

Sakwa, Richard. *Russian Politics and Society.* London: Routledge, 1993.

Schafer, R., and E. Schafer. "Latvia in Transition: A Study of Change in a Former Republic of the USSR." *Journal of Baltic Studies* 23:2, 1993, 161–72.

Schneider, Gertrude. *Journey Into Terror: Story of the Riga Ghetto.* New York: Ark House, 1979.

Segal, Zvi. "Jewish Minorities in the Baltic Republics in the Postwar Years." *Journal of Baltic Studies* 19:1, Spring 1988, 60–6.

Senn, Alfred Erich. "Perestroika in Lithuanian Historiography: The Molotov–Ribbentrop Pact." *The Russian Review* 49:1, January 1990, 43–56.

Shafir, Gershon. "Relative Overdevelopment and Alternative Paths of Nation-alism: A Comparative Study of Catalonia and the Baltic Republics." *Journal of Baltic Studies* 23:2, Summer 1993, 105–20.

Shtromas, Alexander. *The Soviet Method of Conquest of the Baltic States: Lessons for the West.* Washington, D.C.: Washington Institute for Values in Public Policy, 1986.

Silde, Adolfs. *Resistance Movement in Latvia.* Stockholm: Latvian National Foundation, 1985.

Smith, Graham E. "The Impact of Modernization on the Latvian Soviet Republic." *Co-Existence* 16:1, April 1979, 45–64.

"Latvians," in Graham Smith (ed.), *The Nationalities Question in the Soviet Union.* New York: Longmans, 1990.

Sontag, R. J., and J. S. Beddie (eds.). *Nazi–Soviet Relations 1931–1941.* Washington, D.C.: US Department of State, 1948.

Spekke, Arnolds. *History of Latvia: An Outline.* Stockholm: M. Goppers, 1957.

Sprudzs, Adolfs (ed.). *The Baltic Path to Independence: An International Reader of Selected Articles.* Buffalo, N.Y.: William S. Hein and Co., 1994.

Sprudzs, Adolfs, and Armins Rusis (eds.). *Res Baltica.* Leiden: A. W. Sijthoff, 1968.

Stamers, Guntis. *Latvia Today.* Riga: Latvian Institute of International Affairs, 1993.

Starrels, John M. *The Baltic States in Transition.* Washington, D.C.: IMF, 1993.

Strods, Heinrichs. "The National Partisans: Their Ranks and Weapons (1944–1956)." *Humanities and Social Sciences Latvia* 1:1, 1993, 40–5.

Taagepera, Rein. "Lithuania, Latvia and Estonia 1940–1980: Similarities and Differences." *Baltic Forum* 1:1, Fall 1984, 39–52.

"Who Assimilates Whom? – The World and the Baltic Region." *Journal of Baltic Studies* 18:3, Fall 1987, 269–82.

"Estonia's Road to Independence." *Problems of Communism* 38:6, Nov.–Dec. 1989, 11–26.

Estonia: Return to Independence. San Francisco: Westview Press, 1993.

Thomson, Clare. *The Singing Revolution: A Political Journey Through the Baltic States.* London: Michael, 1992.

Thorborg, Marina (ed.). *Women Around the Baltic Sea, Part 1: Estonia, Latvia and Lithuania. Work Report on Baltic Issues.* Lund, Sweden: Lund University Department of Education, 1993.

Toynbee, Arnold, and Veronica M. Toynbee (eds.). *Survey of International Affairs 1939–1946,* vol. XI, *The Initial Triumph of the Axis.* London: Oxford University, 1958.

Trapans, Jan Arveds (ed.). *Toward Independence: The Baltic Popular Movements.* Boulder, Colo.: Westview Press, 1991.

"Averting Moscow's Baltic Coup." *Orbis,* Summer 1991, 427–39.

"The West and the Recognition of the Baltic States: 1919 and 1991. A Study of the Politics of the Major Powers." *Journal of Baltic Studies* 25:2, Summer 1994, 153–73.

United States. Commission on Security and Cooperation in Europe. *Elections in the Baltic States and Soviet Republics.* Washington, D.C.: US Government Printing Office, 1990.

Valkonen, Tapani, Juris Krumins, and Peteris Zvidrins. "The Mortality Trends in Finland and Latvia since the 1920s," *Yearbook of Population Research in Finland,* vol. 29. Helsinki: The Population Research Institute, 1991.

Vardys, V. Stanley. "Modernization and Baltic Nationalism." *Problems of Communism* 24:5, Sept.–Oct. 1975, 32–48.

"The Role of the Baltic Republics in Soviet Society," in Roman Szporluk (ed.), *The Influence of East Europe and the Soviet West on the USSR.* New York: Praeger, 1976.

"The Role of the Churches in the Maintenance of Regional and National Identity in the Baltic Republics." *Journal of Baltic Studies* 18:3, Fall 1987, 287–300.

"Lithuanian National Politics." *Problems of Communism* 38:4, July–August 1989, 53–76.

Vardys, V. Stanley, and Romuald J. Misiunas (eds.). *The Baltic States in Peace and War 1917–1945.* University Park: Pennsylvania State University Press, 1981.

Vebers, Elmars. "Demography and Ethnic Politics in Independent Latvia: Some Basic Facts." *Nationalities Papers* 21:2, Fall 1993, 179–94.

(ed.). *The Ethnic Situation in Latvia.* Riga: Ethnic Studies Centre, 1994.

Veinbergs, Alexander. "Lutheranism and Other Denominations in the Baltic Republics," in Richard H. Marshall, Jr. (ed.), *Aspects of Religion in the Soviet Union, 1917–1967.* Chicago: University of Chicago Press, 1971.

Vizulis, Izadors. *The Molotov–Ribbentrop Pact of 1939: The Baltic Case*. New York: Westport, 1990.

von Rauch, Georg. *The Baltic States: The Years of Independence 1917–1940*. Berkeley: University of California Press, 1974.

Westing, Arthur H. (ed.). *Comprehensive Security for the Baltic: An Environmental Approach*. London: Sage Publications, PRIO and UNEP, 1989.

The World Bank. *Latvia: The Transition to a Market Economy*. Washington, D.C.: The World Bank, 1993.

Zagars, Eriks. *Socialist Transformation in Latvia 1940–1941*. Riga: Zinatne, 1978.

Zemribo, Gvido. "The Judicial Power of the Courts in Latvia." *Humanities and Social Sciences Latvia* 1:2, 1994, 29–37.

Zepa, Brigita. "Public Opinion in Latvia in the Stage of Transition. The Dynamics of Views of Latvians and Non-Latvians." *EMOR Reports* 2:3, July-September 1992 (Estonian Market and Opinion Research Centre, Tallinn).

Ziedonis, Arvids. *The Religious Philosophy of Janis Rainis: Latvian Poet*. Waverly, Ia.: Latvju Gramata, 1969.

Zvidrins, Peteris. "Changes in the Ethnic Composition in Latvia." *Journal of Baltic Studies* 23:4, Winter 1992, 359–68.

PERIODICALS

AABS Newsletter, quarterly, Hackettstown, New Jersey, Association for the Advancement of Baltic Studies.

Atmoda [Reawakening], weekly, Riga, 1989–92. Since 1992 published irregularly.

Atmoda Atputai [Reawakening for Leisure], weekly, Riga.

Baltic Forum, biannual, New York, 1984–89.

Baltic Independent, weekly, Tallinn, 1991–.

Baltic Observer, weekly, Riga, 1991–.

The Baltic Review, quarterly, Tallinn, 1993–.

Briviba [Freedom], Latvian Social Democratic Party.

Cina [Struggle], daily, Riga. Replaced by *Neatkariga Cina* (see below).

Diena [Day], daily, Riga. Published also in Russian.

Dienas Bizness [Business of the Day], semi-weekly, Riga.

Dzimtenes Balss [Voice of the Homeland], weekly, Riga. No longer published.

Elpa [Breath], weekly, Riga.

Estonian Kroon: Finance, Economy, quarterly, Tallinn, 1993–.

Foreign Broadcast Information Service (FBIS), daily, Washington, D.C.

Humanities and Social Sciences Latvia, quarterly, Riga, 1993–.

Izglitiba [Education], weekly, Riga.

Journal of Baltic Studies, quarterly, Hackettstown, New Jersey, Association for the Advancement of Baltic Studies, 1971–

Jurmala [Sea-Side], weekly, City of Jurmala, Latvia. Also published in Russian.

Labrit [Good Morning], daily, Riga. No longer published.

Latvia – Baltic State, quarterly, Riga, 1990–.

Latvijas Jaunatne [Latvian Youth], daily, Riga. No longer published.

Latvijas Vestnesis [Latvian Herald], daily, Riga. Official newspaper of the Latvian government.

Latvijas Vesture [Latvian History], quarterly, Riga.
Latvijas Zinatnu Akademijas Vestis: Humanitaras Zinatnes [Latvian Academy of Sciences Proceedings: Humanitarian Sciences], monthly, Riga.
Lauku Avize [Rural Newspaper], weekly, Riga.
Liesma [Flame], monthly, Riga.
Literatura un Maksla [Literature and Art], weekly, Riga.
Lithuania in the World, bimonthly, Vilnius, 1993–.
Lithuania Today, monthly, Vilnius, 1992–.
Neatkariga Cina [Independent Struggle], daily, Riga.
Padomju Jaunatne [Soviet Youth], daily, Riga. No longer published.
Padomju Latvijas Komunists [Soviet Latvian Communist], monthly, Riga. Also published in Russian. No longer published.
Rigas Balss [Voice of Riga], daily, Riga. Also published in Russian.
Sieviete [Woman], monthly, Riga.
Skola un Gimene [School and Family], monthly, Riga.
Skolotaju Avize [Schoolteachers' Newspaper], weekly, Riga. No longer published.
S. M. Segodnya [Soviet Youth Today], daily, Riga.
Svetdienas Rits [Sunday Morning], weekly, Riga.
Tev [To You], weekly, Riga.
Tevzemes Avize [Fatherland Newspaper], weekly, Riga. No longer published.
This Week in the Baltic States, weekly, RFE/RL publication.
Vakara Zinas [Evening News], daily, Riga.
Veseliba [Health], monthly, Riga.
Zvaigzne [Star], monthly, Riga.

DATA COLLECTIONS

Baltic Chronology: Estonia, Latvia, Lithuania. 1989–1994, monthly, New York: BATUN.
Latvia, Republic of. Ministry of Industry and Energy. *Industry and Energy Republic of Latvia*, Riga: 1992.
Latvia, Republic of. Ministry of Welfare, Labour and Health. *Health in Latvia*, 2nd ed. Riga: Rotaprint, 1992.
Latvia, Republic of. State Committee for Statistics. *Bulletin of Latvian Economic Statistics*, January–March 1994.
Latvia, Republic of. State Committee for Statistics. *National Economy of Latvia in 1990: Statistical Yearbook* (text in English). Riga: 1991.
Latvijas Republikas Valsts Statistikas Komiteja: State Committee for Statistics of the Republic of Latvia. *Latvijas Statistikas Gadagramata, 1993: Statistical Yearbook of Latvia* (bilingual volume). Riga: 1994. (Similar yearbooks in both languages published for 1991 and 1992.)

Index

Index

213